The Open University

GW00708070

D103 SOCIETY AND SOCIAL SCIENCE: A FOUNDATION COURSE

BLOCK 7
SOCIAL SCIENCE AND SOCIETY

THE OPEN UNIVERSITY

D103 PRODUCTION TEAM

John Allen
James Anderson (Chairperson)
Robert Bocock
Peter Bradshaw
Vivienne Brown
Linda Clark (Course Secretary)
David Coates
Allan Cochrane
Jeremy Cooper (BBC)
Neil Costello
Clare Falkner (BBC)
Stuart Hall
Susan Himmelweit
Jack Leathem (BBC)
Richard Maidment
Doreen Massey
Gregor McLennan
Andrew Northedge
Kay Pole
Marilyn Ricci (Course Manager)
Paul Smith
Richard Stevens
Elaine Storkey
Kenneth Thompson
Diane Watson
Margaret Wetherell

External Consultants
Tom Burden
David Deacon
David Denver
Caroline Dumonteil
Owen Hartley
Tom Hulley
Robert Looker
Angela Phillips
Colm Regan
Richard Sanders
Neil Thompson
Patrick Wright

Tutor Assessors
Alan Brown
Lyn Brennan
Mona Clark
Ian Crosher
Donna Dickenson
Brian Graham
Philip Markey
Norma Sherrat
Jan Vance

Tom Hunter, Chris Wooldridge, David Wilson, Robert Cookson, Nigel Draper, David Scott-Macnab (Editors); Paul Smith (Librarian); Alison George (Graphic Artist); Jane Sheppard (Designer); Sue Rippon, Mollie Hancock (Project Control); Robin Thornton (Summer School Manager); John Hunt (Summer School IT); John Bennett; and others.

External Academic Assessors
Professor Anthony Giddens, Cambridge University (Overall Assessor)
Dr Geoffrey Harcourt, Cambridge University (Block III)
Dr Patrick Dunleavy, London School of Economics (Block IV)
Dr Hella Beloff, Edinburgh University (Block V)
Professor Brian Robson, Manchester University (Block VI)

The Open University,
Walton Hall, Milton Keynes,
MK7 6AA.

First published 1991. Reprinted 1992. Copyright © 1991 The Open University

Designed by the Graphic Design Group of The Open University.

Typeset by The Open University and printed in the United Kingdom by The Alden Press, Oxford

ISBN 0 7492 0043 X

For general availability of supporting material referred to in this text, please write to Open University Educational Enterprises Limited, 12 Cofferidge Close, Stony Stratford, Milton Keynes, MK11 1BY, United Kingdom.

Further information on Open University courses may be obtained from the Admissions Office, The Open University, P.O. Box 48, Walton Hall, Milton Keynes, MK7 6AB.

BLOCK INTRODUCTION AND STUDY GUIDE

Prepared for the Course Team by James Anderson

CONTENTS

1   PULLING IT ALL TOGETHER

Congratulations, you've made it to the final block! You'll be glad to know that the overwhelming majority of students who get this far complete the Foundation Course successfully. I'm sure you now know a lot more about society, social science and how to study than you did when you started Block I all those months ago. Ideas which then were unfamiliar, even strange, may now be almost second nature to you. But you still have some way to go.

Block VII pulls together the main strands of D103. It consolidates what you have already learned and will help you to revise the course and prepare for the exam. But it also builds on earlier course work, providing some stimulating new material and fresh insights.

The block spans six study weeks, and then there are a couple of weeks for revision before the exam. But Unit 27 is short so that you can catch up if your study routine was disrupted during the summer, and the suggested study times for the block are less than the 'normal' twelve hours per week. I hope the new material and the experience gained at Summer School will help you to keep going, and that you are returning to your local tutorials with renewed enthusiasm.

TV14 and Unit 27 show that the four *traditions of thought* continue to exert powerful influences in contemporary society, though often in partial or 'impure' ways or in combination with other ideas. The television programme (see the *Media Booklet* before viewing) builds on two of the Summer School modules in illustrating the presence of the traditions in the environmental or 'green' movement.

In Units 28 and 29 attention switches to the influence of the four traditions within social science itself, their more important aspect for D103. Rather than simply describing their influence, we commissioned four external social scientists, each of whom works within one of the traditions, to present their personal overviews of *UK society* — another strand which has run through D103. By comparing their different views about contemporary problems, you will get additional perspectives on aspects of the UK you have already studied; and you will be able to see for yourself how the different explanatory frameworks provided by the traditions give rise to different explanations and research priorities in social science.

TV15 — 'Social Scientists at Work' — gives some insights into how research is carried out and how social science contributes to modern society. Unit 30 concludes the *social science methods* strand in the review units of previous blocks by discussing how to go about choosing between the traditions and other 'grand theories' or explanatory frameworks. TMA 07 covers the *traditions* and *methods* strands of the course (and hence will be important preparation for the second section of the exam paper).

After TMA 07, Units 31 and 32 and TV16 use the *course themes* as a vehicle for course revision and there is new *study skills* material on revising for and sitting exams.

Thus in pulling together the five strands — the *traditions*, *UK society*, *social science methods*, *course themes* and *study skills* — Block VII both revises earlier material and adds new dimensions to it.

1.1   TRADITIONS IN SOCIETY

The four traditions — liberalism, conservatism, marxism and social reformism — 'can themselves be seen as *ideologies* "in action" within society' (Unit 17: 1.1). They inspire political and social movements and have residues in popular culture and everyday common sense (Reader, Chapter 22). They pervade contemporary society, affecting people's thinking — your thinking, my thinking — in all sorts of ways, whether they — or we — are always aware of it. Their influence may not be obvious because in society they don't usually manifest themselves in 'pure' or 'undiluted' forms. More commonly, elements from different traditions are combined together or they are incorporated within other bodies of thought or particular social movements, such as religions, nationalism, the feminist and 'green' movements.

The traditions are thus important objects of study for social science, and Unit 27, along with TV14, provides a tradition spotter's guide. Using examples from earlier in the course and some new ones, it focuses on the politically important 'New Right' which combines elements from liberalism and conservatism, and it discusses how the traditions often cross-cut and divide various social movements.

1.2   OVERVIEWS OF THE UK

However in D103 we have mainly been concerned with how the different explanatory frameworks provided by the traditions have influenced social science. In social science, as in society generally, they often appear in partial or 'mixed forms', but in Unit 5 and Chapter 22 we presented them in relatively 'pure' form in order to highlight their distinctive characteristics and the differences between them. This strategy is continued in Units 28 and 29 where the four overviews of *UK society* by the external social scientists are relatively pure expressions of their respective traditions.

The four social scientists were each asked to write 5,000 words on what they considered to be the main *problems* of UK society, their *causes* and *solutions*, and to reflect on why their respective traditions predisposed them to emphasize certain things and not others. The resulting overviews thus continue the 'UK: Continuity and Change' strand of the television series and Blocks I to VI — indeed some deal with issues first raised in Chapter 1 of the Reader.

Perhaps even more interesting is the fact that their very different answers to exactly the same set of questions (see Unit 28) clearly indicate how the traditions can influence what social scientists choose to define as 'problems', and the causes and solutions which they identify. The four overviews are personal and occasionally provocative position statements designed to stimulate a response from you as to which of the four explanatory frameworks you find most (or least) illuminating. But all four have a refreshing directness. Hearing directly from 'true believers', seeing their different answers juxtaposed and comparing them in *Activities* (which are quite demanding but well worth the effort) will give you a clearer understanding of the importance of explanatory frameworks.

There are of course other frameworks in social science besides the 'pure' traditions, and sometimes their influence is implicit rather than explicit. Some social scientists draw on more than one tradition, or they are influenced by other bodies of thought in society (e.g. feminism or religion). Some of these other frameworks are discussed at the end of Unit 29 and in Unit 30.

1.3   SOCIAL SCIENCE METHODS

Unit 30 — 'Choosing explanatory frameworks' — concludes D103's methods strand which started back in Unit 4 and continued through the review units at the end of each block. These units discussed how social scientists *contextualize* events, *classify* evidence and use *concepts*; how they construct *models* or *theories*, and how they get *evidence* and combine it with *theory* to produce *explanations*. You will have used some of these 'tools of the trade' in your TMAs and tutorial discussions, and they are all important when we come to evaluate general *explanatory frameworks*.

Unit 26 suggested criteria for choosing between particular theories (e.g. theories to explain regional inequalities), but Unit 30 moves to a qualitatively different level in discussing people's choice of 'grand theories', especially the different conceptions of society and general frameworks provided by the traditions. You've probably already got ideas about which framework you find most useful, but Block VII and Unit 30 will help you to reflect on the choices and your own conception of society.

You might conclude that while the traditions are interesting as intellectual history they bear little relationship to your own conceptions and what you 'really believe' about the human condition. Perhaps some other bodies of thought give you a better framework? That is one reason why Block VII goes beyond the traditions. But there is another reason. If you prefer some other framework, it is worth reflecting on the extent to which it may embody elements from some of the traditions. They, after all, have been around for a long time. One way or another we have all been influenced by them quite independently of any formal study.

1.4   COURSE THEMES

Public and Private, Local and Global, and *Representation and Reality* have been used in a variety of ways in Blocks I to VI, to organize factual evidence and raise questions about it. The review of these themes in Units 31 and 32 and in TV16, with selected examples from the different blocks, will help you to consolidate what you've learned and revise for the exam; and you can also use the *Glossary Index* to locate where the themes and other concepts have been discussed in particular units.

1.5   STUDY SKILLS

Block VII concentrates on the study skills of preparing for and coping with the exam. You will need to work out a revision strategy that suits your particular situation. As usual there are few 'magic formulae' but there is basic advice, such as noting the structure of the exam paper, *not* concentrating your revision too narrowly, using the *Glossary Index* and the *Summaries* in the units for revision purposes, and allocating roughly three-quarters of an hour to each of the four questions in the three hour exam. These basic points may seem obvious but they're easier said than done. Any practice you can get at writing 'mock' exam answers will pay off in the exam itself.

You really do learn best by doing it for yourself and so Units 31 and 32 emphasize study skills *activities* (and as an integral part of the units rather than in separate study skills sections). They will help consolidate skills covered earlier in the course, particularly essay writing skills. The exam requires essay answers and you'll need to remember the advice you've had on your TMA essays, in the Study Skills sections in Blocks I, III and V, and in *The Good Study Guide*.

2   BLOCK VII STUDY GUIDE

As usual you should check for any updating in the block *Endnotes*. If you have compiled a *Resource File* of cuttings on previous blocks it might be more useful to include them in your revision strategy rather than compiling more cuttings on Block VII. If you have time you could look out for examples of the traditions in the mass media, but the shorter than normal weekly study times are designed to let you catch up after the summer and give you more time for your own revision work.

Block components	Approximate study time (hours)
Block Introduction and *Study Guide*	$\frac{1}{2}$
Unit 27: Traditions in contemporary society	$2\frac{1}{2}$
TV14: The Traditions and the environment	2
Total	5
Unit 28: Liberal and Conservative approaches	$5\frac{1}{2}$
Study Skills Section: A revision strategy	$1\frac{1}{2}$
Tape 7	$\frac{1}{2}$
The Good Study Guide: Chapter 7, Section 4	1
Radio 14	$\frac{1}{2}$
Total	9
Unit 29: Marxist and Social Reformist approaches	6
TV15: Social scientists at work	2
Total	8
Unit 30: Choosing explanatory frameworks	$2\frac{1}{2}$
Radio 15	$\frac{1}{2}$
TMA 07	6
Total	9
Unit 31: Course themes and revision	$5\frac{1}{2}$
The Good Study Guide, Chapter 7, Section 3	$\frac{1}{2}$
TV16: Wrapping up the themes	2
Total	8
Unit 32: Themes and the exam	$3\frac{1}{2}$
The Good Study Guide: Chapter 7, Sections 5, 6 and 7	1
Tape 7	1
Radio 16	$\frac{1}{2}$
Total	6

UNIT 27   TRADITIONS IN CONTEMPORARY SOCIETY

Prepared for the Course Team by James Anderson

CONTENTS

1   TRADITIONS AS IDEOLOGIES

This short unit has the limited objective of helping you to recognize the continuing influence of the *traditions of thought* in contemporary society. To illustrate their political influence Section 2 discusses the privatization policies of UK Governments in the 1980s and early 1990s; and Section 3 deals briefly with their influence on broader social movements and public opinion. The unit builds on, and hopefully will reinforce, some of the material you covered earlier in the course and at Summer School.

The privatization policies of the 1980s substantially altered the *public-private* balance of the UK economy, as you saw in TV06. They were formulated by the New Right, a political combination involving *liberalism* and *conservatism* which rose to prominence by challenging the *social reformism* which had dominated politics in the 1950s and 1960s. So our case study of privatization illustrates the power of ideas derived from the traditions, and it allows us to see the contest between them in their historical context. However it also shows the complex and often 'messy' nature of their influences, so even the limited objective of recognizing or identifying them can be difficult enough.

1.1   RECOGNITION DIFFICULTIES

You've seen that liberalism, conservatism, marxism and social reformism have clearly recognizable views about human society and that they provide social scientists with different explanatory frameworks. But, as influences in the wider society we study, the traditions are also part of the *subject matter* of social science (Reader Chapter 22, Section 4). As Unit 17 indicated, they can be studied as *ideologies*, that is as *sets of ideas, beliefs or assumptions which influence the attitudes and actions of social groups and institutions, which help them make sense of their social circumstances and give them a sense of identity, and which can either legitimize or challenge the prevailing power relations in society* (see *Glossary Index*). However it was also indicated that ideologies can be very 'slippery' and there are a number of difficulties in recognizing the traditions 'as ideologies in action within society'. As Unit 17 (Section 1.2) noted, 'ideas concerning equality or inequality, social justice, freedom and progress are classic grounds for ideological contestation', and it is just such ideas which the traditions contest. But, as you know, all such ideas involve *values* and are open to widely differing interpretations. The contest is as much about interpretations as about whether such things as 'freedom' exist or how they ought to be achieved, and there is no 'neutral' position from which to judge the different interpretations.

Even on the simplest definition of ideologies as *sets of ideas which serve the interests of particular social groups*, there will be disagreements about how the ideas, interests and groups, and the connections between them, should be identified in particular instances. A broad distinction was noted (Unit 17: 1) between *dominant ideologies* which serve the interests of dominant groups and help sustain the existing social order, and *counter ideologies* which challenge it in the interests of subordinate groups. In the UK marxism is clearly in the latter category, liberalism, conservatism and social reformism arguably in the former. For example, it is often argued by marxists that 'liberal ideas of the free market' and 'winner-take-all' attitudes are simply 'ideologies which further the specific interests of the capitalist class' (Unit 17: 1.3). You've seen that writers in the conservative tradition emphasize loyalty and deference to established authority, while social reformists generally pay more attention to the aspirations and needs of subordinate groups and the desirability of getting their

Homeless under Waterloo Bridge, London, in the 1980s

active consent. So even if it is accepted that, when they operate as ideologies, three of our four traditions help sustain the existing social order in the UK, they clearly disagree about *how* it should be sustained, as we'll see in the case of privatization. Although the distinction between 'dominant' and 'counter' ideologies is an important one, ideological battles are rarely a simple two-way contest: there are differences *between* dominant groups, and there are also ideologies which are not directly 'for' or 'against' the existing order.

Moreover ideologies are often most persuasive in society when the appeal they make is to 'the national interest' or the 'common good' of humanity, rather than explicitly identifying with particular social groups. They may indeed deny any ideological content or intent, believing, or having us believe, that (in the manner of positivism — see *Glossary Index*) their interpretations of social reality rest simply on 'facts' rather than values. An ideology can have the effect of serving the interests of particular groups even though that is not a *conscious intent* of the people propagating the ideology. Ideologies are both more interesting and more powerful than simple propaganda. So just what interests are served by a set of ideas in any given social context can be very difficult to decipher and will usually be open to disagreement.

The interests served can vary with different contexts and ideologies often change over time. You saw, for example, that in the early nineteenth century the conservative tradition was opposed to industrial capitalism and to the liberalism of industrial capitalists, seeing them as disrupting the established social order then dominated by landed interests (Unit 5: 3.1 and Chapter 22). But later conservatives came to support the new order of an industrialized society, and later still, in the 1970s and 80s, we find conservatism in a New Right partnership with its old enemy liberalism. Furthermore, contemporary groups or individuals can be wide ranging and inconsistent in their sources of influence, so we need a readiness to be surprised. Self-proclaimed marxists, for example, may turn out to be, or turn into, social reformists in their political practice as many did when the First World War began and some do today; or people holding social reformist views may reveal a strong streak of conservatism. Likewise, conservatives or liberals may in practice favour social reformist solutions to some issues.

Some of the difficulties in recognizing ideological influences arise from the political nature of ideological conflicts. While social scientists have played leading roles — e.g. Hayek and Friedman for liberalism, Beveridge and Keynes for social reformism — the conflicts are played out in the public arena by politicians, journalists, administrators, business people, trade unionists, pressure groups and others. And, whatever the proprieties of academic discussion, in the hurly-burly of public debate or political struggle ideas are often wrongly labelled, both unintentionally and intentionally. For example, some marxists argue that the label 'marxist' given to Stalin's Russia, both by the regime itself and by its opponents, was a gross *mis*representation of the tradition established by Marx (Cliff, 1974), even though the marxist tradition had originally been a powerful motivating force in the 1917 Revolution (Unit 5: 2.5). And we shall see that some liberals rejected the label 'neo-liberal' for Conservative Government policies in the 1980s on the grounds that they were inadequately liberal. Ideologies cannot be accepted uncritically at face value, nor should we automatically accept the estimation of them by their opponents. Society is a battlefield of ideas and the 'smoke of battle' often obscures what's happening.

Ideologies are important as guides to action and as justifications or legitimations of actions taken. But they are only part of the story. The actions of social groups or the policies of governments are also shaped by circumstances, by short-term tactical considerations, expediency or pragmatism — 'in the real world no political party or government is likely to move as a unified body in one direction at all times' (Unit 16: 2.2). Actions may be justified by a mixture of elements from different, even incompatible, ideologies.

Indeed where the traditions are concerned, mixed and partial forms are more common in society than easy-to-recognize pure expressions. Elements from different traditions are combined together in various ways, and they also appear in other bodies of thought such as feminism or environmentalism. Thus political parties, governments and social movements typically reflect the influence of several traditions and, in the early 1990s, it was noticeable how all the main parties had fairly suddenly incorporated elements of 'green' thinking from the environmental movement. Conversely, as TV14 demonstrates, elements from the traditions are influential in the environmental movement itself.

1.2   A TRADITION SPOTTER'S GUIDE

Any strategy for recognizing the influence of the traditions has to take account of the difficulties involved, the varied forms the traditions take and the different levels in society at which they operate. Above all, we need a clear understanding of their pure forms coupled with a realization that pure forms are rarely to be found in society.

So, faced with a particular 'set of ideas, assumptions, beliefs or images', we could begin by asking: 'Do they reflect any of the characteristic views and values of one (or more) of the four traditions?' (using Table 1 from Unit 5, opposite, and what you found out in Module VII at Summer School).

The forms the traditions take in society can be classified on a 'purity' scale:
- clear expressions of a single tradition;
- combinations involving elements from two (or more) traditions; or
- partial and perhaps subordinate elements in other bodies of thought which sometimes present themselves as alternative 'world views'.

Similarly, the different levels at which they operate can be classified in terms of different social agents or actors — political organizations, social movements, and the broad mass of the population.

These classifications can be combined and further subdivided. Thus at the political level we might want to distinguish between ideological pressure groups or individuals who express relatively pure versions of a tradition (e.g. the Adam Smith Institute, the Institute of Economic Affairs, Hayek and Friedman, in the case of liberalism), and governments (e.g. UK governments in the 1980s) which claim to follow them but whose 'impure' policies also reflect other ideological influences or more short-term practical considerations. In social movements we might distinguish between the ideological pacesetters (e.g. Friends of the Earth on environmental issues) and some of their supporters whose views may be less coherently or less explicitly expressed. At the level of public opinion or everyday thinking, there are again varying degrees of coherence and awareness, with many people accepting ideas as being almost 'natural', simply 'common sense', unaware of their sources in the traditions or other particular ideologies (Chapter 22, Section 4). They may indeed deny these sources. For example, some women, whose attitudes have been profoundly influenced by the feminist movement of the 1970s and 80s, deny any association with 'feminism'. In some cases this is because they identify feminism with a 'radical feminist' rejection of men which they don't share. However, 'radical feminism' is only one strand of a many-stranded movement: there is also 'liberal feminism', and a 'socialist feminist' strand which incorporates elements of social reformism and marxism. Social movements typically contain different strands and looking at their divisions and disputes is often fruitful for spotting different traditions at work.

Table 1   Four Traditions: a summary of characteristic views and values

	Liberalism	Conservatism	Marxism	Social Reformism
Human Nature	Generally seen as constant, though different writers put more stress on the selfishness or altruism of individuals'.	Human nature imperfect and varies from person to person. Inequalities are innate, and hence inevitable in society.	People can change their nature depending on social circumstances and their own activities.	Human nature varies with social circumstances and can be improved by better social conditions and education
State and Society	Society composed of individuals born with rights which the state should protect, but also respect by keeping its interference in social life to a minimum. Stress on freedoms of speech, religion, the press, etc; and on 'state interference' as a cause of social problems.	Society a historically evolved organism held together by leadership and discipline, institutions such as the state, the church and the family, and by the shared customs and traditions of 'community' and 'nation'. Social problems are due to the erosion of these institutions and traditions, and the undermining of mutual obligations and duties.	Capitalist society is inherently unstable because of the conflicting interests of its different social classes. As in previous class-divided societies the state is an organization for the control of society by the dominant class. Social problems are due to class domination and conflict.	Society composed of a variety of institutions and social groups. They pursue their own interests with the state acting essentially as a 'referee' to manage conflicts which arise. Social problems are due to the complex and changing nature of modern society and inadequate institutional arrangements.
State and Economy	Competitive markets with minimal involvement by the state and other collective groupings such as cartels and trade unions, are the best means of allocating resources and ensuring economic growth.	Similar views to liberalism, though with less opposition generally to state involvement.	Production in capitalism is for profit; it ought to be according to people's needs. Workers who produce society's wealth ought to have democratic control over what to produce.	Private enterprise has to be publicly controlled by state regulations; and supplemented by state welfare provision, and, where necessary, by state-run industry.
Social Change	Markets ought to be liberalized if distorted by collective institutions such as the state. Individual initiative should be rewarded and failure penalised.	Continuity is more important than change. Change where necessary ought to be managed by strong leadership.	Radical changes required to achieve the ultimate goal of a classless society in which the oppressive state is no longer necessary. Class struggle by workers and other subordinate groups.	Change ought to be gradual and managed by the democratic state.

Ford machinists equality strike picket, Dagenham, 1984

Picketing the Court — a woman had been murdered by her husband

ACTIVITY 1

From earlier units, the Reader, television programmes or Summer School work, can you think of policies, actions and attitudes in the UK which exemplify the influence of the traditions — on political organizations, social movements and everyday thinking? See how many boxes you can complete in the following grid, which combines social 'levels' with the 'purity scale' discussed above. See if you can include at least one example for each tradition.

(To jog your memory it might help to refer back to the grid for Activity 4 in Unit 17: 2, especially the 'related associations', 'current interests served', and 'impact' columns. In filling in the boxes below, as in Activity 4, don't be afraid to add question marks — examples in this 'slippery' area tend to be debateable rather than clear cut.)

	Examples of a single tradition 'in action'	Examples where elements from two (or more) traditions are combined	Examples of tradition elements in other bodies of thought
Political organizations			
Social movements			
Everyday thinking			

How did you get on? Don't worry if you couldn't cover all four traditions or fill in all the boxes. This unit will give you more examples.

You may have found the 'counter ideology' of marxism more difficult to exemplify than liberalism, conservatism, or social reformism which have served the interests of dominant groups. In the UK marxism has in fact always played second (or third?) fiddle to social reformism, and other forms of what marxists call 'bourgeois ideology', within the trade union and labour movement. In general its influence has been quite marginal. However, it has been significant in brief periods of heightened political and industrial action by workers — e.g. in the decade of 'Red Clydeside' and of solidarity with revolutionary Russia which ended with the defeat of the General Strike in 1926; and in the agitation against unemployment in the 1930s — for instance, republicans inspired by the Irish marxist, James Connolly, managed to forge a short-lived unity between Protestant and Catholic members of the Belfast working class. More recently, in the aftermath of the Paris uprising in May 1968, the biggest General Strike in European history, and with widespread demonstrations against the Vietnam War, thousands of west European students and workers turned to a reinvigorated marxism for political guidance. Marxism has also been influential in *liberation theology* which identifies with the poor, especially in the Third World; while in the UK marxist influences have a long history in

'Right to Work' rally, London, 1970s

some trade unions, the coal miners' union for example. Marxists have on occasion formed the backbone of rank-and-file trade unionism (generally in conflict with a social reformist trade union bureaucracy), and they have played a key role in some anti-racist and anti-fascist campaigns (e.g. the Communist Party members who were in the forefront of the campaign against Moseley's fascists in the 1930s; the Socialist Workers' Party which initiated the Anti-Nazi League against the National Front in the 1970s). But in these situations marxists were generally in alliance with more numerous social reformists. It can be difficult to differentiate specifically marxist ideas from social reformist ones, particularly as the limited objectives of most campaigns don't directly involve the key differentiating question of whether revolution is needed or capitalism can be reformed.

You probably found it easier to exemplify the traditions of liberalism and conservatism because of their longer histories in Britain and their revival in the 1980s in the New Right partnership at government level. With the 'Repeal of the Corn Laws' in 1846, liberal ideas became established as the 'common sense' of nineteenth century Britain (Chapter 22, Section 4), and they have become inscribed at all levels of society, from privatization policies to what Unit 17 referred to as individualist 'I'm all right Jack' attitudes in everyday thinking. Conservative ideas have even earlier roots in UK society and a similarly pervasive influence, exemplified for instance in respect for traditional values and authority, and in recent worries about moral standards, social cohesion, national sovereignty, and the need for 'stewardship' of the environment.

2 PRIVATIZATION IN THE UK

Our case study sketching the rise of the New Right and its privatization policies in the 1980s and early 1990s has several purposes. It should help towards your revision of the *public and private* course theme and Blocks III and IV; it emphasizes the combined influences of liberalism and conservatism on government policy; but it also deals with the social reformist opposition and with criticisms which were made of privatization. These criticisms came from social reformists and marxists and, perhaps more unexpectedly, from within the liberal tradition. The case study thus illustrates the interaction of all four traditions in the political arena and the often 'messy' and contested nature of their influences. It shows how old ideas can regain political dominance in changed circumstances, and that ideological conflicts can only be understood in their historical context.

Putting the ideas and policies in context inevitably means including factual details but the details don't have to be memorized and some are in separate 'boxes' which can be quickly skimmed.

2.1   THE NEW RIGHT VERSUS SOCIAL REFORMISM

Social reformism and the ideas of Keynes and Beveridge were the shared currency of the three main political parties, the Trades Union Congress and much of industry, for a generation in Britain after 1945 (Chapter 22, Section 4). Although there continued to be opposition from economic liberals, social reformism became the dominant political ideology, partly because of the necessity and positive experience of state intervention during the Second World War, and partly because of fears of a return to the mass unemployment and misery of the 1930s and memories of the marxist-influenced workers' movements which followed the First World War. To paraphrase one Conservative Party politician at the time: 'If we don't give them reform, they'll take revolution'.

The dominant view was that the liberal economic policies of the 1930s were a disaster, and John Maynard Keynes' strategy for saving capitalism from itself through government demand management was widely accepted. So were a variety of other types of state intervention, such as the 'welfare state' and regional planning; and the nationalization of some key industries in 1946–9 (Table 2) was one of the most significant responses to the market failures of the private sector evident from the pre-war period (Mohun, 1989, pp.73–4).

The crisis of the 1930s had been generally expected to re-emerge after the war. Instead — from about 1950 to the early 1970s — capitalism enjoyed its longest ever boom, and the tendency to crisis was seen as having been solved by Keynesian policies (at least by Keynesians, for marxists and others disagreed — see Section 2.2, below).

Table 2 Public-private ownership changes, UK 1946–78

To public ownership	To private ownership
1946–49: railways, road haulage, major airlines, coal, gas, electricity and steel industries, and Bank of England.	
	1953: road haulage 1953–63: steel industry 1960: national airline monopoly ended
1967: steel industry re-nationalized 1973: Rolls Royce nationalized	
	1971–73: Thomas Cook travel agency and Carlisle breweries privatized, and some national airline routes granted to a private airline.
1975–78: British Leyland, British National Oil Corporation, British Shipbuilders, British Aerospace, ICL and INMOS in computers, and holdings in 'high tech' companies such as Ferranti, Amersham International, and Cable and Wireless.	
	1977: some British Petroleum shares privatized

However, the long-running problem of the UK's relative decline (see Reader Chapter 1) hadn't been 'solved', reversed or even halted. In 1973 Edward Heath's Conservative Government had to nationalize Rolls Royce, once a 'flagship' of British industry but then a 'lame duck', and after 1974 the Labour Governments of Harold Wilson and James Callaghan carried out the largest nationalization programme since the 1940s, again mostly of internationally uncompetitive enterprises, including shipyards, car plants and computer firms (Table 2). The government had to borrow from the International Monetary Fund (IMF) in 1976 and was forced to cut public expenditure, reduce the money supply and abandon the generally accepted post-war commitment to full employment policies (Unit 12: 4.2). As an IMF-induced 'sacrifice', Labour also decided to sell off some state-owned British Petroleum shares, thus setting a precedent for the privatization policies of Margaret Thatcher's Government after 1979.

The social reformist consensus was undermined by the ending of the post-war boom in the early 1970s. Keynesianism, from getting the credit for boom, now increasingly got the blame for recession, and for the failure to halt decline in the boom years. And (as you saw in Unit 16: 2.2) there were some fears in ruling circles of the state being 'overloaded' by popular demands it couldn't deliver, with a consequent danger of 'ungovernability'. The result was a growing political polarization in the 1970s: Labour's left-wing generally blamed private capital for the decline of industry in Britain, and Keynesian intervention for being too indirect and half-hearted to halt or reverse it; the Conservative Opposition, now led by Margaret Thatcher, argued in contrast that the state interfered too much in the economy and that salvation lay in 'rolling back' its interference.

These then were the basic circumstances in which Britain's New Right emerged as an important political force. It drew heavily on liberalism to develop its arguments (some of which you've seen earlier in the course):

- the state sector is too large and inefficient;
- the private sector is more efficient;
- the state doesn't reward or encourage enterprise and individual initiative;
- it lacks the discipline of market place competition to punish inefficiency;
- it distorts competition and market operations;
- public borrowing 'crowds out' private borrowing;
- taxation to finance state activities reduces private profits, investment and incentive;
- trade unions, encouraged by social reformist policies in the 1960s and 70s, artificially heightened wage levels and supported inflexibilities in the work force;
- state welfare benefits also artificially heighten the minimum wage at which individuals are prepared to work;
- market failures occur but they are less significant than economic failures due to government policy;
- monopoly profits in the private sector are transitory and market competition eliminates them in the long run.

A formidable list — but at a popular level some of the arguments were disarmingly simple: increasing state intervention had caused Britain's decline from greatness in the *laissez-faire* nineteenth century: a return to *laissez-faire* would restore economic success (e.g. Howe, 1978).

ACTIVITY 2

From what you have learnt in previous course work (e.g. Units 11 and 16, TV06), what is your immediate response to each of these points in the 'private versus public' debate? You'll be aware they involve values and assumptions rather than being simply points of 'fact'. If you jot down some responses you can compare them with other arguments later in the unit.

The New Right emphasis on markets and on supply side measures became an international phenomenon in the 1980s (as you saw in Units 11 and 12), but at least in its British version (then dubbed 'Thatcherism') it also drew substantially on conservatism (Unit 16: 2.2). Its rise within the Conservative Party was facilitated by linking free market ideas with a 'more congenial Conservative emphasis on a stronger state in the fields of defence, and law and order, and a strengthened family' (Gamble, 1985, p.139), together with a stress on community, the preservation of national sovereignty, and a reassertion of traditional morals, discipline and respect for authority against what it saw as the 'permissiveness' of 1960s radicalism. For example, Enoch Powell combined economic liberalism with a strongly conservative attitude to sovereignty (TV07). Historically, however, the conservative tradition had condemned liberalism as inflexibly doctrinaire and it was hostile to *laissez-faire*; occasionally there were major disagreements within the New Right (e.g. over national sovereignty and European integration). Yet what Levitas refers to as 'the self-evident contradiction' between a liberal emphasis on 'freedom' and a conservative emphasis on 'authority' did not automatically weaken the New Right —

Delegate to Conservative Party Conference, Blackpool, 1983

indeed she argued that 'given the lack of logical coherence required by common-sense ideologies, contradictions may be a strength rather than a weakness, enabling the New Right to switch the grounds of its legitimations at will' (Levitas, 1986, pp.6, 11). That would be a further reason for expecting ideological inconsistency and 'impurity' with respect to the traditions in the political arena (see Section 1.1, above), but we shall see that the contradictory nature of the New Right helps explain inconsistencies and weaknesses in its privatization policies, and accounts for the liberal criticisms of privatization. Privatization is often seen as a purely liberal policy but some of its objectives were more in line with the conservative tradition.

However the rise and political fortunes of the New Right, as of any ideology, cannot be explained only in terms of its ideas, their consistency or otherwise. After all, the basic ideas were not new and had been around when social reformism was dominant. Circumstances were crucially important, particularly the failures attributable to Keynesianism, a general awareness that 'things had to change', that 'something needed to be done', and, later, the electoral realities of a divided opposition in a 'first past the post system', which enabled the Conservative Party to win large majorities in a further two elections in the 1980s with just over 40 per cent of the vote. But circumstantial opportunities had to be grasped for the New Right to win out over other more left-wing answers to the UK's problems, and old ideas had to be interpreted to fit new circumstances. Here the New Right had an impressive array of research organizations and pressure groups, some already established, some new (Table 3):

Table 3 New Right organizations

Economic League (founded 1919)
Aims of Industry (1942)
Institute of Economic Affairs (1957)
Centre for Policy Studies (1974)
National Association for Freedom (1975)
Adam Smith Institute (1979)
Conservative Philosophy Group (1975) } (produced *Conservative Essays* (1978)
Salisbury Group (1977) } an attack on liberalism's 'freedom')
The Salisbury Review (1982)

Source: Levitas, 1986, pp.3, 4

From the mid-1970s through to the 1990s there was a sustained attack on social reformist ideas and institutions, and a flow of policy proposals which shaped the political agenda, some of them (e.g. the community charge or poll tax) eventually forming part of official government policy. They covered a wide variety of fields, from trade union legislation to local government reorganization, from the operations of broadcasting to privatization as a cornerstone of economic strategy. In 1975 the Centre for Policy Studies, sponsored by Keith Joseph and Margaret Thatcher, asserted that 'state enterprises in the UK have not served well either their customers, or their employees, or the taxpayers. For when the state owns, nobody owns; and when nobody owns, nobody cares' (quoted by Letwin, 1988, p.10).

2.2 FROM PUBLIC TO PRIVATE OWNERSHIP

The UK's privatization programme launched in the 1980s was the world's largest and internationally most influential. Riddell (1989) reviewing 'The Thatcher Decade' concluded that privatization was 'the most striking policy innovation since 1979' — by 1989, 40 per cent of state-owned industries had been sold to the private sector, and by the early 1990s the figure would exceed 60 per cent. In addition to the major industrial privatizations (see Table 4), over one million local authority-owned 'council houses' were sold to their tenants, and (as you saw in TV06) privatization took a number of different forms. These included 'public share offers' through the stock exchange (e.g. British Telecom, British Gas and the Electricity Boards); 'trade sales' to existing private companies (e.g. the Rover Group); 'management and employee buyouts' (e.g. National Freight); the 'contracting out' of public services (e.g. hospital cleaning, the provision of school meals, and refuse collection); and the 'deregulation' of activities to allow private companies to operate services previously confined to the public sector (e.g. the deregulation of bus services in 1986).

Table 4 Major industrial privatization sales, 1981–91

Company	Year(s) of sale
British Aerospace	1981 (and 1985 for remaining shares)
Cable and Wireless	1981, 1983 and 1985
British Sugar Corporation	1982
Amersham International	1982
Britoil	1982 and 1985
National Freight	1982
Associated British Ports	1983 and 1985
Enterprise Oil	1984
British Telecom	1984
Sealink	1984
Inmos	1984
British Gas Wytch Farm	1984
British Gas	1986
British Airways	1987
Rolls Royce	1987
British Airports Authority	1987
British Steel	1988
Water Boards (10)	1989
Electricity Boards (12)	1990
National Power and Power Gen (2)	1991

The proceeds in revenues for the state of all privatization sales totalled over £30 billion by 1991; and in the ten years up to 1989 the number of shareholders in the UK (excluding unit trusts) rose from three million — 7 per cent of the adult population — to nine million — 20 per cent of adults, an impressive increase. 'The overwhelming marketing success of the British Telecom offer, partly through its underpricing, made wider share ownership ... and popular capitalism a central theme of Thatcherism' (Riddell, 1989, p.117).

Most of the running in the 1980s was made by the New Right, but social reformists and marxists made significant critical challenges to privatization, some of which influenced subsequent policy. For instance, they pointed out that the impressive figures for increased share ownership masked its 'thinness': many investors simply make 'a quick killing' on their underpriced shares shortly after privatization (e.g. the 2.3 million BT shareholders had dropped to 1.3 million by 1987); 5.4 million or 56 per cent of the nine million shareholders had shares in just one company; and most holdings were very small — the majority under £2,500, many under £1000 (Riddell, 1989, 119). Similarly with worker shareholdings. Involving employees in company policy making was 'a stealing of the clothes of the left by the right' in the words of one advocate (Letwin, 1988, p.48), but their generally tiny stake gave them no control — National Freight with 80 per cent employee ownership was very exceptional, BT's under 2 per cent much more typical. And 'For all the ministerial talk about popular capitalism, the proportion of UK shares held by individuals ... continued to decline' — to below 25 per cent in 1987 (Riddell, 1989, p.119). In 1988 only 24 per cent of total equity market value was owned by individuals, whereas in 1981 the figure had been 28 per cent and in 1963, 54 per cent; furthermore, there were marked regional variations in share ownership (e.g. South East England 25 per cent of adults, Scotland only 12 per cent) something seen as having electoral consequences in degrees of support for the Conservative Government (Thompson, 1990, p.145).

CONFLICTING OBJECTIVES

Equally telling criticisms were made of the fact that the different objectives of the privatization programme conflicted with one another, and here the critics included liberals (which reflected the contradictory nature of the New Right — see Section 2.1, above). Some supporters of privatization saw potential long-term economic gains being sacrificed for short-term political advantage — the programme was being undermined by 'British empiricism' — pragmatic flexibility in one view, 'muddling through' in another — something which is more in line with the conservative tradition than with liberalism.

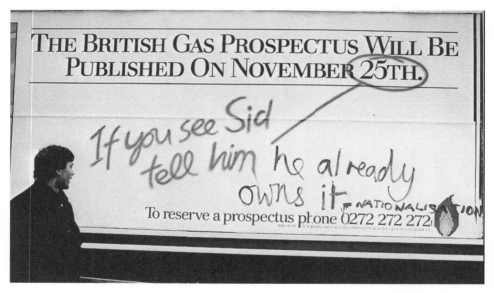

Official and unofficial view of gas privatization

'Popular capitalism' was seen as a neo-conservative policy aimed at increasing social cohesion and loyalty to the established order; providing the state with 'once-off' revenues had the short-term objective of reducing the annual public sector borrowing requirement (e.g. in 1986 revenues from the British Gas sale made up 4 per cent of public expenditure). But in practice both these objectives clashed with the liberal objective of increasing market competition and improving efficiency. Liberals and social reformists argued that the privatization of entire public monopolies, such as British Telecom and British Gas which almost totally dominated their respective markets, was an obstacle to achieving greater efficiency. But, with the 'popular capitalism' objective in mind, BT and British Gas were judged to be much more attractive to individual investors if sold off as single entities, and breaking them up into smaller competitive units before sale would have meant a long delay which conflicted with the short-term objective of providing state revenues. In the event, public monopolies became private monopolies and the Government had to set up regulating bodies (e.g. OFTEL and OFGAS) to police their prices in the absence of effective competition. Criticisms of this led to the electricity industry being sold off as a number of separate companies in 1990–91 (Table 4).

Some critics, including liberals, had concluded that a change from public to private ownership was neither necessary nor sufficient for improving efficiency. They produced empirical evidence to show that privatized enterprises were not necessarily more efficient than those which remained in the public sector; furthermore, that much of the improvement in privatized firms was due to reorganization *prior* to privatization rather than to any new-found disciplines of market competition (Riddell, 1989, pp.93–5). Others saw a contrast between the New Right's ideological commitment to 'deregulation' and the growth of various state regulatory bodies (e.g. OFTEL and OFGAS): 'One of the most remarkable features ... (was) the paradoxical emergence of extensive *re*-regulation of economic activity in a period supposedly typified by drastic *de*-regulation ... the Conservative governments since 1979 ... presided over what can only be characterized as a renaissance of intervention.' (Thompson 1990, p.135). It was a case of the relationship between the public and private being altered, rather than state intervention as such being removed.

While agreeing with these criticisms, marxists interpreted them in terms of class interests; and they widened the debate to analyse the ending of the post-war boom and the subsequent recession, which they saw as having weakened social reformism and allowed privatization onto the political agenda.

Rearmament for the Korean War in the early 1950s and the heavy military expenditure by states during the Cold War were among the explanations for the boom, rather than simply giving Keynesianism the credit. Conversely, Keynesianism wasn't asked to shoulder all the blame when the boom ended. Marxists argued that despite the *laissez-faire* rhetoric of 'Thatcherism' and its U.S. counterpart 'Reaganism', state intervention and Keynesianism were not abandoned in practice; that, for example, it was only massive state funding of the banking system which prevented a 'Wall Street Crash' of 1929 proportions in October 1987; that the economic recovery of the mid-1980s was a triumph for 'John Maynard Reagan' and his 'military Keynesianism'; and that in other countries, including the UK, economic growth was also essentially due to government action stimulating demand (Callinicos, 1989, pp.138–41).

According to marxists, the New Right held together despite these contradictions because both liberalism and conservatism had a shared antipathy to the working class and to the public sector which in the UK was identified with 'socialism' (or more accurately with social reformism). Here the marxist argument was that privatization altered the nature of state intervention to benefit private capitalists and higher level management at the expense of the majority of employees, and one of the initial objectives of privatization had indeed been to weaken public sector trade unionism.

Whether you agree with some of these criticisms or support privatization, there can be no doubt that in the 1980s the New Right succeeded in fundamentally changing the public-private balance of ownership in the UK. So much so that the Labour Opposition retreated from its policy to *re*nationalize the privatized firms (Letwin, 1988, pp.13, 14), partly because of the sheer scale of state revenues which would be required, and partly because of electoral calculations about the extent to which the New Right had succeeded in changing public opinion.

SUMMARY

The case study of privatization exemplified the ideological and political power of liberalism and conservatism while revealing some of the contradictions in their New Right partnership. Criticisms of the policy as implemented came from within the liberal tradition as well as from marxists and social reformists. To understand the often partial and contested influence of the traditions it was necessary to see how they interacted in particular historical circumstances.

3 PUBLIC OPINION AND SOCIAL MOVEMENTS

The issue of New Right influence on public opinion raised the question of whether or not the general population goes along with *dominant ideologies* (Unit 17: 1.7). Some commentators argued that New Right and particularly liberal individualistic ideas had become the new 'common sense' of the 1980s; others that the majority of the population remained wedded to the collectivist social reformist attitudes which had been politically dominant before the rise of the New Right. A detailed attitudes survey in the mid 1980s tended to support the latter view:

> The working class has been relatively immune to the blandishments of free enterprise ... since 75 per cent of our respondents in 1983 favoured government intervention to create jobs, it is rather more likely that there has been a move to the left than to the right ... the bulk of the electorate remains in the centre, favouring some measure of job creation and income redistribution but with ambivalent views towards both nationalization and privatization ...
>
> (Heath, Jowell and Curtice, 1989, pp.299, 300)

The nationalized industries had not been particularly popular (partly because they had been managed on orthodox capitalist lines and were generally seen as unresponsive large bureaucracies, partly because in the 1970s nationalization involved saving some not very attractive 'lame ducks'). But other New Right targets such as the National Health Service retained firm majority support; and a subsequent survey (Jowell, Witherspoon and Brook, 1990) showed increased popular opposition to a range of New Right ideas including the privatization of health care and education.

Public opinion is not 'passively helpless' in the face of politically dominant ideologies. As Unit 17 (Section 1.7) indicated, people may be simply apathetic or alienated from 'elite' ideas, and they are influenced by their own experiences and by broad social movements as well as by political parties and governments. Ideas which dominate in the party political arena do not necessarily dominate at other levels in society.

An unofficial view of water privatization

Influences from all four traditions, together with a variety of other ideas, may co-exist in social movements, as the environmental movement demonstrates (see *Media Booklet* and TV14). It has had a big impact on public opinion, some of its strands relating closely to the traditions while others reject the traditions and the Enlightenment legacy of belief in 'progress'.

We don't have space for case studies of other social movements but we can generalize from the environmental movement in preparation for a 'tradition-spotting' Activity.

SUMMARY

- Broad social movements typically contain different ideological elements some of which are drawn from the traditions.

- The traditions manifest themselves in other bodies of thought propagated by particular movements. The manifestations vary in their 'purity' or the extent to which they are mixed with other ideas.

- The very different values and conceptions of society embodied in the traditions cause tensions and conflicts which sometimes lead to splits and divisions in social movements. Focusing on disagreements within a movement can be fruitful for spotting the influence of different traditions.

- Other bodies of thought have a 'life of their own' and some strands in a social movement may reject the traditions and present themselves as alternative 'world views'.

- The autonomous power of other bodies of thought is seen when they have an impact back on the traditions (e.g. Chapter 22 indicated feminism has had this impact), and when they influence and cross-cut *each other*, again sometimes causing divisions in social movements.

ACTIVITY 3

Remembering the 'tradition-spotter's guide' (Section 1.2), choose some *other* social movements or bodies of thought (such as the peace or anti-racism movements, nationalism, feminism, or a religion), and see if you can come up with examples covering the points in the Summary above.

If you know about Welsh, Scottish or Irish nationalism, they could probably provide all the examples you need. Nationalisms provide an identity which can 'overcome important social differences which might otherwise separate fellow nationals' (Unit 17: 3.1). For conservatives who emphasize the need for social harmony and the nation as an organic entity, nationalism is a powerful way of securing the chief political virtue—allegiance to established authority (Unit 17: 3.2). But 'as with most ideologies, nationalist identities frequently cross-cut one another' (Unit 17: 3.3)—something you saw in TV10. There are white and black British, Catholic and Protestant Irish, working class, middle class and aristocratic Scots, Welsh who speak Welsh and those who don't. The identities of ethnicity, religion, class and language cross-cut and give different meanings to 'the national identity' among people who adhere to 'it', quite apart from the further complications which arise from one national identity being rejected for another (e.g. many Northern Irish Protestants see themselves as British rather than Irish, some West Indians in Britain—there was one in TV04—identify themselves as West Indian rather than British).

At the Falklands victory parade

So it's entirely unsurprising to find that nationalist movements and parties are often riven by contradictory ideologies. Scottish nationalism, for instance, can stoke its fires with memories of battles between feudal barons at Bannockburn (AD1314) and Flodden (1513), or, as Unit 17 suggested, it can draw inspiration from the 'Red Clydesiders' and the working class nationalism of the Scottish marxist John Maclean in his later years. Various 'right/left' divisions have indeed been the rule rather than the exception in contemporary nationalist organizations such as the Scottish National Party, Plaid Cymru and Sinn Fein.

There are marxist, social reformist, and liberal strands in feminist thought, feminists who rely on liberal democratic legislation to end women's oppression and feminists who think a fundamental change in the social structure is necessary. The churches too have internal divisions which may relate to the traditions. For example, some church leaders denounced the New Right's emphasis on individualism and reliance on private charity, for which Margaret Thatcher had claimed a Christian underpinning (see extract from the *Guardian* on page 28).

The Church of England may have been 'the Tory Party at prayer' but during the 1980s some of its leading members were among the strongest critics of Tory policies, and the measures advocated for inner cities in its *Faith in the City* were inspired by social reformist ideas. On the other hand, there were clerics (often conservatives?) who believed the Church should 'stay out of politics' and confine itself to spiritual matters. Marx considered religion 'the opium of the people … the soul of a soulless world'; many liberation theologists draw inspiration from marxism. And they are opposed by other theologians ranging from a conservative Pope (opposed for example to effective birth control for Third World women), to evangelical Protestants (some of whom have an affinity with the New Right).

Religious divisions are often 'politics by other means' (e.g., in Northern Ireland where they have precious little to do with theological matters), and they reflect

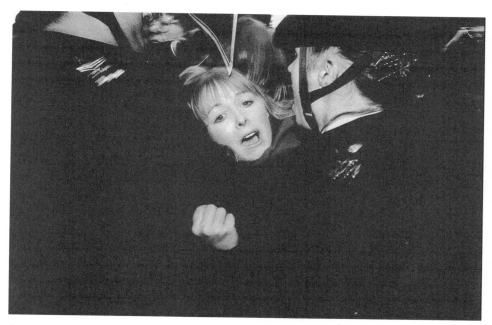

Arrested demonstrating for abortion rights

different political ideologies including the traditions. But religions also pre-date our four traditions (something which is particularly clear in Islamic fundamentalism for Islam is less secularized than western religions) and they clearly have a 'life of their own', capable of independently influencing other bodies of thought. Thus some environmentalists draw inspiration from eastern religions which preach harmony with nature and reverence for all forms of life, which contrasts strongly with western ideas about conquering or 'mastering' nature. Another example of the other bodies of thought cross-cutting each other is the influence of feminism on religion — it was involved in disputes over whether or not there should be women priests.

Deaconess and parishoner after morning service

The battle for the pews

Mrs Thatcher's claim to have a Christian underpinning for her policies has been denounced by the new leader of the Methodists, the church of her childhood. **Walter Schwarz** reports

MARGARET Thatcher was brought up a strict Methodist. Now the Methodists have turned against her. Their new leader, Dr John Vincent, has decided to use his year of office to attempt the strongest religious challenge to Thatcherism since the Anglicans' Faith in the City Report — or at any rate since the Bishop of Durham called Thatcher's policies wicked.

"I reject as un-Christian all taxation and other policies that increase the wealth of those who already have and worsen the poverty of those who have not," Vincent told the Methodist Conference in his inaugural speech on Saturday. "I oppose all policies, such as the poll tax, which victimise any members or groups of society."

Vincent's campaign could hurt. It hits at Mrs Thatcher's consistent claim to a Christian morality of her own, based on individual choice, prosperity, responsibility and charity. Methodists number 450,000 — Britain's largest nonconformist denomination. Many have probably been voting Conservative. Now, by an overwhelming majority, they have elected a turbulent priest as their own leader.

Last year, counterattacking against the Church of England's criticism, Mrs Thatcher delivered her "Sermon on the Mound" before an astonished Church of Scotland Assembly in Mound Street, Edinburgh. She argued:"Christianity is about spiritual redemption, not social reform."

Thatcherite Christianity teaches that individual choice is the key to morality. On Saturday, Vincent retorted: "The new 'choices' of school or medical care or places to live will be made, gladly, by those with power and money — the non-rich will take what's left."

Rejecting Thatcher's private theory — revealed to Woman's Own in 1987 — that "there is no such thing as society, only individuals and their families," Vincent thundered to his flock in Leicester: "The true glory of all our political parties in Britain's recent past is that they have tried to uphold the common good as being of first importance. Current policies are a betrayal of this tradition. They are not, as they claim, Christian tradition, but a perversion of it. They will, I believe, die of shame."

No applause, because Methodists debate in silence.

Vincent's campaign has been long prepared. Even before the Thatcher years he laid claim to be the radical conscience of Methodists as they climbed the ladder of worldly success and began, increasingly, to vote Conservative.

As an antidote, Vincent published a hymn to the tune of the Red Flag:

God's Kingdom's flag is deepest red,
O'er strugglers now and marytyred dead.
Christ calls disciples still today,
Take up my cross, walk in my way.

The hymn was sung at a street-corner fringe meeting at the 1987 Conference, where Vincent was still seen as the over-the-top leader of the Alliance of Radical Methodists. But the tide was moving his way, and the following year's assembly elected him Conference President — the top Methodist job, held for only a year.

Vincent thinks liberation theology is not only for Latin Americans. In Sheffield he runs a permanent study group on the subject — the Urban Theology Unit. Trying to put this into modest practice, his Inner City Ecumenical Mission converts old churches — which he regards as a waste of money and space — into social centres for the underprivileged.

Going further on Saturday, Vincent called for a new use of church buildings as "centres of Christian counter-culture. Our ludicrous, inappropriate, wasteful, pretentious buildings, invariably totally determine what we do." He said the poor should become "the priority, above everything else. in our use of resources."

Naturally Vincent has critics. Some of the Methodists' embattled inner-city workers in the project they call Mission Alongside the Poor think of Vincent as a middle-class windbag.

And the Conservatives among his flock can be as vocal as he is. Yesterday David Wilshire, the Tory MP, said he had reacted "with a huge amount of hurt and a great deal of anger."

Wilshire told BBC radio: "Vincent should try to unite us, not cause offence. He's saying that all you have to do is help the poor and then do what you like. That's as much a caricature of the Gospel as the one he accuses us of."

But Vincent could be speaking for a growing number of Anglicans as well as Nonconformist churchgoers when he insists that Christianity is not, as Thatcherites would have it, about personal morality alone. "Neither is it any business whatsoever of Christian churches to be keeping the people passive and morally well-behaved while all the major questions of their lives are settled by others."

(*Guardian*, 26 June 1989)

4 CONCLUSIONS

The Traditions influence political organizations, social movements and every-day thinking. Their power in the political arena was exemplified by the case study of privatization where we saw that to understand their influences it was necessary to analyse their interactions in their historical context. As ideologies in society the Traditions take a variety of pure and impure or partial forms, often being mixed in with other ideas, and it can sometimes be difficult to identify their influences.

―――――――――――――――――――― ACTIVITY 4 ――――――――――――――――――――

A DIY conclusion:

Activity 1 (in Section 1.2) asked you to identify examples of their influences by drawing on earlier course material. Now on the basis of having studied this unit it would be useful to go back to Activity 1 and see what additions or revisions you think are appropriate.

We chose the four traditions on the basis of their influence as explanatory frameworks for social science, not simply because they are influential in society more generally. So, in Units 28 and 29 we return to our primary concern with the traditions as explanatory frameworks, to see how the frameworks lead social scientists to different answers about the UK and its problems. But at the end of Unit 29 and in Unit 30 we again consider other bodies of thought because they, too, influence social scientists (e.g. feminism influenced the choice of topics in D103) and they may well influence your particular choice of framework.

REFERENCES

Anderson, J. and Ricci, M. (eds) (1990) *Society and Social Science: A Reader*, Milton Keynes, The Open University.

Callinicos, A. (1989) *Against Post-modernism*, Cambridge, Polity Press.

Cliff, T. (1974) *State Capitalism in Russia*, London, Pluto Press.

Gamble, A. (1985) *Britain in Decline*, Basingstoke, Macmillan.

Heath, A., Jowell R. and Curtice J. (1989) 'Ideological change in the electorate', in Anderson, J. and Cochrane, A. (eds.) *A State of Crisis: The changing face of British politics*, London, Hodder and Stoughton.

Howe, G. (1978) 'Liberating free enterprise: a new experiment'. Speech made to the Bow Group, 26 June 1978. (Text from Conservative Central Office, News Service, 856/78.)

Jowell, R., Witherspoon S. and Brook L. (1990) *British Social Attitudes — the Seventh Report*, Aldershot, Gower.

Letwin, O. (1988) *Privatizing the World*: *A study of international privatization in theory and practice*, London, Cassell.

Levitas, R. (ed) (1986) *The Ideology of the New Right*, Cambridge, Polity Press.

Mohun, S. (1989) 'Continuity and change in state economic intervention' in Cochrane, A. and Anderson, J. (eds) *Politics in Transition*, London, Sage.

Riddell, P. (1989) *The Thatcher Decade*: *How Britain has changed during the 1980s*, Oxford, Blackwell

Thompson, G. (1990) *The Political Economy of the the New Right*, London, Pinter.

ACKNOWLEDGEMENTS

Grateful acknowledgement is made to the following sources for permission to reproduce material in this unit:

Text

Schwarz, W. (1989), 'The battle for the pews', *The Guardian*, 26 June 1989.

Tables

Table 3; Levitas, R. (1986), *The Ideology of the New Right*, Basil Blackwell.

Photographs

p.11: Neil Libbert/Network; *p.14*: (top), Maggie Murray/Format, (bottom), Suzanne Roden/Format; *p.16*: Steve Benbow/Network; *p.20*: Pam Isherwood/Format; *p.22*: Joanne O'Brien/Format; *p.24*: Pam Isherwood/Format; *p.26*: Barry Lewis/Network; *p.27*: Paul Lowe/Network; *p.29*: Chris Kell/Network.

UNIT 28   LIBERAL AND CONSERVATIVE APPROACHES

Essays prepared for the Course Team by David Deacon and Owen Hartley.
Introduction and commentary by David Coates

CONTENTS

1 INTRODUCTION

In this unit we want to consolidate your understanding of two of the four traditions of thought used throughout D103, and in Unit 29 to undertake an equivalent exercise on the other two. In Unit 28 we will look at liberalism and conservatism. In Unit 29 we will examine marxism and social reformism. We also want to develop with you an important set of study skills — on ways of comparing and evaluating arguments. In addition, we want to explore ways of putting the traditions to use, and of going beyond them in the pursuit of as refined an understanding of the nature of contemporary UK society as we can manage .

To do all this, we are going to ask you in a moment to look in detail at four position statements which we commissioned from four experienced social scientists. The four were chosen because each had come to the view that just one of the traditions of thought used in D103 provided most of the concepts, theories and values positions required to make sense of the contemporary world. One is a committed liberal (as we have defined liberalism in Chapter 22 of the Reader), one is a committed conservative, one a marxist, one a social reformist. As it happens, all four are also committed teachers with OU tutoring experience — and for that reason would normally be just as effective in laying out positions with which they disagreed as they are here as advocates of just one tradition of thought. But we asked them on this occasion not to lay out other positions with equal rigour. We asked them instead to develop a position statement — to demonstrate for us how a committed liberal, conservative, marxist or social reformist might go about analysing the UK and its contemporary problems.

The exercise we set them — the results of which we are now asking you to consider — was not an easy one; and each of our authors would have been happier if the constraints under which they operated could have been more generous. But because of limits of time and space, we had to set them a tight word limit, and ask them to restrict their argument to a consideration of just four questions. Given a freer hand, they might have chosen to organize what they had to say around slightly different questions. They would undoubtedly have wanted to put in much more supporting evidence than space allowed here. They would certainly have written at greater length; and they might well have qualified and refined the assertions to which they were driven by our insistence on brevity and terseness. But nonetheless what they have produced are four fascinating personal statements on the nature of the contemporary UK, organized as a set of answers to four questions: namely

1 What are the main problems of contemporary UK society?

2 What are their main historical and contemporary causes?

3 What should be done about the problems and by whom? and

4 What is it about your tradition which predisposes you to highlight these particular problems, causes and solutions?

We now want *you* to do a number of things with these four essays. Obviously the main thing we will ask you to do is to read them. But we also want you to:

• relate them back to the traditions from which they come;

• pick out from each essay the main arguments being used;

• compare those arguments; and

• evaluate their relative strengths and weaknesses.

In the process of doing all this, we hope to consolidate with you what may already by now be your normal way of handling the material with which you are asked to deal: a way which enables you to make that material your own through a process of study built around:

- the careful extraction of key arguments
- the summarizing of key positions
- the location of key differences; and
- the evaluation of key assertions.

To *extract*, *summarize*, *compare* and *evaluate* material takes time, and is hard. But if the material on which you are working is as central to the course you are taking as this material is, it is always worth doing — and doing as well as you can. So let's do it together now.

2 LIBERALISM

Let's begin with 'A Liberal approach to the UK' by David Deacon.

──────────── ACTIVITY 1 ────────────

Read the essay through quickly once, and then go through it more slowly, marking what you think are its key words and arguments.

A LIBERAL APPROACH TO THE UK
by David Deacon

INTRODUCTION

In the 1970s and 80s there was a resurgence of liberal ideas which made it respectable again for academics to be liberals. For many, like me, this was a relief after a long period of domination by the 'superstitions' generated by Marx and Freud: 'superstition' that is in Hayek's sense of people believing they know and understand more than they actually do (F. Hayek, 1979, p.176). But the liberal position has to be held against the embrace of conservatism and the simplistic critique of socialists. The aim of liberalism remains what Adam Smith called the 'Great Society', a spontaneously generated social order permitting and encouraging the highest degree of personal freedom and individual development.

Some in the New Right have claimed a kinship between conservatism and liberalism based on a shared interest in such things as the rule of law and a common hostility to socialism, but the conservative's overstated respect for tradition and commitment to a fixed morality, both stifling to individual freedom and development, continues to divide them. Thus, the New Right Thatcher Government of the 1980s was among the loudest proponents of the market and its virtues but their advocacy has been 'divorced from a wider commitment to personal freedom' (S. Brittan, 1988, p.215), if only because the goal of the conservative is order rather than freedom.

The socialist claim that liberalism means 'individualism in the sense of everybody for himself' (F. Hayek, 1976, p.151) is a mirror image of the conservative's misuse of the market approach, rooted in the idea that conscious human action and organization offer

F.A. Hayek, born 1899, Nobel
prize for Economics 1974

the best approach to problems. This 'superstition', based on contrasting an ideal but not actually existing socialist state with a real market system such as the UK's, understates the contribution of the free market in goods and ideas and ignores the failure of socialist experiments in the twentieth century such as that in the USSR. Socialism refuses to draw the appropriate conclusions from the consequences of creating social and political organizations which develop interests and purposes of their own, open to manipulation by sectional interests and inimical to personal freedom.

Socialism and conservatism share a narrow economic view of the market. They lack interest in that personal freedom which liberalism has at its core and which makes the market merely an instrument of its objectives. They lack the liberal's sensitivity to the dangers of political power.

WHAT ARE THE MAIN PROBLEMS OF CONTEMPORARY UK SOCIETY?

In at least one respect a liberal view of social 'problems' is quite distinctive. It questions whether it is useful to talk of 'society' at all. According to Hume 'A nation is nothing but a collection of individuals' (S. Brittan, 1988, p.316), and to my mind the twentieth century inclination to collectivist thinking creates the danger contemporary liberal Robert Nozick alerted us to when he argued that talk of 'society' and the 'social good' merely provides excuses to use one person for the benefit of another (R. Nozick, 1974). Other perspectives treat society as a real and living entity, but a liberal should only use the term if recognizing it as a wholly artificial conception. Claims for this or that organization (such as the state), to 'represent' society or express its will, go beyond what is meaningful and endanger individual freedom.

For the liberal, many 'social problems' are purely individual matters for which there cannot or should not be collective solutions. Some 'problems' are neither 'problems' nor susceptible to solution. There is an argument for a degree of redistribution to prevent absolute want and misery, but the presentation of inequality and unhappiness as 'social problems' which the state can solve is an inflation of rhetoric and of the state's role. These intensify the problem rather than produce solutions. Economic inequality is a necessary result of a market system and an incentive in its operation. It can be eliminated only at vastly disproportionate cost in' growth and progress and then replaces economic differences with power inequalities and oppression. Many 'social problems' are the result of 'solutions' from the past. Thus minimum wage legislation produces unemployment among youths by pricing them out of work; rent control worsens 'housing problems'; 'solutions' to racial problems limit options and create dependencies for minorities.

In considering the problems of the contemporary United Kingdom, then, I shall focus most particularly on the operation of the order as a whole and on ways which limit its capacity to free individuals to develop their own lives and solutions, both singly and in spontaneous association with other individuals; in short the factors frustrating the development of the 'Great Society'.

Given the liberal's stress on the importance of the private sphere and market solutions, the development of a massive state in the twentieth century constitutes a major problem. For the liberal, government should be restricted to the enforcement of the minimum of rules needed for individuals to go freely and safely about their business, plus a minimum provision for the least fortunate. Hayek has likened this function to the maintenance squad in a factory, helping to keep the plant going but not part of the production process itself (F. Hayek, 1973, p.57). Unfortunately the state has taken over vast sections of production, 'crowding out' and discouraging, or even forbidding, private activity, 'weakening the autonomous institutions of civil society' (J. Gray, 1989, p.10). The state continues, despite attempts at reform in the 1980s, to take too large a share of the GNP for itself, to intervene in far too many aspects of individual life, and to impose heavy burdens of taxation to support itself.

Despite talk of 'rolling back the state' it has not gone far, and in some areas the state has actually advanced. For the liberal, an individual's viewing or reading habits, or sexual proclivities, are an entirely private affair, and the 'nanny state' is as offensive when regulating these activities as censorship of plays or books was in an earlier age. Freedom of speech has been restricted by the state both in its concern in the 1960s and 1970s with attitudes to race and gender, and in the 1980s with excessive concern with state secrets and intolerance of criticism. Paternalistic concerns with health have led to increasing pressure on personal habits such as drinking, smoking and eating. A resurgence of religious power (both Christian and non-Christian), has further constricted what the individual can say or do.

Liberalism means tolerating things I might not favour myself: I don't wish to live in a tepee, but freedom was diminished when a 'hippy' tepee village in west Wales was crushed out of existence by bossy local and central bureaucracy. I don't wish to listen to non-stop pop, but oppose a decision by the Home Secretary that all radio stations must carry news bulletins because people 'ought to know what is going on'.

The behaviour of the state would be less of a problem if it did not appear to reflect the attitudes of wide sections of the people for whom a sort of 'dependency culture' has become second nature. People look first to the state rather than endeavouring to find solutions themselves, individually or in association with other free individuals. Although Thatcherism has produced some marginal shift in opinion among the young, the overwhelming mass of people still support state institutions which frustrate the purposes for which they ostensibly exist. The National Health Service provides a clear example of a massive bureaucracy which has failed to perform adequately, treated its customers patronisingly, and consistently shown itself unable to generate adequate resources. Yet efforts to supplement it with private funding and provisions and make it more responsive to customers have met bureaucratic obstruction which finds ready response in a public for whom it has become a shibboleth and who appear willing to endure its inadequacies rather than contemplate their own alternative provision. Public squalor is preferred to private affluence. A poor standard for all is seen as natural in preference to the concentration of limited public resources on the really needy. Individual responsibility is curiously lacking — people who will happily make vast expenditures on their own houses are persuaded that their bodies are someone else's concern. Charities and spontaneous voluntary efforts find limited support as genuine alternatives to the state.

Mass attitudes are underpinned by the limited penetration of liberal ideas among elites. Large sections of the professional and intellectual establishment cling to the ideas of the interventionist and paternalistic state. Higher education and the media remain dominated by opponents of liberalism as do the churches, in what can be described as a modern 'treason of the intellectuals' (J. Benda, 1969). The treason lies not in the commitment to a particular set of ideas, but rather the presentation of these ideas as *the* expression of the public good, when in fact they serve to protect pockets of comfortable conservatism and privilege. Doctors resist the reform of health provision, lawyers of the legal system, and broadcasters of the media, educators of education. In each case a paternalistic and self-serving bureaucracy resists change which might undermine its privileges and open up the organization to consumer pressures and demands; and it does so in the name of the very public whose interests it actually damages. The same sort of activity is to be found in the state bureaucracy itself: the frustration by DES bureaucrats of proposals for a voucher system for schools in the early 1980s is a striking example.

Continued high levels of state intervention, public acceptance of them, and elite efforts to sustain and even increase them, all serve to highlight the biggest problem of all — the failure of attempts to reform these conditions. In the 1980s the New Right Thatcher Government presented itself, and was presented by its enemies, as seeking precisely to change these conditions. That there was some success is undeniable, but it was marginal. The state was not significantly 'rolled back'. Where changes were made they were often either cosmetic, or they took a form which had little value, such as the privatization of state industries in ways which merely transformed public into private monopolies and limited the potential for competition.

In *The Free Economy and the Strong State* (1988), Andrew Gamble has written of the failure of the Thatcherite 'hegemonic project', by which he means the inability of the Thatcher Government to gain widespread acceptance of its ideas, and the evidence does suggest that the thinking of most people was left unchanged. Liberal values are not popular, and thus what change had been made is isolated and vulnerable. The entrenched interests suffered little reduction in their power and continued to exert great influence on government and its policies. Which explains some of the other failures. Finally reform failed, or was not even attempted except in cosmetic form, in government itself. Rather than reducing and limiting the government machine, the Thatcher administration made it more powerful and centralized in many ways, undermining lower levels of government, nearer to the people, and producing a more bossy and interfering state.

The contemporary UK is less conducive to freedom and diversity than ever, the condition seems to cause little concern, and claimed attempts to change the situation have failed and even made the situation worse. The liberal argument is not that economic growth and employment are unimportant, but that they will be greater in the long term under a free market. The defeat and frustration of liberalism in the ways identified here is also the defeat of that sort of progress.

WHAT ARE THEIR MAIN HISTORICAL AND CONTEMPORARY CAUSES?

It will be evident that the approach to the identification of the problems of contemporary Britain adopted here also reflects very considerably on their causes. We can now turn to these more directly.

The social order of western liberal democracies is that most conducive to the maintenance of the personal freedom which liberals value, but liberals do not imagine that these systems are the product of human planning or inevitable natural development, or

Adam Smith 1723–90,
creator of the liberal vision
of the 'Great Society'

that they are bound to endure and progress. The arrangements and ideas which developed in Britain in the seventeenth and eighteenth centuries — liberal values, a rule of law and a developing economic market system which balanced and checked political power — were a serendipity — a happy accident — in that the complex combination of circumstances involved was unplanned and unusual (perhaps unique). That the elements of these arrangements were adopted and further developed by others does not alter their unplanned or fragile nature.

By the same token the creation of or survival of anything approaching the liberal Great Society is a very fragile, vulnerable plant. The freedom of ideas, dependency on the market as the primary mechanism for economic decisions and communications, and the limitation of the role of government to a limited range of functions, are principles which have been spontaneously developed but which are vulnerable to interference particularly from those who fail to understand the nature of the system.

One set of ideas which grew out of liberalism stressed the idea of society as an artefact which, if not made by men, could be remade and perfected by them according to some plan which rested on the ability to know and understand and thus re-order the social whole. This false confidence was boosted by a link with democracy, with the latter seen not merely as an expression of individual freedom and choice but as an establishment of unlimited power and will. In this way, the power of government is not seen as subject to the rule of law and concerned with the performance of a limited range of functions but as the unlimited power of a sovereign legislature which because it claims to speak in the voice of the people is able to use power in whatever way and for whatever ends it wishes. Thus one strand of liberalism led to a socialist aspiration to reconstruct society and an unlimited government. In the twentieth century this produced the collectivist interventionist state which threatened individual freedom. In part it did so through the false mechanism of redefining freedom or liberty. The liberal values of individuals choosing and pursuing their own course of development and involving freedom of speech or assembly were identified as 'negative liberties', which were seen as somewhat limited values and needing supplementing by 'positive' liberties such as the right to work, or to health care. The combination of this notion with unlimited mass democracy produced a situation which threatened the very existence of a liberal order.

It is the influence of these socialist and social reformist ideas which plays a considerable part in shaping the contemporary United Kingdom and produces the highly interventionist state which we know. The recent tide of liberal ideas might be expected to influence developments in the other direction and in ways indicated by talk of 'rolling back the state', and to indicate the importance of what Burton has called 'intellectual entrepreneurs' (J. Burton, 1989, p.7). That this has happened to such a limited degree means we have to be aware of other forces at work.

While some contemporary liberals have seemed to place almost all the stress on ideas — others have given interests much more prominence and seen them as both a central driving force in modern society, and the cause of most of the problems (J. Buchanan, 1989). According to this view, special interests exploit the idea of unlimited government power, and democratic willingness to extend government activity and make laws applying to and penalizing or benefiting this or that group. In this view, interests manipulate unlimited government power to their own benefit and at the expense of the mass of individuals or particular sections of them. In this game the institutional bureaucracies participate:

> Reforms that enlarge options and allow the individual to decide are a great threat to a wide variety of special interests. Social workers become superfluous if the government 'just gives money' to the poor. Public schoolteachers and administrators are endangered by voucher systems which allow parents and children their choice of where to attend school. Moral crusaders would lose the power to shape other people's lives according to 'higher' principles.
>
> (T. Sowell, 1975, p.225)

Sowell's remarks provide clues as to the contemporary causes of the problems and particularly the failures of social reformism. In the first place the argument that ideas rule is seen to be modified by the role of interests. We may speak, with John Burton, of 'the dilemma of ideas blocked by interests' (J. Burton, 1988, p.9). It is not enough for liberal ideas to play an important part in the thinking of those enjoying political power if they are faced by entrenched interests resistant to liberal reforms. This is precisely what we observed when noting the failure to roll back the state, to expand the role of the market, and to change elite attitudes. Without these, the capacity to enlarge public attitudes is much reduced if only because what is delivered falls disappointingly short of what was promised. Indeed failures, reduced efficiencies and economic difficulties will serve to provide arguments for more government action not less. Distortions caused by one set of failed social policies will provide the basis for more, not less, of the same. The highly conservative mechanism which develops proves remarkably resistant to change, particularly change which threatens its interests. The long term result of this process has been analysed by Olson in his *The Rise and Decline of Nations* (1982), where he shows how entrenched interests (what he calls 'distributional coalitions' such as doctors, lawyers, teachers etc. in Britain), reduce national efficiency and capacity to respond to change in a way which reduces economic growth and prosperity. I find this argument useful in throwing light on Britain's economic decline over the last century and particularly since the Second World War.

It is insufficient, however, to place all the stress on the frustration of liberal ideas by interests. It is important also to recognize the problems raised by the fact that where liberal ideas have been implemented in Britain in recent years this has generally been by those whose commitment to them is at best partial. Thus in explaining the failure to cut the state's share of the GNP significantly, or to produce a genuinely competitive privatization scheme for telephones or electricity, we have to understand both the compromise with institutional forces opposed to such developments, and the lack of conviction and full commitment to the market of those pursuing the policies.

Sowell's remarks about 'moral crusaders' serve to remind us how often those who use the rhetoric of the market are old fashioned conservatives in their social and moral outlook: their narrow endorsement of the market accompanies a moral and social paternalism which is restrictive of liberal ideas of freedom, and probably not conducive to genuine involvement of the mass of people in acceptance of liberal values. In the final analysis politicians of this stripe, dominant in Thatcherism, baulked at the creation of a fully liberal and market system — in the media for example.

Most of these comments concern the lack of defence of a genuinely liberal society and its foundations. It is also of value to look at the general strategy of those who have claimed, or been claimed, to be seeking a more liberal UK. In the 1980s the Thatcher Government may have been judged to have made considerable if flawed progress in implementing liberal inspired reforms. Its strategy for dealing with interests, however, took the form of legislation which dealt with distinct policy areas and operated a bit-by-bit system of reform, as with trade unions, or a compromise or buy-out of interests, as with managers in many privatized sectors. The results were not only the imperfect implementation of what were anyway rather vague long-term objectives, but also the possibility that really fundamental changes and the entrenchment of changes was overlooked. It can be argued that this approach exploited effectively the 'unlimited' power of the parliamentary system, and the limited checks on the use of that power by a majority government, but by the same token the changes were left open to reversal by a successor majority, or even by chance developments. Thus the reduction of trade union power, undertaken without establishing an enduring system of individual rights or an entrenched limitation of that power, is highly vulnerable to the effects of the 'demographic time bomb' set to explode in the 1990s when the size of the labour force declines. One cause of the problems of the contemporary UK then may be seen as the failure to take the opportunity for fundamental and enduring changes when this seemed to arise in the 1980s, or perhaps even to prepare for that opportunity. It is said that one Senior Tory minister, Keith Joseph, was still looking for liberal economic advisers a year after the 1979 election, underlining the absence in Britain of a genuinely liberal party and the limited reach of liberal ideas.

WHAT SHOULD BE DONE ABOUT THE PROBLEMS AND BY WHOM?

The depth and severity of the problems identified, the fact that their causes are generalized rather than specific, and that previous attempts at reform have made little progress, means that finding solutions is no easy task. At best the work has to be done at a number of levels, notably policies, organizations and ideas.

With respect to policies Patrick Minford offers the liberal a useful starting point:

1   All services should be privately provided.
2   The help should be given in the form of vouchers.
3   The vouchers should discriminate as little as possible against 'natural' sources of help (i.e. the family in most cases)' (P. Minford, 1987, p.80).

I don't suggest we should follow Minford's prescription unquestioningly but do support the presumption that we should be in favour of private provision where possible. The state should be a 'last resort' provider.

If state power and its openness to distortion by interests are to be minimized, its role as provider has to be diminished. Only a few services are insusceptible to the injection of private provision. Opposition to it is largely a mixture of tradition and sheer prejudice such as the assumption that the pursuit of profit is automatically corrupting rather than a useful test of efficiency and a stimulant to sensitivity to consumers. Of course where the state is paying it does not mean that it must also operate a service.

The use of vouchers should not become a fetish but it can be of value in ensuring that expenditure is on the good for which it is designed, e.g. education, while still placing the

Patrick Minford, Professor of Applied Economics at the University of Liverpool

final selection in the hands of the consumer. Ideally support should be in cash and not in kind, and vouchers are a half-way to the more desirable arrangement where payment is strictly in cash and individuals make choices entirely on their own account but, with a proper education in sturdy independence, do so in ways neither feckless nor self-disregarding.

Such changes, possible in many or most present state services, would massively reduce the size of government and bureaucracy. Concentrating support on those genuinely in need would help shape a system in which reduced taxation encouraged the mass of individuals to seek their own solutions to their needs.

Such arrangements do not imply a lack of a safety net though insurance might help to remove whole groups from those likely to need one. Nor do they deny a role for the state at an early stage. Changes cannot be made overnight, though they can be made with more vigour and commitment than was the case under the Thatcher Government in the 1980s. What the state can do is stimulate and 'pump-prime' the development of voluntary groupings to undertake functions. For example, the subsidy of health insurance tax relief for a period during which the habit spreads may exceptionally be justified. So may the creation or cooperation with and floating of bodies to undertake the provision of services. On the other hand it is clear that house ownership is so wide-spread and engrained a life style that continued tax subsidies to housebuyers are neither necessary nor justified, and their removal could cut prices and help the less well-off.

In a different sphere, government policy should be to permit the free generation and dissemination of ideas on all but a minimum of state affairs, with the very minimum of regulation of the media. The system of censorship and pursuit of organizational stability should be abandoned. In the same way, individual behaviour should cease to be the concern of the state except for the most pressing reasons of public safety.

Such a programme has the air of utopian rhetoric, and so it would be if it was proposed merely at the policy level. While there have been failures of boldness and opportunity with respect of policy it is not there that the problem really lies. Critical to different policy is the question of organizations. Interests will probably continue inexorably to seek to pervert public organizations to their own purposes, changes in ideas notwithstanding. That is why the liberal wants to strip government of superfluous functions: small government presents less of a target for interests: the less it does, the less that action can be distorted. Reduced size is not, however, the whole answer.

The only sure way to limit the susceptibility of government to exploitation and distortion by interests (including its own bureaucracy), is to confine it within clear legal mechanisms. This means the adoption of a binding written constitution, a bill of rights establishing fundamental rights, and clear limitations of expenditure and legislation. Only by removing the temptation will interests be controlled and an atmosphere conducive to a long-run change in public attitudes be established (Hayek and Buchanan are examples of liberals who have constructed powerful arguments on these lines).

Such mechanisms are more familiar to the American than to the British political system, but they are not necessarily the worse for that. Britain's accession to the European Community both involves effective acceptance of the principle of limitation of Parliament's power and the shift towards new and more legalistic arrangements. The debate on a Bill of Rights has been going on for a long time. When expressed by Hayek these ideas have been called utopian but the need and the example is there. Utopian may simply mean difficult to get implemented, not impossible. Certainly these ideas would suggest a change in strategy on the part of those seeking liberal reforms: the Thatcher Government sought them through policy changes which were potentially merely temporary, the only adequate solution is through organizational and constitutional changes which are deeply entrenched. These changes might be accompanied by reforms in British government which ensured the separation of the bulk of the state bureaucracy into agencies which implemented policy and were distinct from the small policy-making bodies in which a small number of professional bureaucrats were supplemented and balanced by political advisers supporting politicians and with a greater chance of pushing through policy reforms. More decentralization of power to lower levels of government and community bodies would also be desirable.

At bottom the solution to the UK's problems is to be found in a change of ideas, in a long term generation and dissemination of liberal ideas not by politicians but by 'intellectual entrepreneurs' at all levels. Britain has been relatively poor in 'think tanks', but the Institute of Economic Affairs, the Adam Smith Institute and the Centre for Policy Studies have made an important and growing contribution. There is a dearth of 'popularizers' like Milton Friedman in the USA. The force of circumstance — such as the consequences of relative decline and inefficiency — may make the audience more receptive (the changes in the USSR under Gorbachev provide an interesting instance here). The closed circle of British thinking will soon be opened up and disrupted by technological and commercial developments which lead to uncontrolled media coverage: globalization can have its benefits. Solutions will be found in the long term, first in thought and its dissemination and only finally in political action. Entrenchment of changes will give more time for experience of and acceptance of changes but only with widespread acceptance will a liberal Great Society be built.

Samuel Brittan has claimed that the European Community provides that rule-based political order where the battle for liberalism can best be fought. This attractive idea overlooks the extent to which it is beset and colonized by interests, and, stimulated by the ideas of social reformism, in the business of petty intervention and restriction of individual freedom. Ultimately the problems identified may have to be fought out at that level — must to some extent be so now — but immediately the task is to create a liberal Britain.

WHAT IS IT ABOUT THE LIBERAL TRADITION WHICH PREDISPOSES YOU TO HIGHLIGHT THESE PARTICULAR PROBLEMS, CAUSES AND SOLUTIONS?

The answer to this question cannot be divorced from why the liberal position is adopted at all. This decision rests firmly on values and leads to the conclusion that liberalism is a form of ideology among others; but it is not necessarily the worse for that, once it is recognized that this places it in no weaker a position than its opponents (including marxism), and that it has claims to be more universalizable, and to have a wide appeal based on experience and its own internal logic which should serve to make it attractive.

Liberalism begins with a concern for the individual identified with 'negative liberties' (the freedom from state constraints on action), such as freedom of speech, thought and personal behaviour. The term 'negative' has been coined somewhat misleadingly to imply that there are additional, perhaps even superior, 'positive' liberties concerned with social 'rights' (state guaranteed jobs, housing, medical care etc.). This terminology is misleading in two ways. First, because it might be argued that while a certain level of enjoyment of 'positive' liberties may be desirable in order to permit proper enjoyment of negative liberties they are by no means identical or equal in kind. A full belly is no more a substitute for freedom of speech than freedom to say what one wishes is sufficient when one is starving to death. The relationship is perhaps hierarchical: history suggests the well-fed slave or, until recently, the Soviet dissident is likely to wish for the negative freedoms to complete his life and to be satisfied with nothing less. This may serve to justify the guarantee of a certain minimum alleviation of material deprivation but will not admit of placing material needs at such a premium that they are attained at the cost of negative liberties.

Second, behind an emphasis on positive liberties frequently lurks the substitution of a general set of alternative values such as 'equality' or 'social justice'. Clearly there is nothing wrong with arguing for alternative values, but the talk of 'positive liberties' creates a very misleading linguistic confusion. Thus equality is a quite different quality from what the liberal means by liberty, and it is possible that it can only be bought at the cost of liberty i.e. the two are incompatible, not different sides of the same coin as some would have us believe. For this reason the term 'liberty' is best restricted to those liberal virtues known as 'negative' liberties.

The pursuit of a Great Society in which individual freedom and development is maximized brings us quickly to the role of the market. For the liberal the market is what experience has shown us, developed through fortunate accident, to be the most universally applicable mechanism for the peaceful reconciliation of divergent purposes: the system which permits people to live together peacefully without uniformity of ideas or outlook. It has the advantage that it is highly conducive to the creation of wealth, whose distribution may necessarily be unequal but which tends over time to have the general effect of lifting the level of prosperity of all. Marx's immiseration of the proletariat under capitalism has simply not emerged.

The market has a number of distinct strengths for the liberal. In the first place, it substitutes for government action based on the idea of a conscious construction of society and its future such as offered by marxism. The experience of the twentieth century has so discredited this idea that it is only the astonishing capacity of human beings for self-delusion, and the blind inexorable faith of some in the power of human reason, that keeps such ideas alive. What the liberal observes is that such action is necessarily arbitrary in its action, replacing the rule of law with a more subjective concern for a particular willed outcome at whatever cost. And the cost is generally in terms of human liberty. Equality, or something approaching it, can only be attained, by creating a machinery which makes the condition of individuals more similar by restricting their opportunities and actions — at the cost of the individuals particularly concerned and of all others who suffer from the resulting less efficient and less creative society — one in which political power replaces property as the root of a more dangerous inequality. No wonder that Keynes argues (in his underlying liberal rather than his more widely publicized social reformist vein): 'It is better that a man should tyrannise over his bank balance than over his fellow citizens; and while the former is sometimes denounced as being but a means to the latter, sometimes at least it is an alternative' (J.M. Keynes, 1936, p.188).

The foundation of private property underlying a market system provides a bulwark against an overblown state, and its functions reduce the need for the expansion of that state. The pursuit of 'equality' or 'social justice' on the other hand leads to socialism and totalitarianism in one form or another: there is no real room for middle ground. Nor does the recognition of the need for a level of minimum provision indicate the acceptance of an argument for social justice. The pragmatic acceptance of a minimum provision where carefully justified serves merely to assist the widest degree of involvement in the market rather than to supplant it.

It has to be emphasized that the market is not simply an economic instrument. This is true both because the market is a synonym for a free competition in ideas and life-styles as well as commodities, but also because seeing it in terms of economic ends is misleading. Economic activities are means to ends rather than ends in themselves and people are in the market place as part of their desire to serve purposes which are ultimately non-economic. Critics stress 'profit', one aspect of the market, but neglect the fact that all participants contribute and extract, and that the neutral and rule-directed market permits each individual to think their own thoughts and use the market for their own purposes, without accepting the ideas or styles of others with whom they deal, or because of differences having to avoid them. It is not surprising that in contrast Hayek has pictured socialism as an atavism involving a return to 'tribalism', the desire to impose a uniformity of outlook and behaviour on the diversity that the market makes possible (F. Hayek, 1976, p.14), or that Ortega y Gasset has identified liberalism as: 'the supreme form of generosity' (J. Ortega y Gasset, 1923, p.83).

Hall has argued that in a sense people can choose between ideologies because there are common human qualities which mean that, for example: 'except in extraordinary cases, people who are starved or beaten know that they are suffering' (J. Hall, 1988, p.188) and because we are now part of a world order in which isolation of ideologies is no longer possible. The first helps to explain the survival of libertarian instincts in the darkest days of communist totalitarianism, and the latter the stimulus to their resurgence when suppression of market, diversity, and liberty produced economic stagnation and decline. With this in mind the liberal will necessarily be optimistic for the long-term prospects of the United Kingdom and perhaps believe as I do that the imaginary individual posited by the philosopher John Rawls as choosing a society without knowing in advance what position he would occupy in it would surely incline to a liberal market order.

REFERENCES

Benda, J. (1969) *The Treason of the Intellectuals*.

Brittan, S. (1988) *A Restatement of Economic Liberalism*.

Buchanan, J. (1986) *Liberty, Market and State: Political Economy in the 1980s*.

Burton, J. (1989) *Reaganomics, Thatcherism and Classical Liberalism*.

Gamble, A. (1988) *The Free Economy and the Strong State*.

Gray, J. (1989) *Limited Government: A Positive Agenda*.

Hall, J. (1988) *Liberalism: Politics, Ideology and the Market*.

Hayek, F.A. *Law, Legislation and Liberty* — (1973) Volume I: Rules and Order; (1976) Volume II: The Mirage of Social Justice; (1979) Volume III: The Political Order of a Free People.

Keynes, J.M. (1936) *The General Theory of Employment, Interest and Money*.

Minford, P. (1987) 'The Role of Social Services: A view from the New Right' in M. Loney: *The State and the Market* (1987).

Nozick, R. (1974) *Anarchy, State and Utopia*.

Ortega y Gasset, J. (1923) *The Revolt of the Masses*.

Rawls, J. (1972) *A Theory of Justice*.

Sowell, T. (1975) *Race and Economics*.

---------------------------------- ACTIVITY 2 ----------------------------------

Make a copy of the matrix printed below on a separate sheet of paper. It will probably be worth while drawing the boxes larger than shown here, so that you can get in as much information as possible. We shall be using this matrix again when we discuss each of the three other essays, so you might want to make three extra copies now, substituting 'conservatism', 'marxism' and 'social reformism' for 'liberalism' at the top.

I have inserted in brief the Four Questions in column 1. In the boxes in column 2, I want you to insert the key words and arguments which the author has used to answer each of the questions. Let's see how you get on.

Liberalism on:	
1 Main UK problems	
2 Main causes of problems	
3 Main solutions	
4 Strengths of tradition	

There are always questions of judgement in this. What you put and what I suggest will not necessarily be exactly the same. But I hope that the general tenor of my suggestions matches yours; if it doesn't, it will be worth while going back through the essay to see the points I suggest and that you have missed.

My suggestions are as follows:

On question 1:

- misunderstanding of the nature of society;
- inflated role of the state, crowding out private activity, interfering in private affairs, inflicting heavy tax burden;
- too much looking to the state for help, 'public squalor preferred to private affluence', especially in elite circles;
- weakness of Thatcherite liberalism.

On Question 2:

- caused by state 'solutions' in the past i.e. 'continued high levels of state intervention, public acceptance of them, and elite efforts to increase and even sustain them';
- previous liberal phase unplanned and fragile. One strand of liberal thought led to socialism;
- role of special interests ('distributional coalitions'). Persistence of conservative, paternalistic attitudes even in liberal politicians.

On question 3:

- new policies — to increase private provision and reduce role and size of the state. To leave just a safety net. State to encourage replacement of its superfluous functions by voluntary organizations, and to let ideas flourish uncensored;
- bill of rights to stop state encroachments. Break up of central state bureaucracies;
- spread of liberal ideas.

On question 4

- central concern with individual freedom and development;
- strength of market and private property as guarantors of freedom.

When your matrix on liberalism is complete, there are only two other things that for the moment you need to do. One is to do some reading, the other is to tackle an Activity.

═══════════════════ READER ═══════════════════

The reading I want you to do is to go quickly through the liberalism section in Chapter 22 of the Reader — to see if there are any points that you might want to add if you were making a matrix that was more representatively liberal than David Deacon's position appears to be. That is worth doing because in the end the value of this exercise will lie in its capacity to indicate the strengths and weaknesses — not of David Deacon's argument as such — but of liberalism as a whole. If there is much of a gap between David Deacon and other liberal positions, it will also enable you to distinguish those strengths and weaknesses that are his alone from those that are more generally applicable to liberalism as a tradition. Indeed if the gap is enormous — if David Deacon is truly idiosyncratic — you might even be able to build a liberal critique of what he has to say — a critique from *within* the tradition rather than from *outside* — a critique that in effect marks him down for not being liberal enough, for not being sufficiently true to the tradition of thought he espouses.

In fact I will be very surprised if you do discover much of a gap. David Deacon has written a position statement from the very heart of classical liberalism. The quickest way to establish that — indeed the quickest way always to sweep through a piece of writing as long as Chapter 22 — is to use any summaries and concluding remarks as a first guide. There are three bits of summary in the liberalism section of the traditions essay. I have reproduced them here to save you time.

The individual in liberal thought

1   All traditions of thought are workings out of basic assumptions about human nature and human knowledge.

2   Liberal thinkers made a sharp break with previous modes of thought by taking as their starting point the existence of self-interested individuals.

3   Early liberal thinkers disagreed about the degree of human sociability, and about the role of intuition and reason in the formation of individual action: but they shared a common view of society as composed of individuals in the pursuit of their own ends.

Power and the State

1   Liberal thought specified individuals as free and equal, and judged the acceptability of political systems by the degree to which states respected and enhanced individual liberty. Liberal thought divided the world into private and public spheres, and privileged the private — linking its understanding of freedom to that of privacy.

2   Liberal commitments to representative government did not make early liberal thinkers democrats; and even today, liberal thought is uneasy about the tendency of democratic governments to 'over govern'.

3   Early liberal thought equated 'the individual' with 'the male', and either denied, ignored or down-played the rights and freedoms of women.

Economy and Society

1   Liberal thought came to see 'the market' as an effective and impartial allocator of economic resources and an invaluable arbiter of conflicting interests.

2   The over-riding appeal of markets is that they work without human direction, as an 'invisible hand' enabling a multiplicity of purposes to be reconciled and attained.

3   This defence of markets can be applied to international trade as well as to domestic economic activity; and continues to be a major theme in contemporary thinking on state and economy.

When you set these against the summary you made of David Deacon's argument, you will see how close the two are. There is even an echo in the Deacon piece of the unease with democracy when he writes of collectivist thought — in his discussion of causes — 'this false confidence was boosted by a link with democracy'. The same silence on questions of gender is also there. As far as I can see, David Deacon has written so representative a piece of liberal argumentation that there seems no need to add anything to the matrix we have already put together. But you may feel that you can embroider the matrix — fill it out and make it slightly more nuanced — by adding the odd sentence from the summaries of the liberalism section of the essay, or indeed from the body of the essay itself.

So that was the first of the two things it is worth doing to round off your reading of the David Deacon piece. The other is the following Activity.

——————————— ACTIVITY 3 ———————————

Make a preliminary list of the strengths and weaknesses of the case David Deacon makes. What part of Deacon's argument looks particularly persuasive to you? What doesn't? Can you think of any social phenomena that seem in tension with it? Does it seem an adequate explanation of things you have come across in the course — poverty, for example, or unemployment? Does it seem an adequate explanation of things we have not directly examined — for example, law and order, industrial unrest … ?

———————————————————————————

All this Activity requires you to do is to think of *bits of evidence* that you might want to use to test the adequacy of the position. To obtain that evidence you need to draw on your own experience. After all, we all live in the society David Deacon is describing and analysing. You need to draw too on what you have read and seen — in the course material, in Deacon's own essay, in newspaper and on television. It doesn't need to be a long list. It just is always useful to jot down any thoughts you have. Thoughts are always too precious to waste! And then you can come back to them later.

It is perhaps worth saying on this that when I am evaluating arguments I am normally quite difficult to live with (unlike the rest of the time, I insist). That is because thoughts don't come all at once. I normally find that I cover the house with paper and pencils, to scribble down thoughts as and when they arrive. You will be amazed at what moments of intimacy and privacy you suddenly think 'oh yes, the weakness of the Deacon position is…' Well — if that happens — just stop whatever it is you're doing, and write your thought down. And then put it safe somewhere — in a file or whatever. Your loved ones may no longer be speaking to you by the end of the week, though by then you will have developed absent-mindness and pre-occupation to a fine art. But at least you'll have the basis for a good answer to 'what are the strengths and weaknesses of liberalism'. Such is the price of scholarship!

3   CONSERVATISM

We will come back to liberalism later. But now let's repeat the exercise on Conservatism.

——————————— ACTIVITY 4 ———————————

Please read the essay 'A Conservative Approach to the UK' by Owen Hartley, remembering that you will have to fill in the matrix when your reading is over.

———————————————————————————

A CONSERVATIVE APPROACH
TO THE UK

by Owen Hartley

INTRODUCTION

Conservatives are by natural inclination sceptical of big themes and ideas. They are not much in favour of general speculation, least of all on 'conservatism' itself. Things are as they are and, since a conservative is inclined to believe that people are naturally conservative, further clarification is rarely relevant. Some conservatives will offer 'conservative principles' for discussion, but they seem to be no more than elaborated proverbial wisdom, so that 'look before you leap' becomes 'a preference for gradual change'. Such exercises by conservatives arise merely because conservatives are led to *react* to certain contemporary pieces of delusion and error in ways that are both pragmatic and appeal in a fairly loose way to the beliefs that conservatives hold.

The essential, and perhaps the only, conservative principle is 'to consider all broad claims and hopes with sceptical scrutiny' and especially whether the results are as the claimants predict. The evaluative test on the results that a conservative uses here is whether some form of social order and stability is encouraged or discouraged. A conservative has a strong preference for social order, largely because it is observably a preferred state of the world by most human beings.

In this essay I wish to identify those features of contemporary British society that worry me as a conservative. It is balanced by an equally long list of features that please me, largely because they are the ways in which these problems will be changed from worries into mere concerns. Conservatives usually combine an intellectual scepticism with a realistic appreciation of the fallibility and foibles of human beings, but this does not lead them to despair. The resources to reform what is wrong with our contemporary world are at hand, and will be used (despite human fallibility) because human society is extraordinarily resilient and self-healing.

A conservative is not a reactionary. A conservative might think that some things were done better in the past, but there are clearly things in the present that are as good as anything in the past. Conservatives react to the world as it is, identifying both the negative and the positive elements. If the exasperation of a conservative with the negative elements in the world seem to predominate it is because conservatives are, in truth, serious reformers, eager to improve on disorder and maintain the existing good.

WHAT ARE THE MAIN PROBLEMS OF
CONTEMPORARY UK SOCIETY?

The primary feature of contemporary British society is disorder. It begins in the hearts and minds of individual people, spreads to their communities and governments, and then pervades their existence. The evidence for the disorder to which I am reacting is largely contained in *Social Trends,* published annually by HMSO, containing statistical data which I read in a conservative spirit for which the Central Statistical Office compilers are not responsible.

At the individual level, disorder can be identified in two areas: in the decline of religious and secular faiths, and in the rise of personal selfishness. A conservative seeks to locate individuals within larger human groups, since these 'communities' can help and sustain individuals through the inevitable problems that confront individual lives. When individuals do not see their own social nature clearly, then nothing social above the individual level can thrive and the individual will suffer further. Faith, for most British conservatives, will be Christian faith, but other religious faiths, or even secular faiths like Marxism, which share a belief in supernatural entities (like God or the Proletariat) and which might have an effect on the individuals in such groups, can also be included. All have suffered a decline.

Most conservatives would claim a connection between the loss of faith and the rise of personal selfishness, but it is not a necessary connection, and the disorder generated by this is certainly affected by some factors not affecting faith (such as changes in legal requirements). The rise in the numbers of criminal offences leads a conservative, who can see in criminality evidence for individual failings as well as social failings, to draw the conclusion that all is not well. Similarly, when over 20 per cent of births are illegitimate, nearly 10 per cent of women aged 18–24 are cohabiting, 13 per cent of all dependent children are in one parent families, divorce rates in Britain are the highest in Europe and abortions are rising most rapidly in the 20–34 age group, the evidence, for a conservative, of a preference for socio-economic selfishness and irresponsibility in Britain is clear.

The disorder at the personal level spreads to communities and governments. Communities for a conservative are founded on the loyalty of human beings to each other, giving mutual support and encouragement in both individual and collective action. They are ultimately sustained by faith with both personal and public dimensions. Such communities are most readily found in families, neighbourhoods, linguistic, cultural and work groups. Larger communities or 'nations' can also exist. It is these communities that are also disordered in Britain.

Consider first of all the largest community we can consider — the United Kingdom itself (the 'European Community' is so obviously a fiction we will not feel the need to discuss it). A conservative would observe that 'Britain' is a creation in 1707 as a union of England (and Wales) with Scotland. Apart from a common political head, a fact that had not since 1601 led to unity, the link was one of religious faith, broadly Protestant. Reduce that Protestant faith and 'Britain' will be likely to disintegrate. The community of Protestant faith has been undermined not merely by the loss of personal faith but also by the diminution of Protestant faith as a binding force in favour of another vision, of a multi-faith community, the like of which has rarely flourished whenever it has been attempted. The attempt to include Roman Catholic Ireland in the Union after 1800 failed, but Roman Catholics were enfranchised after 1829 and since then membership of the community of Britain has not included any substantial faith test. The unsurprising consequence is that 'Britain' barely holds together at all as a single community. Scotland. Wales, Northern Ireland, Northern and Southern England, all seem set on going their own way. These are geographic alternative communities, but inside Britain alternative faith or group communities (Muslim, Afro-Caribbean, and so on) define themselves as their members' real community and not 'Britain'. Britain as a community barely exists and consequently can do very little for those who at some point want to claim that their essential character is 'British'.

This may not matter if the groups that provided alternative communities were themselves coherent groups in which the dissolving effects of lack of faith and personal selfishness were diminished. But this is not so. The geographic communities are as internally divided as 'Britain' is, and the other alternative faith or group communities are noisy promotions of special interests without being particularly creative as communities. The groups that are successful in Britain are not those that sustain community but those that reward their participant members with the most material rewards. Linguistic groups like the Welsh take a monopoly of teaching posts in parts of Wales, cultural groups such as opera lovers seek taxpayers' money for their sophisticated indulgence, while work groups like unions and professional bodies maintain a superficial rhetoric of community while taking advantage of those who are not members.

We cannot retreat, as some would have it, to the smaller communities of neighbourhood and family. Family as a community is beset with the issues that were identified as evidence of individual selfishness. Neighbourhood is much more plainly a device whereby architects, planners, teachers, social workers, and police seek to *invent* structures that make their professional tasks easier. The resulting 'neighbourhood communities' are

The Lord Chancellor followed by the Law Lords proceeds to the House of Lords for breakfast

sustained only by such professional interest: remove it and they collapse. When such neighbourhood groups occur through a threat to community values (a new road, a gypsy encampment, the closure of a school) they are dismissed as hopelessly selfish. The consequences of this disorder of community, falls back to individuals again. Without being part of a community, individuals cannot speak for anyone other than themselves. They may claim to do so, and leaders have to claim to do so, yet the claim is an empty one that, whenever tested, fails.

Two particular disorders, as a consequence of our disorder at individual and community level, are of special concern to the conservative, since they are such substantial obstacles to the overcoming of disorder: the decline of 'the rule of law', which includes the end of a stable financial system, and the belief that strong government is itself the answer.

The decline in 'the rule of law' which can easily be accepted as at last a decline in the power of lawyers, is more serious when it involves the abandoning of a description of a way of conducting public affairs that required rules and the acceptance of rules as binding. Neither individuals nor groups understand that rules are a guide to conduct. Following rules is a virtue even, or especially, when it is not in our interests to do so. The tendency, at a political level, is to make the passing of laws not an opportunity to obtain agreement upon community objectives but as a coercive measure. We lack a framework of rules and prefer instead the trials of strength that makes might right. One consequence of this is an end to a stable monetary system. Conservatives are not on the whole very interested in economic affairs except to ensure that they are orderly, and that order may have different characteristics from time to time as different mechanisms are tried and tested in practice. However order is now lost. This is because of the tendency to ignore rules of economic prudence, and also because once such order is lost, all individuals and groups protect themselves from economic chaos.

The second particular element of contemporary disorder is the identification of governmental power as the salvation for our disorder. 'The government should do something' becomes a standard cry. Concentrate the power of changing into governments and then the power will, it is thought, be used to 'solve' the problems of modern Britain. This view neglects the obvious difficulty that government has no strong interest in solving some problems: funny money helps governments win elections; the rule of law is much more onerous on governments than on powerless oppositions; and for a government to encourage a community of faith would arouse immediate political objections. Government then is more often a willing ally to disorder than a corrective to it.

Traditionally, conservatives have been associated with a belief in strong government and the exercise of authority, even 'authoritarianism'. However, I suggest that conservatives are ambiguous about authority in government. On the one hand conservatives see the necessity for government (as opposed to anarchy), on the other, governments are prone to error and must therefore be held in check by some devices, either formal rules or internal moral persuasion. Conservatives have historically been adept at creating arrangements which while allowing governments and leaders of governments freedom to act (and especially in chaotic conditions) nevertheless have put limits on that freedom. They have considered rebellion, purged 'failed' leaders, and acted as the enemies of established but ineffectual or tyrannical order. Government is a trust or covenant allowing government to act within limits. It is an element of present disorders that such limits on governmental activity are neglected or treated lightly. Government is not, by virtue of being government, best enabled to know how children should be educated, how the economy should grow, or whether a cure for AIDS can be found. This is a special, political, disorder. It is to the causes of these problems that attention must now turn.

WHAT ARE THEIR MAIN HISTORICAL AND CONTEMPORARY CAUSES?

The prime cause of disorder for a conservative will always be found in the nature of human beings. Humanity is essentially flawed, inclined to selfishness, taking advantage of others, neglectful of common human purposes. Humanity is capable of being refined and transformed to do better than this. For a conservative the mechanisms or devices that enable this transformation to occur are a practical problem that will be solved in a community of faith. If however it is these communities that are themselves in need of transformation, then what can be done will be a mixture of exposing the reality of the situation by intellectual means, and encouraging faith and emotions in wishing to amend the situation to a better one.

Thus, in considering the disorder of modern Britain, the rise of personal selfishness requires no particular explanation from conservatives: it is what human beings are quite naturally like unless they decide to be otherwise. The decline of faith however has more mixed causes. In some ways it is a consequence of human nature: those who are selfish may not easily see the need for faith or for communities of faith. But in other ways it is often the case that such selfishness is sustained by a network of ideas, institutions and persuasive individuals, who will see in disorder, liberty, and in its consequences, better worlds.

The causes are of two types: one, the ideas and techniques that are used to justify and encourage disorder and two, the groups and individuals that profit from disorder and have no particular shame about their behaviour.

In the realm of ideas, the most destructive of human society are those which combine the three propositions that human beings are perfectible, that human history exhibits the rise of greater perfections, and that governmental power ought to be used to make human beings more perfect. Taken individually, these three propositions are dangerous enough, together they have in this century been the warrant for genocide and tyranny by Hitler and Stalin and a host of imitators. The propositions are not always asserted but taken as assumptions not to be questioned in our daily lives. Of course, human beings can become better but too great an expectation of human capacities is certain to lead to grave disappointment. This is particularly so when the claim is made that if only a particular obstacle were removed, then all will be well (an old example would be those suffragettes who believed that having the vote would liberate women in all other areas too). Reading history as the story of how humanity is rising to greater heights is a story that is often true of science and technology, but less clearly so of human capacities either individually or collectively. The tendency to complacency about human efforts, the belief that such and such is medieval or barbaric, and therefore cannot reappear is sadly disproved by events both big like the Holocaust and small as in child abuse.

However, ideas encouraging disorder do not exist independently of people. We must identify those individuals and groups who have an interest in encouraging disorder. Who profits from contemporary disorder? In one sense, we all do. We all enjoy freedom from certain kinds of restrictions on our ideas, behaviour, and future plans, which a more orderly Britain would certainly require of us. We can though identify some groups who particularly benefit from disorder.

Two types of group can be identified. The first comprises those unhappy characters who, glassy eyed with enthusiasm for distant causes and intolerant of others, gather in groups to persuade us that there is indeed a different, better, world if only their solutions to our problems would be accepted. Let us, such groups, say, increase the misery of our time, increase the disorder of contemporary Britain, so that our favoured solution seems by contrast ever brighter and better. A simple example are the numerous 'revolutionary' groups whose individual members often attain leadership positions inside organizations like the trade unions of miners or actors — and whose hearts may be in the right place but whose heads see this level of disorder as a political advantage.

The second group overlaps a little with the first: it comprises those who assume that everything else is orderly but in their particular case (e.g. university teaching) some other rules of disorder might be applied for alleviation of a problem. 'Only a little disorder', they cry, 'for a greater good'! A simple example is strike action taken to hurt bystanders or the innocent so that those against whom the action is directed feel the need to protect others by concessions to the demanders. When university teachers threaten not to mark examinations they do the moral equivalent of kicking the cat having quarrelled with the spouse.

Such groups expose themselves quite easily. However the characteristic technique they use needs also to be identified. This is the vilification and shaming of those who stand in the way of 'progress' or whatever slogan is thought fit to hide the disorderly claims. The attempt is made to suppress discussion of some topics like immigration or capital punishment by such devices. At least some part of the disorder of modern Britain arises from the denial of public legitimacy to public fears.

A key role is played here by the social sciences. Insofar as certain things are held to be facts or truth an effective censorship on contrary views may be sustained as the prestige of 'science' is deployed to exclude what are alleged to be the equivalent of flat-earth views. This is particularly important since the social sciences have often fallen into the assumption that human society is 'progressing' in an ameliorative and improving fashion — that is, it takes as given the second of the idea-propositions that conservatives regard as dangerous.

WHAT SHOULD BE DONE ABOUT THE PROBLEMS AND BY WHOM?

What then will a conservative see as solutions? Plainly the answer here is to encourage orderly beliefs, ideas, persons, and institutions and the encouragement of resistance to other seductive but ineffectual alternatives. Exposure of the situation is in part sufficient, but it would be by winning over those seeking reassurance that their moral sentiments are not without logic or foundation that transformation might occur. In the modern British situation it may be that it is the encouragement of a fairly natural British 'bloody mindedness', or, put more technically, a sceptical and distrustful temper, that is needed.

The programme of action to be undertaken to deal with the causes of present disorder, would, on the intellectual exposing side, be to reject a large part of the intellectual baggage with which establishment Britain has been afflicted since the 1750s. It would relegate most of the social and political theorists (Mill, Marx, and such like) to be unread in dusty library basements, require a rewriting of textbook British domestic history from about 1850 when such ideas began their baleful influence, as a tragic decline, and require a positive re-evaluation of some themes and theories and an assertive condemnation of the awfulness of 'the Commonwealth' and 'Europe'. This intellectual task is an immense one, but it is already being undertaken and the intellectual foundations for established doctrines rest on such sandy soil that the cheerfulness of their defenders is touchingly heroic.

On the more positive side, of encouraging faith and emotional commitment, the programme of action is more modest. It would be easy for a conservative of my temper to urge the virtues of a Protestant reformation as the core of a revived Britain, a Protestantism not hostile to other faiths (as historically it has not been to Jews, Roman Catholics, or, in imperial situations, other faith groups). However, such a grand design is both impracticable and unnecessary. To work with what is already at hand is much more certain of success. Thus I would wish to build on a list of the positive features of British Society. In descending order of significance these are: Individuals who are moral persons; Families, Communities of Faith; the structure of community relations; the structure of Government; and the conservative political tradition.

The greatest weight for a conservative in creating public order lies with individuals. As Confucius reportedly said 'If a man have not order within him, he cannot spread order about him.' Though a conservative is bound to be pessimistic about human nature it is also the case that human beings are already moral agents, aware of their failings and ready to attempt to do better. Such individual action will help shape proper human relationships, especially those of the family and communities of faith, which will, in turn, support and encourage individual efforts. The trio of individual-family-community of faith taken together provides a particularly rich source of order, partly because of the natural and spontaneous ordering and partly through its own mutually reinforcing activity.

Though families, like all human relationships, are fragile and can degenerate into violence (consider the death of Abel in the first family myth), families represent the best possibilities of human relationships extended over time. The continued existence of the family remains both an aspiration that humans can build to and build from, and a potential rock of order in a disorderly world. All individuals and families can, and do seek to belong to communities, of neighbours, friends, acquaintances. Such communities observably require a structure of faith to sustain them over time and through crises for the community. Churches have traditionally been the basis of such communities of faith, though other factors, such as common language and rituals, physical nearness of members, are also significant elements in sustaining faith. Such communities exist, some indeed are growing, but many need the effort of individuals and families to revive them.

A conservative thus will seek to encourage individuals, families and communities. Creating order in this trio, while having the advantages of actual spontaneity has some disadvantages. It is not easily accessible to outsiders; it is essentially private and away from a public sphere; it cannot be programmed and organized. This is why the task before anyone seeking to sustain order is to encourage faith and an emotional attitude which will inspire at this level. It is not possible to create the order by administrative or political instructions, and even education may wash by this area of human life without affecting its character. For this reason, also, the capacity to respond to order has not been dulled or bureaucratized away.

Of the other three positive features of British Society which can tend towards order more can be said. They are concerned with public policy. In these it is possible to discern those points which develop public order.

First of all, the structure of community relations has three inter-connected elements: a basis of debate and discussion from which action may come; expectations of elements of future stability (and especially in finance); and the capacity and ability to form associations for mutual support and benefit, and also representation to other associations. Without these three elements there cannot be any community relationships established or sustained. All these structures of community relationships are present in modern Britain.

All could with little effort on the part of individuals, families, and communities of faith, be developed further. This will be a test of leadership and vision within each community. To maintain debate and stability and to create associations is of particular significance if the community of 'Britain' is to be sustained.

Secondly, structure of government. The obsessive concern of those intent on disorder has been to distort the structure of government and make it too strong and powerful. Conservatives over the years have sometimes assisted in this by their distrust of human capacities, so that they have exalted the capacities of leaders or of constituted authority at the expense of the appreciation of the capacities and experiences of ordinary people. Thus government's power to control disorder has been exaggerated by conservatives too. Even so, there is in the British traditions of government sufficient material to counter the overweening self-importance of British Government as now constituted. No conservative should put too much faith in the capacity of government to achieve much, but within a 'rule of law' environment, limited government might be capable of encouraging order by discouraging the ambition to coerce and control. The elements of this limited structure of government are the rule of law itself, understood as a self-imposed limitation on government to act within rules, a 'mixed' constitution whereby the different parts are capable of influencing each other into moderation and self-limitation, and, as a part of that mixed constitution, a preference for self-government by communities of all kinds (but especially local ones).

One problem of our structure of government is the overwhelming strength of a party with a majority in the House of Commons. A more mixed eighteenth century constitution in Britain gave equal weight to the Monarch and the House of Lords. In the absence of these balances after the 1911 Parliament Act, British government has been too inclined to exercise enormous authority unchecked. Some have wanted to find an equal balance in associations (churches, trade unions and so on) or in the judiciary (with a 'Bill of Rights') or in devolution (so Scotland, Wales and English regions can avoid Parliamentary controls). What solution commends itself eventually is difficult to determine: that the search should be engaged upon is clear.

The final item in which one can take contemporary pleasure in Britain is the survival of a real conservative tradition — a way of considering issues that has not been overtaken by fashionable 'liberalism' or 'socialism' or fallen back into being (as they now are) mere celebrations of past triumphs. The scepticism about power and its uses, a willingness to engage in debate and discussion within a framework of rules, and an acceptance of the ultimate need for limited government, have deep and lively roots in at least the English political culture, and from these presuppositions about political action may come sufficient impetus to allow for those legal changes that open up the possibilities of individual, family, community, and association renewal. This conservative tradition is widely shared and no conservative, being sceptical of broad claims and sure that everyone is ultimately a conservative, would be surprised to discover that the soundest conservatives today may be found in a Labour Party and not in a 'Conservative' Party. The conservative tradition thus has a capacity to renew both itself and Britain.

WHAT IS IT ABOUT THE CONSERVATIVE TRADITION WHICH PREDISPOSES YOU TO HIGHLIGHT THESE PARTICULAR PROBLEMS, CAUSES AND SOLUTIONS?

I started this essay with the observation that conservatives were by natural inclination sceptical and that the only enduring conservative principle was to continue that scrutiny through everything. Yet in writing as I have it is clear that a conservative *believes* quite a lot of things and suspects many more. The conservative is probably always to be found trying to reconcile the tensions between sceptical doubt and absolute certainty, between believing that humanity is corrupt and that it is capable of transforming change, that things

Edmund Burke 1729–97,
a founding figure in the
Conservative Tradition

were once better than the present, that the present is better than some futures, and that future may, or may not, be different from the past. *The* 'conservative tradition' then is a nicely elusive thing, capable of containing a variety of elements and emphases, which, given a disposition to be critical of big themes and ideas, selects among its repertoire of ideas those elements and emphases that suits a present pragmatic purpose best of all.

As a brief illustration of this, consider the great names David Coates identified as being in the conservative tradition — Burke, Coleridge and Carlyle. What I have written owes very little to Coleridge or Carlyle, large parts of whose writings appear to me to be utterly mistaken, and only something to the later rather than younger Burke. A conservative is reluctant to have to defend a particular 'ism' or pantheon of heroes.

Moreover a conservative has a particular problem — the existence of a very successful 'Conservative' Party. No sensible conservative would wish to be required to defend all a Conservative Party or especially a Conservative Government says and does. The practical necessities of political life will lead a political party to experiment widely with practical possibilities, as well as making deliberate compromises with other factions and perspectives. A conservative will normally feel more comfortable with a Conservative Party than with any other, but the party has always included diverse elements, as with a liberal 'New Right', which seem to provide solutions to particular problems, and conservatives will accept such tensions as normal.

Even so, there are two aspects of this essay which would seem characteristic to conservatives. The first is the identification of problems and solutions at a highly *personal* level which is a very regular element for a conservative: people and their characters, not ideas, are at the centre of concern. At its most extreme this becomes an obsession with leaders and their characters, but is more normally expressed through a concern for the binding together of public and personal aspects of human life. Personal failings are taken as public failings too.

The second aspect is that the framework of analysis is always around a theme of order-disorder. Order is regarded as a possible state of affairs however much human beings drift towards disorder. Conservatives are not in practice always sure that an orderly society is one they really want, but as a better vision than contemporary disorder it will always attract. They are thus always interested in reforming contemporary society.

Welcome back from your reading again. Now let's use the matrix to identify Hartley's key words and arguments in the same way as we did with Deacon.

—————————————— ACTIVITY 5 ——————————————

Answer the following question using your 'Conservatism' version of the matrix (as in Activity 2):

What does Owen Hartley say in answer to Question 1, 'What are the main problems of contemporary UK society?'

Use the first box for your answer.

It seemed to me that the Hartley argument is harder to grasp, both overall and in detail, than was the essay on liberalism. So don't be surprised if you have more difficulty with this exercise. The answer I came up with, for Hartley on question 1, was this:

- Disorder: in individuals, communities, society. Manifested in individuals as a decline in faith, rise in selfishness. Manifested in UK society as disintegration of community into regional and group loyalties. General lack of community.
- Decline in the rule of law.
- Decline in proper constraints on the role of government.

—————————————— ACTIVITY 6 ——————————————

Now go through the Hartley essay, locating his answers to Questions 2, 3 and 4 — on causes, solutions and the strength of conservatism as a tradition — and write them into the matrix.

(You will find a possible set of answers to these at the end of the unit. But try not to 'cheat'. The benefit (as well as the pain) comes from doing this yourself first, and then checking your answer against ours. If you do find a big divergence, don't be too shaken. It is quite hard to pin the Hartley argument down. What you get and what I extracted could very easily differ quite a lot.)

Next you need to situate the Hartley piece in the wider conservative tradition — to see what kind of a conservative Hartley is. The tradition is a broad and opaque one. A *lack* of organizing principles is one of its defining features, as Chapter 22 of the Reader said; so it should come as no surprise to find that the Hartley position is representative of only certain kinds of conservatism.

—————————————— ACTIVITY 7 ——————————————

Check the Hartley answers to the four questions against the summaries of conservative thought to be found in Chapter 22, and reproduced for you here.

The bases of Conservative thought

1 Conservatives tend to be reluctant to theorise, reacting instead to the proselytizing of others. Conservatives are wary of excessive rationalism, and conscious of the dangers of radical social engineering.

2 Conservatism is a philosophy of imperfection. It rejects liberal optimism in progress and human reason, emphasizing instead the limits on human capacities, the importance of the past, and the risks involved in rapid social change.

Economy and society

1 Conservative attitudes to industrialization changed over time: from initial hostility to eventual advocacy of market forces. Conservatism no longer possesses any developed and distinctive economic theory of its own.

2 Conservatives recognize the inevitability of social inequality and the necessarily organic nature of all complex societies. They accordingly attach importance to leadership and to the maintenance of social order.

Power and the state

1 Conservative thinkers tend to treat the family as a natural social order, and to leave unexamined the gender relationships within it.

2 Conservative thinkers give an important role to the state as a guarantor of social order and of minimum standards. Conservatives attach central importance to the maintenance of political authority and to the rule of law. They do not look to the state for grandiose schemes of social improvement.

There are clear echoes of those summaries in the arguments of Owen Hartley: the reluctance to theorize, the emphasis on human fallibility, the indifference to economics, the concern with social order, the prioritizing of the family. But in two respects at least the Hartley presentation of the conservative case looks less than fully representative of the core of the tradition: in his attitude to Protestantism, and in his remarks on government and the state. He gives a particularly Protestant interpretation of what is a more generally conservative theme — of the importance of religion and morality in the stabilization of society — and as he says himself, he does not entirely share the traditional conservative view of the desirability of strong government.

So if we are to build a Hartley/conservative position we might want to add:

- The decline in religion in general, and not just Protestantism, as a problem in answer to Question 1, or a cause of problems in answer to Question 2.

- Firm government as one conservative solution, in answer to Question 3.

——————————— ACTIVITY 8 ———————————

Now build your list of the strengths and weaknesses of the conservative position, by thinking again about bits of evidence with which it seems to deal well, and bits that give it greater difficulty.

The final task of the week is to put the two matrixes together, and to pull out their main lines of agreement and disagreement on each of the four questions in turn. My list of agreement came out as

Question 1:   Not much overlap here — similar unease with role of government.

Question 2:   Both uneasy about ideas that encourage state action.

Question 3:   Both keen to roll back and set legal limits on the activity of the state.

Question 4:   Both keen to focus on the individual.

So the two essays do demonstrate an overlap of concerns — one indeed that manifests itself in the tone of much New Right thinking in the Conservative Party. But it was the disagreements that stood out more strongly for me.

Question 1:   Liberal emphasis on the need to let individuals get on with things free of government interference — contrasted with conservative emphasis on disorder and moral decay (including the personal selfishness of liberalism's individuals).

Question 2:   Liberalism's keenness to place the blame squarely on too much government contrasts sharply with conservatism's analysis of the wider social origins of a loss of moral community.

Question 3:   Liberalism's emphasis on rolling back the state as the key solution contrasts with conservatism's search for new bases of moral order.

Question 4:   Liberalism's faith in the individual contrasts with conservatism's sense of human fallibility. Liberal optimism contrasts with conservative scepticism.

There are choices here. Is the problem that of excessive government, or of moral disorder? Is the cause excessive faith in government action, or a generalized loss of faith? Is the solution a return to market forces, or the establishment of a new moral community? Keep these questions with you, for consideration again at the end of Unit 29.

But for the moment, on to marxism and to social reformism.

ANSWERS

POSSIBLE ANSWERS FOR QUESTIONS 2, 3, AND 4 IN THE HARTLEY MATRIX

Question 2: causes	• flawed human nature, natural selfishness; • erosion of faith by spread of ideas that encourage social disorder in the pursuit of human perfectibility; • the way these ideas are disseminated by revolutionary groups and individuals, and by special interests (including social sciences themselves) associated intolerance and dismissal of important conservative concerns.
Question 3: solutions	• encourage orderly beliefs, ideas, persons, institutions. encouragement of a sceptical and distrustful temper; • exposure and rejection of ruling orthodoxies in social science and history; • encouragement of faith and moral commitment: in strong individuals, in the family as a vital social institution, and in other communities of faith; • subordination of government to the rule of law — creation of a mixed constitution to restrain party government; • reassertion of already existing conservative tradition.
Question 4: conservative strengths	• useful balance between scepticism and certainty; • reluctance to be labelled as a tradition; • a willingness to anchor social problems and solutions at the personal level, concern with individuals, not ideas; • recognition of the dangers of contemporary disorder.

STUDY SKILLS SECTION: A REVISION STRATEGY

Prepared for the Course Team by Neil Costello

(D103 EXAMINATION ALERT: please read this section now. It is important to consider your revision strategy early so that you can do yourself justice in the exam.)

The reason I have put up an 'examination alert' is the concern I have that, under the pressure of other course work, you will begin to think about revision too late. To be done effectively your revision should start now. That does not mean you should drop everything in a scramble to learn the course! But it does mean you should begin to think about a *revision strategy* and that you should work out a realistic timetable to enable you to carry out your revision satisfactorily — and that both these things should be done in the next few days if you have not yet started on them.

The purpose of this section is to help you to work out a satisfactory revision strategy and it links to the last two units in the course, Units 31 and 32, which consider the nature of examination questions in more detail. To some extent good revision is a matter of personal taste and the model which suits you best will depend upon how you, as an individual, like to learn. However there are a number of points which apply to virtually everyone and these are the topics which we shall cover here.

In Block VI you were asked to look at Chapter 7, Section 1 of *The Good Study Guide*. It would be helpful if you could cast your mind back to the points made in that chapter. You will remember that it considers the nature of examinations and explains the value of taking them. I think it is also worth stressing that the skills which you need in examinations — the ability to think quickly and to respond concisely and in a relevant way — are ones which are valuable in many contexts outside the exam room itself. What we must recognize is that they are skills which you can acquire, if you do not yet have them in abundance, and they are not things which just a few lucky people happen to be born with. To acquire them means working out systematically what is required and then taking appropriate actions. That is what I suggest we should do now in the specific context of the D103 exam.

I   WHAT ARE WE TRYING TO DO IN REVISING?

I suppose that seems like an obvious question. In revising are we trying to remind ourselves of everything that is in the course? Is that true? *Everything* that is in the course? Word for word? No, clearly we cannot do that. What we want to do when we revise is to prepare ourselves as well as we possibly can for the tests which the examiners are going to set us. Now that is a more manageable proposition. And we can begin to work on that more systematically. I hope you don't feel dreadfully daunted by this task. For many people revision is a stimulating activity. It brings together different areas of the course so that linkages can be seen that had previously been unclear and it makes it possible to get a better sense of the different kinds of explanations which are being offered. It would be worth doing even if there were no exam. There is no denying though, that for most of us, it is hard work.

So where do you start? You need to prepare yourself for the tests the examiners are going to set you. The best place to begin is therefore the examination paper.

From the exam paper we can see the kinds of questions which are likely to be asked and the coverage of the course which we are expected to make. Exam questions will be looked at more closely later in the block. At this stage the important point is to check out the amount of the course we are expected to cover.

2   MAKING SENSE OF THE SPECIMEN PAPER

Have a look at the Specimen Examination Paper. You will see it has two sections. Section A contains six questions from Blocks I to VI and Section B has three questions based on course-wide issues — Traditions, social science methods and the course themes. You are asked to answer three questions from Section A and one question from Section B. The questions are intended to make it possible for you to show your understanding of the course. You will be asked questions which are drawn from the course material and which you should be able to tackle if you have a grasp of the main issues addressed by the course. There are no 'catch questions'. However, you are not asked to cover *all* of the course. As a minimum you will be able to answer the prescribed number of questions if you revise three blocks out of Blocks I to VI, plus Block VII for the Section B question. That will enable you to tackle three questions from Section A and one from Section B. So the minimum coverage you must revise is four blocks. The maximum coverage is, of course, all seven blocks.

But what is the wise coverage? In one sense the more you revise the better, since this will give you a greater understanding of the course and its interconnections. For most people, however, this would be unwise. You have only a limited amount of time at your disposal and you are probably better advised to use that time to gain a thorough understanding of a few blocks than to spread it thinly across the whole course. The question is then, how many blocks and which blocks? Only you, and perhaps your tutor-counsellor, know how much time you will need to revise a block thoroughly. I would suggest that to revise less than five blocks is a wee bit foolish — isn't it one version of Sod's Law that if you revise only four blocks those will turn out to be the most difficult questions on the paper? — but to revise more than six is probably giving yourself far too much to do. Four or five blocks is then the number which is appearing, and in my case being a cautious kind of character, I would go for five. This is not cheating! You can fulfil the examination requirements by concentrating on a limited number of blocks. If you do this you will have more time to spend on each of the blocks you choose. It is likely that you will be able to produce better answers on those questions.

Which blocks should you choose? This is a less mechanical question. The answer must depend on your response to the course so far but there are some things you should bear in mind when choosing. The most important by far, I think, is the enjoyment you got from a particular block. You are much more likely to do well if you are answering questions about topics which really stimulate you. Those which link to courses you intend to take in future years probably fall into this category. Do remember, however, that later blocks in the course have built upon earlier blocks. An answer, for example, which looks at the way in which unemployment or 'women's work' is represented in Block III, could be enhanced by drawing in material from Block V. Similarly, answers may often need to go beyond a particular unit into a course theme or tradition. Do try to avoid becoming very compartmentalized in your revision and think about the course-wide links (including summer school) which can be made. This is starting to sound very daunting again. I am not suggesting that you need an overview of the whole course to answer any question! It is worthwhile making the connections which occur to you when you can, however, and perhaps to consider which blocks 'fit' together in some way. I hope all the blocks fit but some are closer than others. There are strong connections between Blocks III and IV, for example, in the way in which both deal with the changing economic and political climate in recent UK experience. If this is something which interests you it would be worth considering these two blocks as part of your examination revision. Your tutor-counsellor can also provide helpful advice on which blocks to choose.

—————————————————— ACTIVITY 1 ——————————————————

It is probably timely for you to make an initial selection of the blocks you would like to revise. Go through the list of unit and block titles here and decide which five blocks you think are the ones you would most like to concentrate on. (It's sometimes easier to start off by deciding which you really don't want to look at again and then choosing from the ones that are left!) Bear in mind you will have to cover every unit in the block. If you leave one unit out that could well be the unit on which the block's question is based.

BLOCK I FOOD FOR THOUGHT
Unit 1   The World of Food Production
Unit 2   The Production of Hunger
Unit 3   The Consumption of Food
Unit 4   Making Sense of Society
Unit 5   Social Science in Society

BLOCK II SOCIAL STRUCTURES AND DIVISIONS
Unit 6   The Idea of 'The Social'
Unit 7   Social Class
Unit 8   Race, Ethnicity and Gender
Unit 9   The Role of Concepts

BLOCK III WORK, MARKETS AND THE ECONOMY
Unit 10   Work and the Economy
Unit 11   Competitive Markets
Unit 12   The Management of the UK Economy
Unit 13   Constructing Models

BLOCK IV POLITICS AND POWER
Unit 14   The Sovereignty of the UK
Unit 15   Power and the State
Unit 16   Power and the People
Unit 17   The Power of Ideology
Unit 18   Theories and Evidence

BLOCK V IDENTITIES AND INTERACTION
Unit 19   Personal Identity
Unit 20   Social Identity
Unit 21   Social Interaction
Unit 22   Investigative Methods

3   WHAT STRATEGY SHOULD I ADOPT?

To decide on an appropriate strategy means first establishing what it is you are aiming to do. Then, secondly, looking at the resources you have at your disposal and marshalling them in such a way that you are most likely to meet your objective.

We have already discussed the objective. It is to be well prepared for the tests the examiners are going to set. Their tests are set out on the exam paper and so the objective becomes one of ensuring we are able to give good clear answers to the examination questions. I know I am labouring this point and the reason for that is to establish that the objective is not to be able to write down all you know about the course. It is to write clear, concise and relevant answers to the questions the examiners set.

It can be useful to think about revision strategy rather like a game of chess. We know that we can convince our opponents to resign if we provide them with clear answers which keep to the point. We then have to collect our chess pieces and other resources together so that we can do that as successfully as possible. We don't want to scatter pieces all over the board in the hope that some might land in the right place. On the other hand, concentrating on too narrow a front can mean that we never break through. The chess board is the examination room in October and we have the period between now and October to practise and train ourselves. The great advantage we have over a chess player is that in this case our opponents positively want us to win and, furthermore, they have already given us much of their game plan in the specimen examination paper. We need to practise our game and to think about broad strategy and detailed tactics.

So we should now consider what it is we have at our disposal.

──────────────────────── ACTIVITY 2 ────────────────────────

Think back over the course and the study skills you have practised, either alone in your period of private study or with your colleagues and tutor-counsellor in the study centre sessions.

What kinds of things came to mind? These are some of the things which occurred to me as I thought about this issue.

- Ways of organizing your time.
- Skills which enable you to obtain information from units, Reader articles, television and radio programmes, and the ability to condense this information into notes and diagrams.
- The skill to read off numerical and statistical information from tables.
- Ways of structuring a coherent and persuasive argument.
- The skill to benefit from, and contribute to, shared activity in study centre sessions and self-help groups — how to select relevant material and present it to others in written or verbal form.
- The skill to construct logical, coherent, informed and well-presented essays and short answers.

This is an impressive array of skills and I am sure your list will contain many of them. Some of you will feel more competent at them than others but that is true for everybody. These skills are acquired only gradually and are constantly refined and developed as new courses and new types of study are taken on. Studying and learning is a continuing process and one that is never complete for any of us.

So those are some of the skills you have acquired or polished during D103. What kind of materials can they be combined with?

─────────────── ACTIVITY 3 ───────────────

Think back over the course again. What specific materials have you gathered together which you might be able to make use of in your revision?

───

The course units, Reader and *Glossary-Index* are the most obvious things which come to mind. My guess is that you will also have notes (whether annotated units or separate pages of written notes) and importantly there are your TMAs. There are probably a number of other things you have acquired in a resource file, or perhaps from an activity at summer school.

These materials in combination with your study skills are the main things at your disposal to help in the forthcoming challenge from the examiners. You can also call upon your tutor-counsellor and your fellow students. Let's think about how you might marshal these resources to help in your game plan. Have a go at the following quiz.

───

QUIZ — SOME STRATEGIES FOR YOU TO THINK ABOUT

You have a strictly limited amount of time to spend on preparing for the exam and many possible ways of using it. Which of the following strategies do you think you will adopt as you set out on your revision of D103?

Please tick the appropriate boxes.

	Yes	No
1 I'll start on Unit 1 and reread the whole course	❏	☑
2 I'll work sixteen hours a day for a week	❏	☑
3 I'll spend the first evening sorting out all my course material and notes into piles	☑	❏
4 I'll read through the *Glossary-Index* and learn every term	❏	☑

5 I'll try to identify central questions that the units are written around and write notes on them	☑	☐
6 I'll go over and over the notes I made earlier in the year and learn them by heart	☐	☐
7 I'll try to reduce my notes on selected units to a single sheet per unit	☑	☐
8 I'll memorize every name that's been mentioned in the course	☐	☑
9 I'll pick one unit per block to specialize on	☐	☑
10 I'll stick to rereading my essays	☐	☑
11 I'll guess what questions will come up and revise around them	☐	☑
12 I'll set myself four practice papers under exam conditions	☐	☑
13 I'll practise jotting down outlines for answers to questions	☑	☐
14 I'll give up the luxury of tutorials	☐	☑
15 I'll arrange with another student that we set each other questions and try answering them	☐	☑
16 I'll spend hours sitting and worrying about how hopeless the whole venture is	☐	☑

Here are some brief thoughts on the options presented.

1 *I'll start on Unit 1 and re-read the whole course*

It is a hopeless task to attempt to reread the whole course. It would take far too long and your mind would be numbed by the tedium of it. You need to take a much more selective and more active approach as you return to earlier sections of the course.

2 *I'll work sixteen hours a day for a week*

Examination folklore is full of legends of people studying 'around-the-clock', especially for finals. However, as a part-time student with several years of exams ahead of you, I suggest that a more temperate approach will serve you better. Make out a *timetable* of your remaining weeks and see how many hours you can reasonably hope to set aside. Do it now! Go on, get out your diary/calendar and mark in blocks of revision time. It's so easily postponed. I'll come back to this in a moment.

3 *I'll spend the first evening sorting out all my course material and notes into piles*

Good thinking. A central feature of revision is getting yourself organized, in terms of *time*, in terms of the *course materials*, and in terms of the *content of the course*. Unless you have a superbly efficient filing system you will have accumulated mounds of assorted bits of paper. Getting clear *what* you have got and *where*, will give you a much clearer run at a spell of constructive revision.

4 *I'll read through the* Glossary-Index *and learn every term*

Concepts gain their significance from the context in which they are used. Formal definitions on their own are often not very helpful, and a task as mechanical as the one suggested would only distract you from *the main task of revision — consolidating your understanding* of the *central issues* of the units and practising *relating* these issues to *exam-type questions*. However, you might focus on some of the more important concepts and try writing them down in your own words; then check them against the Glossary. The indexing has been specifically designed so that you can follow through how important concepts (e.g. course themes, the Traditions and methodological terms) are developed from one unit or block to the next.

5   *I'll try to identify central questions that the units are written around and write notes on them*

This is a far more promising approach. Many units identify the central questions for you, and in other cases you can construct questions of your own. Then try to jot down notes summarizing the main answers each unit gives to its questions. This will focus your mind on the kinds of issues the exam questions will deal with.

6   *I'll go over and over the notes I made earlier in the year and learn them by heart*

This could be a waste of effort. Don't concentrate solely on routine, boring things like dutifully scanning over and over old notes. Do something constructive as you read like improving them, or making a new shorter version, and ensuring that your notes are a good summary of the relevant units.

7   *I'll try to reduce my notes on selected units to a single sheet per unit*

This is a much better idea. Work to condense your notes. Try to extract the main points from your notes and from the units at the same time. See if you can produce a system of notes for your chosen blocks. Chapter 7, Section 4.9 of *The Good Study Guide* gives particular recommendations on how you might do this.

8   *I'll memorize every name that's been mentioned in the course*

Bad idea again. You *will* need to know a *few* central names, but in the context of *what* the person said or did, not just as names.

9   *I'll pick one unit per block to specialize on*

Quite the wrong approach. The exam question may well be on different sections of the block.

10   *I'll stick to re-reading my essays*

Re-reading your essays is certainly a good way to remind yourself of how you drew together arguments earlier in the course. However you can't afford to rely solely on your essays, since the exam question may be on different sections of the blocks as mentioned above.

11   *I'll guess what questions will come up and revise around them*

It's certainly a good idea to think up questions you might be asked. When you step over to the course team side of the fence to devise questions it helps you to get into a constructive frame of mind and to take an overview of the course, looking for the broad themes and central issues. But of course you might guess badly, so you can't afford to pin all your hopes on this approach. Your tutor-counsellor could advise you on the appropriateness of your 'invented' questions.

12   *I'll set myself four practice papers under exam conditions*

If you haven't taken exams for a long time it is obviously useful to get some practice at working on exam questions against the clock. On the other hand, I doubt whether many students would get round to a full scale practice more than once. It depends on your own abilities and inclinations as to how much time it is useful to spend in this way. Some students prefer to set themselves a smaller scale exercise now and again — namely writing out an answer to a single question in forty-five minutes. But a word of warning — don't be discouraged if the answers you produce in such exercises look unimpressive. Answers under exam conditions are usually very different from a polished TMA.

13 *I'll practise jotting down outlines for answers to questions*

A quicker exercise, which you can do much more frequently, is to rehearse those first few minutes of answering a question, when you jot down an outline of your answer. All you need to do is spend ten minutes producing an outline, then see what you have left out. This is worth doing many times, since it helps to give you the intellectual agility to succeed in what examiners so clearly want you to do, which is to answer precisely the questions you are set. If you run out of questions from sample papers you can set questions for yourself, or better still exchange questions with another student as suggested in item 15 of the quiz. Units 31 and 32 give further guidance in this kind of essay planning.

14 *I'll give up the luxury of tutorials*

Bad idea. It's easy to get a distorted perspective on your exam preparations. You think your own problems are worse than they really are, or you bias your revision too sharply to one particular view, or to one particular section of the course. The best way to keep a sense of proportion is to talk to other people about what you are doing. Of course I don't want to imply that if you can't get to your study centre your chances are necessarily poor. It's just that if you can go you will make revision a lot easier and more pleasant. It's a mistake to think that time at tutorials is time that could be better spent revising at home. Group revision can be very efficient.

15 *I'll arrange with another student that we set each other questions and try answering them*

At a less formal level than tutorials, it can be very helpful to make contact with another D103 student and work together on your revision, for the reasons outlined above.

16 *I'll spend hours sitting and worrying about how hopeless the whole venture is*

I assume I need make no comment.

THE GENERAL CONCLUSIONS

So what are the general conclusions we can draw from all this?

You have to 'learn' parts of the course but that does not imply rote learning. One of the best ways to learn is to go through your existing notes and to check whether or not you still feel they are a good summary of the relevant block. Look at a section in a unit and then ask yourself, 'Do my notes adequately represent the material in this section?' Once you feel confident that you have a good set of notes you can then begin to summarize them and to try to produce notes on the whole block on just a few sheets of paper. This is a form of active learning in which you are asking yourself to assess and think about the content of the block and the main questions it asks. You may find it helpful to read through the new notes a number of times to try to establish the main ideas more firmly in your memory but this is very different from the idea of simply trying to learn a block. Your TMAs are also a very useful resource which can be used alongside your notes in a similar way.

Choose one of the blocks you intend to revise and think about how you might do this. First of all you should collect your notes and the units together, including notes made for the TMA and the assignment itself. Then it is important to check how accurate a picture you now feel your notes represent. Look at the Contents page of the unit. Could you summarize each section of the unit in the light of your notes? Which section of the unit is concerned primarily with explanation and which with describing a case or example of some kind? Amend the notes so that you feel confident you have clear coverage of all the important points.

Now step back a little and look for the main questions which this block is trying to answer. You will find these by looking at the Introductions to the block and to the units, and by considering the short summaries which are placed at the end of major sections and sub-sections. Do your notes enable you to address those questions and can you provide brief examples to illustrate your answers?

Lastly, how does this block relate to the main themes and traditions in the course? Are there useful cross-references too with other blocks and units?

If you can polish your notes so that they provide you with this kind of coverage you will be carrying out a very useful form of active revision. You will be thinking about the purpose of your notes and the main messages the units are trying to deliver and not limiting yourself to the retention of a list of points to be learned by rote. If you find it difficult to define an important concept you should find the Glossary-Index a useful source.

The next activity is to condense the notes into a more manageable revision tool. They are probably too lengthy, or certainly have some sections which now seem less important and some which probably need more emphasis. The boiling down of notes to extract their concentrated essence is also a valuable way to revise. Try to summarize the notes so that you can put the essence of a unit onto one or two A4 sheets. This helps you to concentrate on the few crucial points you will need in the examination and should enable you to avoid becoming bogged down in detail.

=============   THE GOOD STUDY GUIDE   =============

Section 4.9, Chapter 7 of *The Good Study Guide* discusses this aspect of refining notes and you should read that section now if you have not already done so.

Once you have a set of notes in which you have reasonable confidence it is then better to concentrate on using those notes to answer questions rather than to learn them. You will be asked to answer questions on the blocks and the most successful way to do that is to practise that precise task — answering questions. It will be worth while trying to write out one or two answers in full under exam conditions if you can, but you may have neither the time nor the energy to do that very often. Spend as much time as you can planning answers. Aim to get your planning time down to about ten minutes (approximately the time you will have in the exam) and write out a clear outline of the answer you would intend to give.

Practice makes perfect we are told, but unfortunately that isn't entirely true. Practice makes permanent and it is a good idea to get a second or third opinion, if you can, on whether you are making perfect things permanent or actually consolidating bad habits and misunderstandings! This is where fellow students and tutor-counsellors are so important. You can check your understandings with each other, invent questions for each other and explore the subtleties of different arguments and ideas. If you are unable to get along to the study centre it is well worth while trying to meet with one or two fellow students at other times or to keep in touch by phone or letter.

In Units 31 and 32 we shall take up the idea of planning exam answers in more detail but please bear in mind that this is an activity which you should be moving towards in your revision schedule. One of the scarcest of all resources for most of us is time. It is important to look seriously at the time you have available between now and the examination date in October. You have to build into that time sufficient opportunity to go through the five blocks you chose earlier in this section. Maybe you should rethink. Do you have enough time to revise five blocks? Only four blocks would be more risky but perhaps in your circumstances it is more sensible. You will need to consolidate your notes on each of those blocks and leave enough room to spend time planning (and, if you can, discussing) essay outlines.

I find it much easier to give myself a specific task for each session I revise, rather than to decide I am going to revise for, say, two hours. Then once that task is completed — let's say summarizing the notes on two units — I stop with a sense of satisfaction. If I simply sit down for two hours my mind can very easily wander into all sorts of alternative avenues and I finish up dissatisfied and nervous. So if I was devising a revision schedule for myself, I would divide the relevant blocks into suitable chunks and set aside whatever time I could for each piece. It is often necessary to rework the schedule after a few days! The important point is really to work all this out now, trying to assess how long you will need to sort out your various bits of paper, how long to consolidate your notes and so on, leaving enough time to practise exam questions one you have got under way.

THE GOOD STUDY GUIDE AND AUDIO CASSETTE

Chapter 7 of *The Good Study Guide* picks up these points in Section 4 and you might find it helpful to read the whole of that section now.

You should also listen to Side A of Cassette 7 at this point.

SUMMARY

You should now schedule the following activities to give yourself a revision period which takes into account your skills and resources, including the time you have available. You need to do 3 things within the next few days:

1 Study the structure of the exam paper carefully by looking at the specimen paper.
2 Select the parts of the course you intend to revise.
3 Make a timetable for revision.

Your timetable must include time for the activities listed below and you should begin to carry out these tasks soon. We have tried to incorporate sufficient time for you to undertake revision within the allocations for the Block VII units. At the end of Unit 32 you will find more suggestions on coping with the exam itself.

Revision strategies:

- Seek out the central questions in each of the parts of the course you have chosen to revise and ensure that your existing notes adequately deal with these questions.
- Condense the notes on each of your chosen units into brief summarizing notes.
- Think up questions you might be asked.
- Practise writing down outlines for answers to questions.
- Practise writing out one or two answers in full against the clock.
- Keep in touch with other students and your tutor-counsellor to broaden your ideas and to check your understanding.

(PS Remember the 'exam alert' and don't put off working out your revision schedule too long.)

ACKNOWLEDGEMENTS

Grateful acknowledgement is made to the following sources for permission to reproduce material in this unit:

Photographs

p.34: London School of Economics; *p.37*: Mary Evans Picture Library; *p.40*: Courtesy of Professor A.P.L. Minford; *p.50*: Mike Abrahams/Network; *p.55*: Mansell.

UNIT 29   MARXIST AND SOCIAL REFORMIST APPROACHES

Essays prepared for the Course Team by Robert Looker and David Denver. Introduction and commentary by David Coates. Further commentary by Robert Bocock

CONTENTS

1   INTRODUCTION

In Unit 29 we have three linked concerns. First, we want to complete your journey through the four traditions — by examining how marxism and social reformism can be used as an approach to UK society. Secondly, we want to look in detail at how best to compare and evaluate material of this kind — and in this way consolidate with you a particular set of study skills which you will need on many occasions in your university career. And finally we want to go beyond the four traditions, probing some of the complex ways in which these bodies of thought live alongside other ways of thinking, analysing and acting in the contemporary world. We want, that is, to consolidate, evaluate, and explore the limits of D103's four traditions of thought.

2   MARXISM

THE FOUR QUESTIONS

To save you looking back to the beginning of Unit 28, here again are the questions which form the core to the four essays:

1   What are the main problems of contemporary UK society?
2   What are the main historical and contemporary causes?
3   What should be done about the problems and by whom?
4   What is it about your tradition which predisposes you to highlight these particular problems, causes and solutions?

By now I hope that the basic strategy for extracting and comparing the arguments in the four essays should be second nature to you. So carry on by reading the essay by Robert Looker.

———————————————— ACTIVITY 1 ————————————————

Read his essay 'A marxist approach to the UK', and build up a matrix as you did in Unit 28 on the four questions.

As before, you will find a set of answers at the back of the unit.

A MARXIST APPROACH TO THE UK
by Robert Looker

INTRODUCTION

An analysis written from a Marxist standpoint faces problems in communicating with readers in the UK. In our kind of society, such ideas are often viewed with incomprehension or hostility. Marxism is seen as dogmatic, jargon-ridden, and probably propaganda. Leaving aside the propaganda issue — in my view, existing 'communist states' have nothing in common with communism as envisaged by Marx — I would agree that there is a problem of tone and language in Marxist writings. It arises in part from the way in which the tradition sets about the tasks of analysis. Marxism, more than other traditions of social thought, is explicit in its use of theory and concepts. However, this doesn't mean that it is a dogmatic system or that it secures itself from criticism by reference to some set of 'sacred' texts composed by Marx and selected followers. There is no single Marxist view. Rather, there are vigorous debates between individual Marxists and competing 'Marxisms' which reveal marked disagreements over analyses, methodologies, theories and political commitments. My analysis of modern Britain is therefore only *a* — not *the* — Marxist view.

Given this, I need to indicate what I see as the key assumptions of the tradition. These consist of three elements — *critique; alternative; agency*. First, Marxism offers *a critique* of capitalism as inherently exploitative and oppressive. Its dynamic but unstable processes of capital accumulation and its antagonistic class relationship between capital and wage-labour mean that crises and class conflict are integral to its social order. Second, capitalism creates the material pre-conditions for a radically *alternative* social order, i.e. a genuinely communist society based on the fullest democratic social control over the processes of production and distribution. The result would be a 'society of abundance' free from both exploitation and oppression. Third, capitalism creates its own gravediggers in the shape of a working class which has both the objective interest and collective capacity to act as the *agency* of revolutionary change. If that class can be won to consciously Marxist perspectives, it is capable of creating the conditions for the liberation of the human species as a whole.

WHAT ARE THE MAIN PROBLEMS OF CONTEMPORARY UK SOCIETY?

For Marxists, the main problems confronting the UK flow from its character as a capitalist system whose specific features have been shaped over a long period of historical development. Their manifestation in the late twentieth century takes the form of a complex of inter-related crises which have disrupted the social order from the 1970s onwards.

The first aspect of crisis arose from the poor performance of the UK economy in the world market. Even during the 'Long Boom' decades of sustained expansion in the global economy from the late 1940s to the early 1970s, British capitalism had lower levels of economic growth and a declining share of global production and trade relative to its main industrial rivals. As the world economy moved into a period of crisis and instability from the early 1970s onwards, this relative decline threatened to turn into absolute economic collapse.

Economic crises from the early 1970s onwards set the context for a second crisis — one of the practice and theory of the post-war British state. During the decades after 1945, popular consent for the social order was underpinned by state policies aimed at expanding living standards and providing a welfare state. 'Welfarism' and 'Keynesian interventionism' were central to a 'consensus politics' which united both Labour and Tory governments in these decades. The consensus was shattered by economic crises in the 1970s which directly challenged the credibility of Keynesian strategies for 'demand management'. State expenditures, hitherto seen as the cure for economic crisis, now appeared to contribute to the disease.

A third face of the crisis involved a rising wave of social and particularly industrial unrest within the UK. One powerful appeal of the 'consensus politics' package for significant sectors of the British ruling class in the post-war decades was that it ensured a fair degree of stability and popular support for the social order. It gave Britain the *appearance* of a society that had eliminated fundamental class divisions and conflicts. Yet the 1960s and 1970s saw an erosion of consent. Challenges came from a variety of directions — in Northern Ireland; from student, feminist and other radicals; and through union militancy.

In particular, government economic policies in the period stimulated a rising wave of industrial militancy, culminating in 1973–4 with a miners strike and the collapse of the Tory government. The material and ideological underpinnings of the social order seemed suddenly very fragile.

The cumulative effect of these problems provoked a further crisis in the perspectives which had dominated the post-war political universe of capitalist democracy in Britain. The 1970s was a period of profound ideological crisis which called into question the *social reformist* assumptions of both Labour and One Nation Toryism, and the 'politics of consensus' which they had underpinned. The most visible manifestation of these changes was the triumph of 'New Right' ideas in the Tory Party under Margaret Thatcher's leadership. Conservative electoral victories from 1979 ensured that these ideas — an uneasy mixture of 'neo-liberal' themes of monetarism, individualism and the market, with 'neo-conservative' views on the family, nationalism and traditional values etc — provided the language within which politics were formulated in the 1980s.

In analysing the problems facing Britain, Marxists focus on factors which shape the balance of forces between capital and wage-labour. More specifically, we look at the structure of

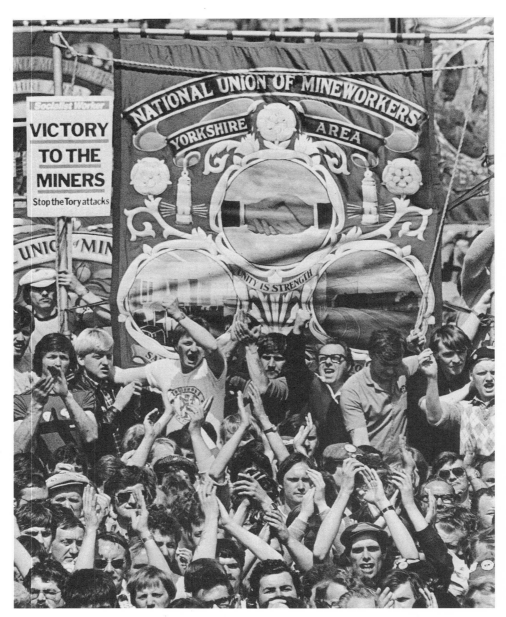

Miners demonstrate against pit closures, Mansfield near Nottingham, May 1984

class inequality, the strength of organized labour, the role of state power, the competitiveness of UK capital, and the ideological framework of the social order. A marxist view of, for instance, Tory government policy in the 1980s therefore focuses on its impact on these dimensions of the British social order.

Government economic and social policy during the 1980s led to a marked increase in the structure of inequalities intrinsic to capitalism. At the top end of the class structure, the *Thatcherite* programme of transforming Britain into 'a land fit for entrepreneurs' ensured that the benefits flowed mainly to the rich. The horrendous social and economic costs of those policies, in terms of unemployment, poverty, homelessness, ill health etc., fell on the working class, with the greatest deprivation and misery being endured by the weakest and most deprived sections of the population. This in turn generated a swathe of 'social problems' — drugs, sexual violence, soccer hooliganism, racial attacks etc. — rooted in the multiple alienations bred in the 'lower depths' of modern Britain.

Tory governments also attacked the industrial strength and political influence of organized labour, most notably through a series of anti-union laws which drastically constricted the space available for legitimate industrial action. Such attacks on the institutions and practices of organized labour clearly had a sharp impact during the 1980s, but their long term effect is uncertain. The government won major victories over key sectors of organized workers — notably over the miners in 1984–5 — and persuaded most trade union leaders to work within the restrictive limits set by the anti-union legislation. Yet though union membership shrank and the number of strikes declined over the decade, arguably this was less a consequence of government policy than of unfavourable labour market conditions. The trend could well reverse if employment and output revive. Moreover the late 1980s saw a growth of union militancy among public sector employees and white collar and even professional workers who had hitherto shunned the languages and practices of trade unionism. The 'enemy within' had been curbed but not crushed by Thatcherite policies.

The 1980s also saw a marked expansion of the coercive resources of the state and an increased readiness to use them. As government policies provoked a wide range of protests, from industrial struggles to inner city riots, the state responded with increasingly authoritarian strategies, 'criminalizing' the conflicts and relying on the police and the courts for their solution. 'Law and order' perspectives also framed its approach to the rising tide of social problems (homelessness, drug abuse, youth unemployment, etc.) and associated crime levels in the decade. Such policies required and legitimated a sizeable expansion in the scale and scope of the coercive apparatus of the state, thus tilting the balance away from consent and towards force in the maintenance of social order. One result was an increase in popular awareness and resentment at the role of 'state power' as distinct from 'democratic government' in underpinning the system. Whether this will work to undermine the legitimacy granted to the social order remains to be seen.

Many Marxists saw the essence of government strategy as an attempt to restore UK capitalism to competitive health by exposing it to market forces. Results here were very mixed. On some measures — increased industrial productivity for example — it seems to have paid dividends. Other indicators — continuing decline in manufacturing output and levels of productive investment, the re-emergence of inflation and balance of payments crises in the late 1980s etc. — suggested that Thatcherite 'cures' for the long-term weakness of the UK economy were more cosmetic than real.

Some commentators on the Left saw the boldest element in the Conservative programme as its ideological attempt to reconstitute the languages of political debate and of sub-political 'common sense' on assumptions derived from New Right rhetoric and practice. Its goal was the construction of an 'historic bloc' or permanent electoral majority for New Right strategies encompassing all sections of society, including key components of a working class traditionally aligned to Labour. Yet while specific aspects of government policy achieved some successes on this front — cuts in direct taxation, the sale of council housing, the Falklands War etc. — there is little evidence that Thatcherism created a new 'common sense' in its own image. Thus government policies had little success in shifting popular support away from the 'social welfare' component of the consensus towards New Right views. Arguably the main success of 'Thatcherite' ideology lay, not in shaping popular consciousness, but in promoting the ideology and practices of an 'enterprise culture' among key personnel in the corporate bureaucracies of the public and private sectors. In this task, it was powerfully assisted by changes which took place in the Labour Party.

Most Marxists see the Labour Party as incapable of bringing about the socialist transformation of British society. Its historical role has been to win benefits for organized labour as a sectional interest *within* the existing social order while blocking attempts by workers to challenge and move *beyond* it. Its highly visible internal divisions — between a Right seeking only a limited reform programme and a Left aspiring to some socialist alternative — obscure the more fundamental agreement uniting both wings of the party. They share a conviction that 'the limits of the politically possible' are set by the constraints of parliamentary politics. Marxists argue that a bourgeois state cannot be used to achieve socialism by act of parliament — capitalist democracy simply won't stretch that far. The socialist aspirations of the Labour Left are therefore negated by their strategy for achieving them. Historically, Labour has papered over its internal divisions by advocating reformist programmes which satisfied the material requirements of the Right while allowing the Left to believe that they were steps along the road to an eventual socialist future.

Labour's version of social reformism reached its high point in the post-war decades when Keynesianism provided it with a coherent intellectual and practical pedigree. When the actual experience of Labour governments in the period showed that 'space' for reform was more limited than either Right or Left supposed, this was attributed either to lack of resolve by the leadership or to pressure of immediate circumstances blowing the programme temporarily off-course. However, the crises of the 1970s were of a different order. The collapse from the mid-1970s of Labour's reformist programme exposed the contradiction at the heart of the Labourist compromise and led to intense internal conflict between Left and Right. Yet the crises also demonstrated the inability of social reformist perspectives, whether of Left or Right, to cope with the changing structure of world capitalism. The result was widespread disillusionment with such strategies and a series of electoral defeats for Labour. Attempts by the party to redesign its policies in the 1980s were forced explicitly to accept the need to 'work with the grain of the market'. By the 1990s, even a modest Social Reformism had become far too ambitious a goal in the eyes of the Labour leadership under Neil Kinnock. For Labour as much as the Conservatives, the requirements of the capitalist market were now the final arbiters of state and party policy.

WHAT ARE THE MAIN HISTORICAL AND CONTEMPORARY CAUSES?

Marxist explanations of the problems facing the UK operate with a hierarchy of levels of causes, from the structural and historical determinants of world capitalism to the balance of class forces within Britain today. They start from the view that the core crises arise from its capitalist character. At the most fundamental level, the capitalist mode of production involves a drive to accumulate capital which produces both dynamism and instability within its social order. Crises and change are written into the system at both global and national levels. However, we cannot infer directly from this to the specific features of the crises of the 1970s and 1980s. Here we need a more specific grasp of both the *local* and the *global* levels and the interplay between them — between the historical trajectory of UK capitalism and the changing structure of the world economy. More particularly, Marxists look at the way these have combined to produce a pattern of long-term decline in the industrial base of the British economy.

Most Marxists agree that the central role played by British capital within the developing global economy from its earliest beginnings has had a profound impact on its degree of involvement within the world market system. Though Britain lost its pre-eminence as the workshop and clearing house of the world from the late nineteenth century onwards, all sectors of its economy — manufacturing no less than commerce and banking etc. — remained deeply enmeshed in, and particularly sensitive and vulnerable to, world market forces. Yet while commerce and banking prospered throughout the twentieth century, industry faced a long relative decline in international competitiveness.

Many Marxists see this long-term decline as a consequence of *peculiarities* in the British social order arising from its position as the world's first capitalist and industrial state. However, *which* feature of that order has been causally decisive here is a matter of much debate. Some see it as a debilitating legacy of prolonged aristocratic rule. Others argue that it flows from the subordination of manufacturing interests to those of the City in the affairs of the nation. Still others see it as part of the baleful legacy of Empire.

Such views see the long-term problems of British industrial capitalism as flowing from its premature, partial or limited development. My own view is that it arises from the *advanced* nature of industrial capitalist development in Britain in the nineteenth century. The long, slow and thorough transformation of the social order produced by the Industrial Revolution gave birth to an unusually large and skilled industrial working class and a powerful and well organized labour movement. This posed major problems for the social order of UK capitalism. Its maintenance required a degree of class 'cooperation' on the political and industrial fronts which could not simply be compelled by state coercion or market discipline alone. Working class interests also needed to be accommodated and channelled into moderate programmes of reform. What emerged was a set of institutions, ideologies and practices — trade unions, parliamentary politics, reformist ideologies — which worked to conciliate class interests and to manage and moderate rather than exacerbate class conflict. The result was to build a 'corporate bias' into the system of political and industrial relations of twentieth century Britain. In particular, it gave organized labour a significant influence over the rate of exploitation, and hence the level of profitability, within the industrial sector of the economy, and helped set parameters for state social and economic policy. At the same time it posed crucial problems for a capitalist economy deeply enmeshed in world markets.

In my view, it is the fusion of *global* and *local* elements — the openness of the British economy to world markets and the defensive strength of organized labour within the social order — which accounts for its relative industrial decline. Indeed, this is the key contradiction which lies at the core of British capitalism. Its history over the past century — particularly since 1945 — pivots on the ways in which the two have combined to limit the effectiveness of reformist politics to satisfy the needs of the working class, while also failing to ensure the profitability and competitiveness of industrial capital.

This was evident even when the post-war decades of the 'Long Boom' allowed some 'space' for both economic growth and the expansion of welfare. The post-war expansion of the world economy provided the material underpinnings for political and social stability throughout the West. Affluence, consensus politics and welfarism (variously mixed together in different states depending upon their internal balance of class forces) prevailed throughout the advanced industrial capitalist sector of the globe. Yet even in these favourable circumstances the weak performance of the British economy set tight limits on the extent to which working class aspirations — for rising living standards, an expanded welfare state, job control — could be satisfied within the existing system. At the same time the achievement of even modest welfare gains and their political entrenchment within a 'social democratic consensus', accompanied by continuing union strength on the industrial front, worked to limit the possibilities for a thorough-going renovation of the industrial capitalist economy.

The increasing preoccupation of governments with problems of low economic growth in Britain from the 1960s onwards only served to intensify and formalize the 'corporatist bias' in the system. This reached its peak under successive Labour and Conservative governments between 1964 and 1976 when tri-partite negotiations between management, unions and the government became the preferred strategy for ensuring union cooperation in a programme of industrial modernization. Yet such *corporatism,* with its attempts to reconcile incompatible class interests within a common framework of agreed priorities, needed a favourable external economic environment for success. Increasingly the international instability from the 1960s and slump and uneven growth from the 1970s onwards removed the material underpinnings for achieving class cooperation for the strategy.

The causes of the international crises are complex and contentious. Most Marxist accounts see the immediate causes of disruptions — the oil price hikes of 1973 for example — merely as symptoms of a deeper malaise within the world capitalist economy. Some argue that the system is facing a long-term decline in rate of profit. Others see the pattern of uneven development in the relative economic performances of USA, Japan and EEC, and between the West and Third World, inducing destabilizing imbalances in production, trade and financial flows between the component sectors of the global economy. Whatever the causes of crisis, the inter-dependent structure of the modern international economy, locking national economies tightly together at the levels of trade, production and finance, effectively restrict the possibilities open for national economic responses to it. Unlike the inter-war slump of 1929–31 which precipitated a decline in international trade and a retreat into economic protectionism, the reaction to crises from the mid-1970s by the major industrial capitalist states was to intensify market competition at all levels. The particular severity of the impact of the crisis on an already vulnerable economy like Britain meant that it required a major re-structuring in order to survive as an effective capitalist player within the highly inter-dependent world market system.

The pressure of international market forces sharply restricted the room available for autonomous decision making by national governments, particularly the economically weaker ones. In Britain by the 1970s, space no longer existed for social reformism of either the Labour or Tory variety. The restoration of capitalist competitiveness and profitability dictated the abandonment of such politics in favour of policies designed to shift the balance of class power from labour to capital in both industry and the state. The emergence of 'Thatcherism' at this juncture was thus part of a wider process reshaping the perspectives guiding the ruling circles of Britain. The crises of the 1970s convinced many of those who staffed the command posts of state, economy and civil society — including sections of the Labour leadership — that the core source of Britain's problems lay in the power of organized labour and its insulation from the 'disciplines' of the market. The emergence of a 'free market' strategy as the preferred solution for the many ills of the UK economy and social order was thus a rational and coherent response to the situation, at least within the logic of capitalism. It was this elite consensus which 'set the agenda' for politics in the 1980s.

In similar fashion, the limited achievements of Tory rule in the 1980s set the scene for the politics of the 1990s and beyond. Thatcherism neither restored British capital to competitive health nor ensured a decisive shift in the balance of power between capital and labour. In many ways, its main effect was to strip away the practical and ideological coverings obscuring the class nature of British society which grew up during the decades of social reformist ascendancy. In the process it has exposed many of the 'raw nerves' intrinsic to capitalist exploitation and oppression without delivering the sustained economic growth which might have headed off the conflicts such policies necessarily produce.

Yet if Thatcherism represented an 'idea whose time has gone', there seems little prospect of seeing a successful return to the politics of the social reformist consensus. The imperatives of the world capitalist order no longer make available the kind of 'space' for national reformism that such a programme requires, particularly for an ailing national capitalism like Britain. Whichever party achieves electoral success in Britain in the 1990s the result will be the politics of Micawberism, hoping for 'something to turn up' — a new 'Long Boom' in the global economy or some European miracle cure — to rescue them from this impasse. In the absence of such a *deus ex machina*, the orthodox politics of capitalist democracy have reached a situation close to ideological exhaustion as far as strategies for resolving the problems of the UK are concerned.

WHAT SHOULD BE DONE ABOUT THE PROBLEMS AND BY WHOM?

Judged solely as a critique of capitalism, Marxism is both powerful and persuasive. However Marxists also aim to identify a viable socialist *alternative* to capitalism and to provide guidance to the social *agencies* which can bring it about. Yet it is often precisely at this point that we feel weakest. For the central problem Marxists face in Britain is the absence of any belief in, or support for such a socialist alternative, not least among its supposedly 'natural' constituency, the working class. Given this, Marxist socialism is not on the current agenda of class politics in Britain and it would require a major shift in the class perspectives to put it there. How then do Marxists explain why their programme for socialism has proved so unappealing in our epoch?

It may be tempting, but ultimately sterile, to ascribe the problem to the prevalence of 'false consciousness' among the working class. This is merely to re-describe the problem, not to explain it. Nor can we argue that the mechanisms sustaining the legitimations of capitalist order have proved too strong for this is simply to sidestep the issue. In any event, one of the most striking features of modern Britain is the visible disenchantment of large sections of the population with the choices they are currently offered. The experienced oppressions and exploitations of capitalist Britain have created 'constituencies' and movements — of women, blacks, gays, environmentalists etc — which both express a marked degree of alienation from the system and a search for radical strategies to transform it. Even within the more orthodox political arena, there has been a continuing search for alternative political agendas of varying degrees of radicalism — from celtic nationalism to Green politics — appealing to different but equally disaffected constituencies. In this welter of ideas and movements, the rhetoric of 'socialism' has not entirely disappeared, but its articulation usually involves a distancing from, or outright disclaimer of lineage with, Marxism. Marxist socialism is encountered only at the periph-

Police disperse striking miners near Sheffield, May 1984

ery, usually in tiny organizations existing at the margins of the processes shaping developments in Britain.

If we confront the problem of the Marxist alternative first, it is not difficult to see why it should appear so unpopular. Bluntly, the major obstacle here is the long term legacy of failure by socialist ideas and practices to create a different and better social order. The socialist promise at the dawn of the twentieth century all too frequently resulted in bureaucratic statism or totalitarianism as the century progressed. Both have failed, and been visibly seen to fail, even in the estimation of their erstwhile adherents. And while much Marxist energy and thought has been devoted to demonstrating that the failures of Social-Democratic and Communist parties in the twentieth century flow in substantial part from their rejection or perversion of Marxist ideas, the result — long term erosion of working class belief that socialism is either possible or desirable — remains undeniable. The revindication of a Marxist strategy thus depends upon re-establishing the relevance of socialist perspectives to the lived experiences and collective struggles of the working class at the dawning of a new century.

The question of class agency raises a further problem. For today, many of those on the Left would deny that it is any longer appropriate to view the working class as the key agency of revolutionary change in capitalism. 'Revisionists' argue that technological and other trends in advanced capitalism involve a long-term decline in the 'traditional' working class. As a result, ideas of 'socialism' constructed by and for that class have lost relevance to the needs of the post-industrial society that Britain is becoming. The prospects for socialist renewal are thus contingent on building a new 'historic bloc' for socialism based on 'new social forces' emerging in the movements of women, gays, blacks, ecologists etc.

More 'orthodox' Marxists like myself acknowledge the importance of these struggles. They address issues rooted in capitalism and potentially contribute to the movement to build socialism. However that movement and its programme is viable only if there is a working class at its core committed to socialism as the practical route for their own self-liberation. We remain optimistic about the long-term prospects for such a development and argue that the changes currently taking place in the working class in Britain and on a global scale promise to expand and strengthen the class over time.

Globally, industry and the industrial working class grows larger every decade. In advanced capitalisms like Britain, shifts within the manufacturing sectors and between it and the service sectors are part of a continual process of restructuring the internal composition and external boundaries of the working class which has been going on throughout the lifetime of industrial capitalism. One key development is the progressive subjection of sections of the non-manual working population to the logic of the capital/wage-labour relationship with consequences for loss of autonomy in the work process, exposure and vulnerability to the operation of market forces on pay and employment etc. 'Proletarianization' of significant sectors of white collar and even professional workers has produced a marked growth in their industrial organization and militancy, particularly in the public sector. In principle, this works to create a more favourable environment for the growth of socialist ideas and in this context, the terminal decline of reformism and of stalinism constitutes as much of an opportunity for Marxist advance as a constraint upon it.

Marxists ultimately believe that the dynamics of the world capitalist system itself will create the openings for conscious socialist intervention. The growing centralization and socialization of capital on a global as well as national scale continues to generate exploitation, oppression and class conflict while restricting the options open to any state to manage and ameliorate them. It also ensures an acceleration in the interdependence of social labour within and across national boundaries and establishes the material basis for a recognition and collective action in pursuit of common class interests. Struggles and conflicts which mobilize workers into collective activity have always been seen by Marxists as the point around which to organize and articulate their politics. The issues may be highly specific — a strike in opposition to racial abuse, sexual harassment or environmental pollution, defying specific government policies — but they provide the context in which concrete gains can be made and where political lessons can be generalized in a socialist direction.

For Marxists, this represents the way forward both in Britain and elsewhere. Economically, politically and ideologically, we live today in a highly inter-dependent world. One sign of this is the way in which various 'national' conflicts in the late twentieth century impact on popular consciousness on a global scale. Struggles led by or relying on the working classes in locales as diverse as South Korea, China, Poland, South Africa and Brazil have an increasing potential for connecting with the situation and perspectives of workers in Britain. Perhaps after all the vision of a socialism as *international* class struggle will place the Marxist programme of social transformation on the agenda in Britain in the twenty-first century.

WHAT IS IT ABOUT THE MARXIST TRADITION WHICH PREDISPOSES YOU TO HIGHLIGHT THESE PARTICULAR PROBLEMS, CAUSES AND SOLUTIONS?

As a Marxist, I have a minimum and a maximum requirement from the tradition to which I subscribe. The former is that it provides a framework of analysis which enables me to make better sense of what is happening in the world than any of its other competitors. The latter is that its goal of an alternative, communist social order is a feasible one and that it provides a guide for realistic strategies to achieve it.

As a system of analysis, Marxism is nothing if not ambitious in the standards against which it asks to be judged. Its goal is *holistic*: it seeks to grasp the social order of capitalism in its entirety and in all its internal complexity. At the same time it is *dialectical*; it sees capitalism as driven by the contradictory logics of capital accumulation and class conflict at work

The choice according to Marx is between Socialism or Barbarism

within it, with all the historical processes of conflict, change and transformation this entails. Further, it is *materialistic* and even *economistic* in its focus on the material practices which constitute a social order and gives particular priority to the economy in explaining the workings of the social order as a whole. Politics and ideology are seen as intimately bound up with economic processes, though they can also exhibit considerable, if relative, autonomy from them. It sees social ideas as 'social products' concerned with practical orientations to the social order. Finally, Marxists do not believe that theories can be used to short-circuit the need for detailed empirical investigations nor can they be applied in such a way as to produce an automatic 'read out' of what is going on. There must be a *dialogue* between *theory* and *history* rather than the subordination of one to the other. I believe that Marxism meets its minimum requirements, though this can only be demonstrated through empirical analysis. But how relevant is its maximum programme in the world today? An ancient Chinese curse runs 'may you live in interesting times'. For better or worse, we as the inhabitants of our planet on the eve of a new millennium are fated to live in very interesting times indeed! Yet the challenge of what the future holds for us — the continuation of our existing exploitative, oppressive and conflict-ridden global social order; its final annihilation through nuclear war or global pollution; or the construction of a truly free and liberating social order built on socialist principles — is less a matter of scientific prediction than of collective political choice and action. Marxists see no inevitability about the triumph of socialism. The options remain, as Marx identified them a century and a half ago, Socialism or Barbarism.

Welcome back from your reading. Now we need to compare the argument in the Looker essay with the summary of the marxist tradition in Chapter 22 of the Reader, to see how typical a piece of marxist writing this is, and to see if anything needs to be added. The summaries from Chapter 22 read like this.

THE REAL PREMISES OF MARXIST THOUGHT

1 Marx rejected liberalism's starting point of 'the individual', insisting instead on the primacy of social relationships.

2 For Marx, individual action was socially conditioned and socially constrained. 'Men make their own history, but not just as they please'

3 Since for Marx human labour is what distinguishes humans from animals, it is the social relationships which surround production which then shape society as a whole. Societies, that is, have an economic base and a social, political and cultural superstructure.

ECONOMY AND SOCIETY

1 Historically, societies have been divided between producers and non-producers, divided, that is, into antagonistic social classes. Different social classes have developed and dominated in different periods. In capitalism the two most important social classes are the bourgeoisie and the proletariat.

2 The contemporary economy is organized on capitalist lines. Capitalism, for Marx, is a system of generalized commodity production based on free wage labour.

3 Capitalism is more dynamic than earlier ways of organizing economic life, but it is also crisis-ridden. The ultimate source of its instability is the proletariat it creates, which comes to have both an interest in its replacement and the capacity to replace it.

POWER AND THE STATE

1 Marxist sensitivity to questions of power relations between men and women has not been great. But Engels did attempt to explain gender divisions as products of the emergence of private property, and — as such — unlikely to survive the demise of private property in socialism.

2 Marx saw the state as the agent of the dominant class, with at most a limited degree of autonomy from control by the owners of the means of production. He expected the proletariat to establish its own dictatorship in socialism, and for all forms of the state to wither away in communism.

3 Later marxists — particularly Gramsci — emphasized the important role played by the state in orchestrating ideologies to legitimate capitalism and alliances of classes to sustain it.

If you compare your matrix on the Looker essay with these summaries from the traditions essay, you will see that again we have a mainstream position on offer. Bob Looker lays much store on the crises of capitalism, the importance of social class, the role of the proletariat as a revolutionary agency, and the way in which state power is constrained by capital. And like the mainstream of the marxist tradition, he doesn't give much chance for the incremental reform of capitalism into something better.

─────────────────── ACTIVITY 2 ───────────────────

Once again, you need to locate the strengths and weaknesses of the essay you have just read. One possible strength is its ability to explain the return of economic crises. One possible weakness is the difficulty it has explaining the lack of support for revolutionary socialist political parties. Can you think of two more strengths and two more weaknesses?

───

There are lots of possible answers, of course. For *strengths*, you might list the insights marxism gives into the distribution of wealth and income in the contemporary UK, and into the capacity of financial institutions to exercise more political muscle than trade unions do. We already touched on issues like that when laying out theories of the state in Unit 18. For *weaknesses*, perhaps there is not enough discussion of gender divisions (as was mentioned in Unit 8) or of the persistence of a large middle class (though marxist treatments of this do exist, as we saw in Unit 7). But marxism is generally thought vulnerable in some of its sociology (its treatment of working class consciousness, its tendency to a two-class model of social stratification, its prioritizing of class divisions over those of gender) but often looks better in its economics and politics (on its crisis theory, and its analysis of the determinants of state power).

3 SOCIAL REFORMISM

Finally, let's do the exercise again on the following essay by David Denver on 'Social Reformism'.

─────────────────── ACTIVITY 3 ───────────────────

Read the essay, then fill out the four boxes on your matrix in Unit 28. Supplement them by reference to the summaries of the tradition in Chapter 22 of the Reader, and list social reformism's strengths and weaknesses.

This one we want you to tackle more on your own. So we will not reproduce all the summaries here. Instead the summaries are there to help you — in Chapter 22 of the Reader. And if you are still in doubt about any part of the social reformist package, you could always check back in

- Unit 7: for the discussion of Max Weber's theory of stratification;
- Unit 12: on Keynesianism; and
- Unit 15: on pluralist theories of the state.

And, as usual, there is a summary of the four answers David Denver provides, attached to the end of this unit.

A SOCIAL REFORMIST APPROACH TO THE UK

by David Denver

WHAT ARE THE MAIN PROBLEMS OF CONTEMPORARY UK SOCIETY?

At first glance a question such as this looks easy enough to answer. Without very much difficulty we could all reel off a lengthy list of problems — battered children, NHS waiting lists, drug abuse, shortages of skilled workers, 'lager louts' and so on. Indeed, samples of the population are regularly asked just such a question by opinion pollsters and they give perfectly sensible answers. At the end of the 1980s, for example, Gallup Polls reported that people believed the most important problems facing the country were unemployment, health, law and order, housing, education, defence, the cost of living and pensions (Gallup Political Index, 1986–88). While it is likely that what an individual perceives as a problem will depend to some extent on his or her situation — few Highland crofters, I think, would immediately fasten upon traffic congestion in the South East of England as a

Homeless in London

matter of grave concern — not many people would deny that the sorts of things mentioned by Gallup's respondents are serious problems.

Comparing the Gallup list with the list that I 'reeled off' at the outset suggests, however, that there are two interconnected difficulties in defining major problems. The first is that the question can be answered at different levels. The Gallup list comprises issues that are pitched at a more general level than are those that I started with. It is not difficult to see how it could be argued that specific problems are merely consequences of some more general problem. Thus a shortage of trained teachers is a fairly specific problem but it might be a consequence of relatively low pay in the public sector, which is a more general problem. In turn, poor public sector pay might be a consequence of the even more general problem of poor rates of economic growth. Clearly this sort of regression could continue until we reached some highly general end point such as human nature, world capitalism or the movements of the planets. There is, then, a difficulty in defining the appropriate level of analysis when defining what problems the country faces.

The second difficulty relates in particular to the kinds of problems that people mention when questioned by pollsters. The matters they refer to are frequently couched in such general terms that it is not at all clear what they think the problem actually is, or what should be done about it. Many people say, for example, that 'Health' is a problem but it is not clear whether they are thinking of general underfunding of the NHS, poor pay for nurses, restricted patient choice, waste and inefficiency or a top-heavy bureaucracy. Clearly solutions will vary with the precise definition of the problem. Even if everyone agrees that underfunding is the problem they might disagree about whether the solution is to divert public resources from other areas, raise taxes or encourage private health care. In raising these sorts of issues I am moving away from thinking of problems as being matters about which there is general concern or unease. I am introducing a causal element into the definition of problems (since solutions imply causes) and also bringing in values (since having a view about what is wrong and what should be done about it implies a judgement about how things ought to be). It is in these terms, rather than in terms of naming areas of concern, that individuals and political and theoretical traditions diverge in their assessments of the major problems facing the country.

Thinking first in terms of the level of analysis, how do people in the social reformist tradition tend to define problems? They clearly avoid high levels of generality. There is little that any individual or group can do about something as general as the global economic system or even the general shape of British society (even though social reformists want to change British society to a greater or lesser degree) and so these tend to be taken as 'givens', the contexts within which problems need to be solved, rather than as problems in themselves. There is a clear difference here with the marxist tradition which frequently leads people to conclude that 'the capitalist system' is, in the end, the problem.

Social reformists, in contrast, usually prefer to deal with problems that are manageable, or at least more limited, and this has led many people to concentrate their attention on very specific concerns. There are numerous interest groups which stem from the social reformist tradition — Shelter, Child Poverty Action Group, Help the Aged, Howard League for Penal Reform and so on — which campaign on behalf of particular groups and causes. At a more middling level of analysis, however, the main substantive focus of the social reformist tradition is upon the management of the economy and the general welfare of the population. (I use 'general welfare' here in a broad sense to include such matters as health, housing and education as well as more specific welfare benefits such as pensions.)

It is not, of course, particularly surprising that social reformists should focus on the economy and general welfare. One does not have to be a marxist to recognize that economic policy and performance are of fundamental importance in any society, and people of all persuasions would profess a concern for the general welfare of the population. Moreover, the issues which ordinary citizens refer to when asked what is the most important problem facing the country are largely 'bread and butter' issues related to welfare and the economy.

It is worth noting that this focus excludes problems relating to the environment — such as the 'greenhouse effect' — which have attracted a good deal of attention in recent years. Individuals within the social reformist tradition are, no doubt, sympathetic to 'Green' issues but these are often seen as 'post-materialist' concerns. That is, they are issues about which people in general become concerned after they have achieved a satisfactory level of material existence — adequate housing, income, standard of living and so on. Most social reformists are still mainly concerned to secure improvements in these areas in order to achieve a more equal society.

I have noted that almost everyone would agree that management of the economy and the provision of general welfare are, in one sense, the major problems facing British society. Where social reformism diverges from other traditions is in the way it defines more precisely what is wrong in these areas and prescribes what should be done about them. For social reformists, there are two main interconnected problems in this sense. Firstly, in recent times there has been an over-reliance on the market as an economic instrument and secondly, the dominant view of the role of the state in promoting welfare has been a negative one. In identifying these as the main problems, modern social reformists are voicing the same concerns as those which exercised two of the great figures in the social reformist tradition — Keynes and Beveridge. Keynes, it will be remembered, saw unregulated markets as the basic cause of economic crises, depression and the accompanying social ills of unemployment and poverty. Beveridge was the principal architect of the post-war welfare state.

Throughout the 1980s, the management of the British economy was increasingly market-oriented and the principles of the market were extended into areas such as health provision, education and other local and central government services. Social reformists are not entirely opposed to market principles but regard their unfettered use in the economy and their application in areas like health as sources of division and gross inequality, as well as promoting essentially selfish values. Accompanying this increased commitment to market principles — and underlying it — was a negative view of the state. Although there were areas in which the role of the state was enlarged or central control increased at the expense of local control, the dominant view of government was that the state was a burden on the people. This led, in general to attempts to reduce the role of the state in providing for the collective welfare of its citizens.

It is clear testimony to the divergence between political and social science traditions that what I have described as the main problems of British society, as seen by social reformists, are precisely the solutions prescribed by economic liberalism. And, of course, economic liberals view the social reformist inclinations of past governments as in part the cause of Britain's problems.

WHAT ARE THE MAIN HISTORICAL AND CONTEMPORARY CAUSES?

My discussion of the main problems facing Britain today clearly points to a short-term cause — the policies of successive British governments in the 1980s. But establishing causal connections in social science — like defining problems — is not as simple as that. It would be naive to suggest that government policies in the 1980s are the source of all our ills and that simply changing the policies will immediately result in a full and satisfying life for all! Problems, in the sense of conditions which cause people concern — unemployment, poverty, bad housing, crime and the rest — have been with us for a very long time. Although I might argue that over reliance on the market and reduced state provision of welfare have made things worse than they would have been otherwise, no-one could or would claim that such social problems suddenly appeared in the 1980s. On the contrary, they have a long history and their very persistence is an indication that their causes are deep and complex. An explanation of persistent regional differences in prosperity within the United Kingdom, for example, would involve consideration of physical geography, regional cultural attitudes, patterns of communication, differences in the scale and form of early industrialization, government polices over a very long period and so on. Not surprisingly, the problem has defied efforts to find a lasting solution.

Social reformists are acutely aware of the complexity of society and of the foolishness of seeking single-cause explanations for the multifarious problems that beset British society. Nonetheless, if I were required to nominate a single long-term factor which could be identified as a key element in explaining current problems, it would be Britain's failure to achieve an adequate level of sustained economic growth. It is worth stressing that this is, indeed, a long-term factor since the British economy has been in relative decline for a hundred years or so.

The failure to secure economic growth is crucial because, put crudely, wealth is required to pay for improvements in health care, education and the rest. The notion that all that is needed is to 'tax the rich' and redistribute the proceeds to the poor has an appealing simplicity but it is inadequate. There are simply too few rich people and too many who are 'not rich' for this to be a viable, long-term solution. Rather, increased wealth must be generated through economic growth. The assumption that there would or could be continuous economic growth underlay the optimism of social reformists in the 1950s and 1960s, and can be observed both in scholarly works (such as C.A.R. Crosland's *The Future of Socialism*) and in party election manifestos.

There is nothing specifically social reformist about identifying long-term economic decline as a fundamental source of current problems, however. Conservatives, marxists and liberals can all agree with that. There is sharp disagreement, however — and not just across traditions — about what has caused this decline and what should be done about it. The problem of explanation has been tackled by economists, historians, sociologists and even psychologists as well as by politicians. Among the long-term causes of relatively poor economic performance which have been put forward are the fact that Britain was the first country to undergo the industrial revolution, cultural attitudes towards work and enterprise, the pervasiveness of class divisions and the consequences of colonialism and two World Wars. It is clear that these sorts of explanations take us rather far away from the major contemporary problems that I have identified. There is nothing much that can be done today about the fact that Britain was the first country to industrialize, for example. It is also clear that the long-term causes of economic decline are more complex than simply a failure to implement Keynesian or free-market or marxist economic policies.

If we turn our attention to the more recent past, it is clear that from the end of the Second World War to about the mid-1970s social reformism was in the ascendancy in Britain. This period has been described as an era of consensus in British politics. There was a consensus (at least among policy-making elites — party leaderships and top civil servants) upon the two central elements in the social reformist tradition — an active role for the state in economic management and in welfare provision. All political parties accepted Beveridge's prescription of a welfare state to conquer 'Waste, Disease, Ignorance, Squalor and Idleness'. All agreed that full employment was a goal to be pursued by governments. Indeed the Conservative party manifesto for the 1951 general election stated that 'We regard the achievement of full employment as the first aim of a Conservative Government' (Kavanagh, 1987, p.40). All governments during this period managed the economy on Keynesian principles. The predominant ethos in British politics was *collectivist*. That is, there was a willingness and even an eagerness on the part of political leaders to pursue state intervention in the economic and social system in order to improve the collective welfare of the society.

In the mid-1970s, however, things began to go seriously wrong. Rising unemployment accompanied by sharply rising prices (a situation characterized as 'stagflation') appeared to indicate that Keynesianism was flawed and had failed. In addition, public expenditure

— spending by the state — was widely perceived to be 'out of control' and the welfare state appeared to be a bottomless pit into which more and more money was being poured. A lengthy period of collectivism, it seemed, had created immense public bureaucracies at enormous public cost but had failed to solve basic economic problems or to make much impact on the numerous social problems besetting British society.

As a result of these developments, social reformist principles came under attack and the tradition went very much on the defensive. Academics argued that collectivist politics had resulted in a situation in which the expectations of citizens about what the state should provide for them far outstripped the ability of the state to deliver and that the state had, in consequence, become 'overloaded'. The only solution was to scale down people's expectations. Politicians on the Right, influenced by the ideas of Hayek and Friedman, reacted against central planning and the 'nanny' state arguing, that not only had Keynesianism failed but also that the state's over involvement in welfare provision had stifled individual initiative and created a 'dependency culture', in which people took no responsibility for sorting out their problems but continually expected the state to look after them. On the Left there was much theoretical confusion, but some turned to marxist or near-marxist solutions — pursuing 'full-blooded socialism' by nationalizing large sections of industry or seeking 'a political transformation of the present institutions and structure of the world system' (Gamble, 1985, p.230).

In this battle of ideas the 'New Right' was victorious. Throughout the 1980s governments sought to 'roll back the state'. In some areas, paradoxically, central state power actually increased (education, for example) but a major policy objective was to reduce the role of the state both in the economy (by privatizing publicly-owned corporations and by decreasing the extent to which market forces were regulated) and in the provision of welfare (by a more gradual erosion of state provision). Social reformist ideas were castigated as 'wet', woolly and wimpish.

WHAT SHOULD BE DONE ABOUT THE PROBLEMS AND BY WHOM?

Whether social reformism is 'wet' or 'wimpish' might be a matter for debate, but there are certainly good grounds for agreeing that it is 'woolly'. It is a theoretically untidy tradition; it lacks the clarity, simplicity and even elegance of liberalism and marxism. For social reformists there is no 'pat' answer to the question 'What is to be done?'; there is no simple solution such as abolishing the private ownership of the means of production or letting the market loose to do its miraculous work. Nor do social reformists have a vision of some utopian society which is the goal towards which they are working. 'More equality' is certainly an underlying value — although social reformists differ about how much more there should be — but this is a guide to the direction of change rather than an end point. Since there are no easy solutions and since society's problems have complex causes, the tradition emphasizes incremental change to deal with concrete problems. Since all problems can never be eliminated, progress consists of steadily trying to make life a bit better for most people. Social reformists regard this as realistic and practicable, in contrast to the solutions proposed by marxists which tend to involve changing the world rather than dealing with immediate problems.

Social reformism is clear, however, on who should tackle the problems of our society. Primarily this is the task of government. Such clear advocacy of political action is a distinctive feature of social reformism. Liberalism, in contrast is distrustful of politics. In classical liberal economics it is an 'invisible hand' not the state which ensures that the economy works well; modern neo-liberalism argues that decisions about the allocation of resources are better made by the impersonal forces of the market rather than by fallible politicians too eager to yield to the (unreasonable) demands of citizens who might otherwise vote them out of office. And classical marxism — on one interpretation, at least — suggests that the development of capitalist societies is determined by inexorable economic laws which will eventually produce a 'final' crisis leading to revolution. Moreover, in the ideal society to which the revolution leads there will, eventually, be no state and no politics. Social reformism argues that, in the meantime, it might be better to use the power of the state to effect more immediate improvements in social conditions.

But what, precisely, do social reformists think should be done? Here again the untidiness and lack of clarity characteristic of social reformism is apparent. In running the economy it is not just a matter of totally abandoning market principles — in many respects the market system works efficiently and well. Most people (including, apparently, many in Eastern Europe) would agree that as compared with the performances of centrally-planned economies, those which have been basically market-led have been staggeringly successful in satisfying consumer demands. In addition, total planning involves a level of restriction of the freedom of individuals that social reformists are unwilling to countenance. What is required is some compromise, some mix of planning and the market, some degree of regulation which preserves the undoubted benefits of the market system but minimizes the costs. Quite what the balance should be, where the line should be drawn, is difficult to determine — and individuals within the social reformist tradition would disagree about this — but a basically market economy regulated by the state in the interests of the society as a whole remains fundamental to social reformism.

As far as welfare provision is concerned, social reformists reject the view that the market should govern such matters as health care, education, public transport and provision for the elderly or disabled. They argue that matters such as these involve social as well as individual responsibility. On the other hand, some of the criticisms made of collectivist politics are well taken. The state clearly cannot undertake a commitment to open-ended spending on welfare. Spending on health, for example, is potentially infinite as new techniques of medicine become available and ever-increasing standards of care are demanded. It is clearly not enough simply to 'throw money' at problems. In addition, the danger that increased social spending may lead to the proliferation of unresponsive and inefficient bureaucratic agencies is a real one. Nonetheless, social reformism continues to advocate a positive conception of the role of the state in providing for the general welfare of the population. The state is viewed not so much as an infringer upon the freedom of people to do what they want but an institution which can help to free people from deprivation and enable them to develop their potential.

As with economic management, the problem is to find the right balance. Individual initiative is to be valued and should be rewarded; too much compulsion by the state can

J.M. Keynes argued that governments must regulate markets to prevent economic crisis

make serious inroads into liberty and must be guarded against; there is much to be admired in the idea of individuals being responsible for their own destiny. In crude and over-simple terms, the problem might be said to boil down to finding the balance between taxation and welfare spending. The search for the right balance is difficult and once again individuals within the tradition have varying views about it. The point is, however, that their answers will be pragmatic rather than be deduced from any set of widely agreed and well-defined set of theoretical principles. Fuzziness and even inconsistency are characteristic of the tradition, but since what is sought is the best of all possible worlds that is understandable.

Although social reformism was clearly on the defensive during the 1980s as ideas associated with the 'New Right' and economic liberals came to dominate in governing circles, it is somewhat paradoxical to note that central aspects of the tradition continued to be alive and well among the population at large. Surveys of public opinion regularly found that there was near-unanimity among the population in support for state provision of core welfare services such as the NHS, education, pensions and services for children and the disabled (although there was less sympathy for the 'undeserving poor'). There was little support for the proposition that public provision of services should be reduced in order to allow cuts in taxation. In 1986 one of a regular series of reports on British social attitudes concluded that 'Collectivism seems to be an integral feature of public attitudes in this country, shared by those of quite different ideological viewpoints on other issues' (Bosanquet in Jowell, Witherspoon and Brook, 1986).

What is galling for social reformists, however, is that a population which professed to share many of their concerns and opinions persistently elected governments which were avowedly hostile to the tradition. How is this to be explained? Analysing the reasons for the electoral dominance of the Conservatives during the 1980s is too big a task to be attempted here. It is, however, worth calling attention to the fact that at no time did the Conservatives get the support of anything close to half of the electorate. In the general elections of 1979, 1983 and 1987 they received 43.9 per cent, 42.4 per cent and 42.3 per cent of the votes. But if we take account of people who did not vote, then only 33.3 per cent, 30.8 per cent and 31.9 per cent respectively of the total eligible electorate supported the Conservatives. One could argue, then, that the attack on social reformism mounted by governments during the 1980s was supported, at most, by only about a third of the British population. This has led some people to conclude that just as early reformers sought political reform — an extension of the suffrage — as a precondition for social reform, so now further political reform — some alteration in the electoral system — may well be required before social reformist ideas can regain their former ascendancy in government.

WHAT IS IT ABOUT THE SOCIAL REFORMIST TRADITION WHICH PREDISPOSES YOU TO HIGHLIGHT THESE PARTICULAR PROBLEMS, CAUSES AND SOLUTIONS?

There is no single 'great work' of political or social theory to which one can turn for a definitive statement of the principles of social reformism. Keynes was, of course, a major economic theorist, but for non-economists his importance lies in the fact that his theory provided practical solutions to the problems of managing a capitalist economy in a way that would avoid recurrent crises and social distress. Similarly, Beveridge was not primarily a social theorist. What he provided was a practical scheme to alleviate squalor and deprivation. Both men were Liberals (with a capital 'L'); neither wanted to sweep away the existing structure of society. Keynes did not want to abolish capitalism but to have it managed differently; the fact that the Beveridge plan emphasized contributory social benefits in a scheme of National Insurance illustrates his concern with preserving an element of individual responsibility. Both were concerned with immediate problems and with finding practical solutions. These sorts of concerns are evident in the way in which, when applying social reformism to modern conditions, I have emphasized (and arguably over-emphasized) the flexible, pragmatic and almost a-theoretical nature of the tradition, despite its underlying commitment to equality.

Social reformism, it would be fair to say, originated with the 'caring' middle classes. The evidence which accumulated about the degrading conditions in which the 'lower orders' lived in late Victorian England simply shocked many middle-class people and, in some cases influenced by religious beliefs, some resolved that 'something must be done'. Moral outrage was, however, complemented by hard-headed realism. 'Doing something' about social conditions was also a sensible precaution to prevent any spread of revolutionary ideas among the newly-enfranchised (male) working-class. Caught between the visible horrors produced by free-market individualism and the potential horrors of full-blooded collectivism, the solution was to alleviate the former in order to secure and reinforce working-class support for the economic and political system as a whole. Only a system which responded effectively to the demands and problems of the working class — who constituted a huge majority of the population — could hope to retain legitimacy. Social reformism was in part, then, a realistic response to the extension of political democracy. International comparisons also provided a realistic stimulus to social reform. Britain's chief international rival, Germany, had instituted a rudimentary form of welfare state in the late nineteenth century. This, it was believed, had improved standards of health and the educational level among the population and had contributed to the increasing industrial and military strength of Germany. Elite opinion in Britain was dismayed by the poor physical condition of recruits into the British army and feared that in any future conflict unhealthy and ill-educated British soldiers would be no match for their German counter-parts. There were, therefore, pressing reasons to improve the general welfare of the population.

Moral indignation still informs social reformism. Whether they derive their values from religious or humanist convictions or from some other source, social reformists believe that it is simply not right that there should be gross inequalities in society; slum housing, homelessness, unemployment and poverty remain morally offensive. Fear of German military strength or of a threat to the legitimacy of the system are, obviously, less in evidence. But, arguably, a poorly trained and dissatisfied workforce does not help Britain to compete effectively in the international economic system and if social conditions are allowed to deteriorate then this may result in alienation from the system (sometimes boiling over into rioting and disorder).

It would be wrong to imply, however, that social reformism is some sort of middle-class plot to keep the workers content. The British working-class movement itself has never shown very much interest in revolutionary ideas or in theory of any kind. Rather, trade unions and the Labour party, despite a good deal of rhetoric about socialism, have themselves largely adopted a version of social reformism in practice. On the whole, they have been concerned with practical solutions to immediate problems, with managing rather than overthrowing the political, economic and social system. Their commitment has been to what some commentators characterize as 'Labourism' rather than to socialism.

Social reformist values are not the property of any one party, however. Since the tradition is somewhere vaguely 'in the middle' between other more clearly defined and coherent traditions, it encompasses a relatively wide variety of views — from mild, cautious reformers to people who advocate thoroughgoing and extensive change. People who are neither liberals nor marxists are strung across the political spectrum from the 'soft' left of the Labour party, through the Democrats to 'wet' or 'one-nation' Conservatives.

All of these, however, would share an aversion to any fixed 'game-plan', any unalterable set of precepts which provides the definitive answer to society's problems. They would all prefer to focus on 'middle-level' problems which can be ameliorated in some degree by political action; to pursue policies that are flexible and incremental; and to seek some balance between conflicting goals and interests. Fundamentally, all would agree that the state should take an active role in managing the economy for the benefit of society as a whole and in providing for the general welfare of the people. And that is the core of the social reformism.

REFERENCES

N. Bosanquet, (1986) 'Interim Report: Public Spending and the Welfare State' in R. Jowell, S. Witherspoon and L. Brook, *British Social Attitudes: The 1986 Report,* Gower.

A. Gamble, (1985) *Britain in Decline,* Basingstoke, Macmillan.

Gallup Political Index, 1986 to 1988.

D. Kavanagh, (1987) *Thatcherism and British Politics,* Oxford, Oxford University Press.

4   COMPARISON AND EVALUATION OF THE FOUR ESSAYS

We began this exercise at the end of the last unit. We saw there that there were serious issues in dispute between liberalism and conservatism. We also saw that there were areas of agreement. Let's just repeat what we said then, starting with the areas of *agreement* between liberalism and conservatism.

Question 1 — Problems: not much overlap here — similar unease with role of government.

Question 2 — Causes: both uneasy about ideas that encourage state action.

Question 3 — Solutions: both keen to roll back and set legal limits on the activity of the state.

Question 4 — Strengths: both keen to focus on the individual.

So the two essays do demonstrate an overlap of concerns — one indeed that manifested itself in the tone of much New Right thinking in the Conservative Party. But it was the disagreements that stood out more strongly for me.

Question 1:   Liberal emphasis on the need to let individuals get on with things free of government interference — contrasted with conservative emphasis on disorder and moral decay (including the personal selfishness of liberalism's individuals).

Question 2:   liberalism's keenness to place the blame squarely on too much government contrasts sharply with conservatism's analysis of the wider social origins of a loss of moral community.

Question 3:   liberalism's emphasis on rolling back the state as the key solution contrasts with conservatism's search for new bases of moral order.

Question 4:   liberalism's faith in the individual contrasts with conservatism's sense of human fallibility. Liberal optimism contrasts with conservative scepticism.

There are choices here. Is the problem that of excessive government, or of moral disorder? Is the cause excessive faith in government action or a generalized loss of faith? Is the solution a return to market forces, or the establishment of a new moral community.

We can now repeat that exercise for marxism and social reformism. There is *agreement* on:

Questiom 1: seriousness of economic situation.
Dislike of Thatcherite liberalism;

Question 2: failure of social reformism to solve basic problems 1945-79;

Question 3: solution requires political action; and

Question 4: shared concern to transform present reality.

But, as with liberalism and conservatism, it is the *differences* which stand out as far more significant than the agreements.

Questiom 1: profound disagreement on how deep the problems run, and especially on how linked to capitalism;

Question 2: social reformism's tendency to give political failures a big explanatory role contrasts with marxism's insistence that the causes are structural;

Question 3: disagreement on the value and possibility of piecemeal reforms;

Question 4: total disagreement on which of the two traditions is the naive one, which the hard-headed.

So our choices widen. Is the *problem* one of excessive government, moral disorder, too little government or too much capitalism? Is the *cause* excessive faith in government action, a generalized loss of faith, a failure of past politics or a product of capitalist contradictions? Is the *solution* a return to market forces, the establishment of a new moral community, a return to government intervention, or a movement towards revolution? Or do the problems, causes and solutions lie elsewhere, undiscovered by any or all of the traditions we have examined?

How then to pick our way through all that. It's very tough, of course, but if we think back to what review units in D103 have told us, we can at least see the various options we face.

- To a degree, as we saw in Unit 18, the choice between the essays can be resolved by a mobilization of evidence, by going back to our lists of strengths and weaknesses, and by seeing how each of them coped. The fit of each essay with the available evidence, and the coherence with which each case was argued, will give us a sense of what Unit 26 called each essay's *explanatory power.*

- We can also resolve their conflicting claims by bringing in evidence and questions that they do not address. We can take another big issue — the issue of gender, for example, or ethnicity, or ecology — and see how each copes with the new agenda. We can explore, that is, each essay's *explanatory reach.*

- We can also go beyond the text of each essay, to make some kind of preliminary judgement on what we anticipate would be their *explanatory openness* — their ability to deal with new situations and to respond to new criticisms.

- Finally, we can also raise an issue that we will discuss in more detail in Unit 30. We can look less at the essays than at the traditions of thought which inspire them. We can examine the presence of the traditions in the world around us — by seeking out the causes with which they are identified, the political systems they seem to favour, and the actual policies they seem to advocate. We can then ask ourselves if we agree with these causes, political systems and policies: and in that way we can check the relationship of the traditions-in-practice with our *values.*

These are very large and difficult tasks, as I am sure you can see. They are never easy to do. They take a lot of time; and the decisions we come to are invariably provisional and tentative in character. Making choices of this importance is never a quick or a permanently resolvable thing. Nor it is something to be done to order. You may not want to do it yet. You may still have vast areas of unease about the choices on offer and the procedures being recommended. That is why we will devote the next unit, Unit 30, to talking about the traditions, the choices they represent, and your relationship with them: and why you would do well to delay any decision of your own about the four traditions until you have read that unit.

What you might profitably do at this stage, however, is a more limited exercise — just part of the task of choosing between traditions of thought. You might try and pull together your reactions — not to the traditions as such — but to the four essays on which, by now, you have done so much work.

————————————————— ACTIVITY 4 —————————————————

Let's explore the *explanatory power* and the *explanatory reach* of the four essays. Think back to what you decided were the strengths and weaknesses of each of them. Think about their coherence, their fit with the evidence, and their ability to handle new issues. Is there one of the four which—against these criteria—seems to you the most impressive? Is there one which you found more persuasive than the others? If there is:

Jot down your reasons for choosing that particular one.

For choosing …	

Then jot down your reasons for rejecting the other three:

For rejecting …	
For rejecting …	
For rejecting …	

Summary of the four essays

	PROBLEMS on question 1	CAUSES on question 2	SOLUTIONS on question 3	STRENGTH OF TRADITION on question 4
Deacon (Liberal)	• misunderstanding of nature of society; • inflated role of the state, crowding out private activity, interfering in private affairs, inflicting heavy tax burden; • too much looking to state for help, public squalor preferred to private affluence, especially in elite circles; • weakness of Thatcherite liberalism.	• caused by state 'solutions' in the past, i.e. 'continued high levels of state intervention, public acceptance of them, and elite efforts to increase and even sustain them'; • previous liberal phase unplanned and fragile. One strand of liberal thought led to socialism; • role of special interests ('distributional coalitions'). Persistence of conservative, paternalistic attitudes even in liberal politicians.	• new policies — to increase private provision and reduce role and size of the state. To leave just a safety net. State to encourage replacement of its superfluous functions by voluntary organizations, and to let ideas flourish uncensored; • bill of rights to stop state encroachments. Break up of central state bureaucracies; • spread of liberal ideas.	• central concern with individual freedom and development; • strength of market and private property as guarantors of freedom.
Hartley (Conservative)	• disorder: in individuals, communities, society; Manifested in individuals as a decline in faith, rise in selfishness. Manifested in UK society as disintegration of community into regional and group loyalties. General lack of community; • decline in the rule of law; • decline in proper constraints on the role of government.	• flawed human nature, natural selfishness; • erosion of faith by spread of ideas that encourage social disorder in the pursuit of human perfectability; • the way these ideas are disseminated by revolutionary groups and individuals, and by special interests (including social sciences themselves). Associated intolerance and dismissal of important conservative concerns.	• encourage orderly beliefs, ideas, persons, institutions. Encouragement of a sceptical and distrustful temper; • encouragement of faith and moral commitment: in strong individuals, in the family as a vital social institution, and in other communities of faith; • subordination of government to the rule of law — creation of a mixed constitution to restrain party government; • re-assertion of already existing conservative tradition.	• useful balance between scepticism and certainty; • reluctance to be labelled as a tradition; • a willingness to anchor social problems and solutions at the personal level. Concern with individuals, not ideas; • recognition of the dangers of contemporary disorder.
Looker (Marxist)	• inter-related capitalist crises: involving the relative decline of the UK economy, the crisis of the Keynesian-welfare state, and the crisis of social and industrial unrest; • crisis too of social reformism, and of the Labour Party as the main political vehicle of that reformism; • shift in the balance of forces against the working class under the Thatcher Governments (growing inequality and social deprivation, anti-union laws and strengthening of the state). Thatcherite ideological assault on ways of thinking of particularly elite groups.	• rooted in capitalist character of both global and local economy, and in the relationship between the two; • UK decline rooted in openness of local economy to global forces and in defensive strength of organized labour. Gives UK politics a 'corporatist bias'; • stresses global crisis too; and the way interlocked nature of national economies blocks national solution of either a social reformist or free market kind.	• lies in a socialist reconstruction of UK society by political forces based in the organized working class; • asserts this in spite of unpopularity of idea of socialism and of profound restructuring of contemporary proletariat; • argues that dynamic of world capitalist system will create conditions for socialist alternative again, this time as international class struggle.	• quality of marxism as analysis: holistic, dialectical, materialist; • way forward offered by marxism out of contemporary barbarism.

Summary of the four essays - Continued

	PROBLEMS on question 1	CAUSES on question 2	SOLUTIONS on question 3	STRENGTH OF TRADITION on question 4
Denver (Social Reformist)	• a vast list of specific and general problems could be given; • prefers to concentrate on problems that can be solved — includes here concerns of particular interest groups and general questions of economic management and welfare provision. These last two are the key problems; • recently these two problems tackled too much by market-based policies — generating inequality and selfishness. Sees liberalism's solutions as social reformism's problems.	• the main short-term cause is government policy itself; • the long term causes of any problem are complex — if one important common cause, it is the failure to achieve adequate levels of sustained economic growth; • social reformism failed, in its period of political dominance, to solve basic economic weakness — and so let in the New Right.	• no simple solutions: but must pursue incremental practical solutions that move towards equality; • this is primarily the job of government; • governments must balance (in the economy) the market and the plan, (in welfare provision) private and state care. The trick is to get the balance right.	• its focus on practical solutions and manageable problems. Anchored in the caring middle classes — moral outrage fused with hard-headed realism; • the way it balances free-market individualism and full-blooded collectivism; • its concern for the general welfare of the people.

5   GOING BEYOND THE TRADITIONS

Prepared for the Course Team by Robert Bocock

There are social scientists who find that working within one or other of the four traditions provides them with a set of concepts, theories and values which gives a guiding framework within which they are able to conduct their work. But I want to suggest to you some of the variety of positions which social scientists occupy in relationship to other positions than the four traditions which you have been studying. It is important to do this in order to correct the false impression that you might otherwise gain — namely that every social scientist works coherently within one of the four traditions and in that one alone. This is by no means the case. Indeed if you reflect momentarily on the units which you have studied in D103, you will realize that many of the social science theories discussed do not relate directly to any single tradition. Frequently the units have referred to more than one of the traditions, or to none of them. If you think back to the first block of the course, for example, you may recall that explanations for the existence of famine in Unit 2 ranged over a number of different explanatory frameworks, some of which related to one of the traditions, some not.

———————————————— ACTIVITY 5 ————————————————

Look back to Unit 2, Section 6 'The Search for Explanatory Frameworks', and Section 7 'Testing the Frameworks'. Remind yourself of the three frameworks discussed there: 'Traditional/Modern; North-South; Core/Periphery'. Check through any notes you made in Activity 12 in Unit 2. How did these frameworks relate to the traditions? Which components of them related to one or other of the traditions?

How did you get on? Here, first of all, are some hints about how the three approaches discussed in Unit 2 link with the traditions:

1   Traditional/Modern. There are some echoes in this framework of Liberalism — the need to move from traditionalism to modern economic and social structures through the socialization into entrepreneurial market activities of some individuals in the 'underdeveloped' societies.

2   North-South. This has some links with Social Reformism in the need to alter the terms of 'free trade' by the governments in the richer North to the advantage of the South. It is Social Reformism applied at a global level.

3   Core/Periphery. This explanation uses the notion of 'exploitation' of the South by the North and a notion of 'unequal exchange' to analyse this process; both notions have echoes of marxism.

There are other features of the three explanations, however, which do not fit so easily into the conceptual structure, or the vocabulary, of the traditions. For instance the distinction between traditional and modern societies in terms of their 'culture' is not part of the usual vocabulary of the Liberal tradition. The global thrust of the North-South type of explanation is a new development which goes beyond Social Reformism applied, as it generally has been, in one country, or in one continent. Although the third explanation draws on marxist concepts, there is a debate about whether 'exploitation' through trade and 'unequal' exchange between countries, as distinct from the exploitation of one class by another in the production process, really is a marxist concept.

As with the presence of the traditions in society, discussed in Unit 27, social science theories may draw on only some elements of a tradition or they may combine them with ideas derived from other sources. They may find that the explanation of a specific phenomenon requires some ideas from one or other of the traditions and some concepts from another framework — perhaps from feminist theory, or from concerns about ecology and the environment for instance.

When social scientists move beyond one of the traditions they try, on the whole, to avoid eclecticism, that is mixing ideas together without regard to the possible contradictory principles underlying them. Nevertheless, they may well find that they wish to make use of concepts derived from more than one of the traditions. For example, in trying to understand famine and hunger in the Third World, it may be that a social scientist would try to combine some of the emphasis on the need for social change in tribal kinship patterns of life in traditional societies — from the Traditional/Modern framework — with the idea of seeking changes in the terms of trade between the First and Third Worlds — an idea derived from the North-South framework. These two frameworks themselves depend, in part, upon Liberalism and Social Reformism respectively. Yet there may be thought to be some gains and advantages in combining some of their ideas together in this way, both to deepen understanding of what contributes to hunger and famine in some societies, and to begin to formulate policies which might alleviate these problems.

Both of the frameworks just mentioned for developing combined explanations of hunger and famine in the Third World assume the continuing dominance of capitalism in the global system. The Core/Periphery framework is more closely linked with the marxist tradition which sees the continuing dominance of capitalism as being a large component in producing hunger and famine in the periphery — but it assumes that capitalism could be challenged or changed. This framework, therefore, is much less easy to combine coherently with either of the others, which work both theoretically and practically on the assumption of world capitalism continuing as a system.

Other social scientists concerned with understanding, and changing, the position of women in modern societies such as the UK, have worked within one or other of the traditions, but some have found that they wish to retain a distinctive theoretical focus, derived from feminism, in order to prioritize gender as a central issue. Although the traditions can each be modified to take account of the position of women in paid work roles, in the family, in child rearing, housework, and care of the sick and the infirm, they have not done so fundamentally enough in the view of some. Let us look at each of them briefly.

Marxism makes class relations a central feature of its conceptual framework, not gender relations. It can take account of gender, but marxism will always push someone towards the view that class and the mode of production need to be seen as of *primary* importance, not gender relations. Liberalism also prioritizes economic matters, in the form of the free market, and does not make gender a central concept in its theory of how markets operate. It too can be modified to take account of gender, by looking at whether men or women form a major part of the paid labour force in particular historical circumstances, but this is not central to its concerns. Conservatism does make the family a central issue in its framework, and it does see gender, especially the role of women, as an important site of debate. On the whole, however, conservatives have stressed the social and psychological benefits to babies and children, to men and to women themselves, of traditional gender relations. Men do paid work; women stay at home to look after the house and the children. Social Reformism has been able to address and incorporate the concerns of women for political, social and economic equality, at least in theory. However it has often remained more concerned with class and racial issues and gender has not been really central to its concerns in practice.

Feminists have argued that there is need for a specific theoretical and practical area of research which addresses the position of women as a central dimension in all analysis. Unless this is done, they claim, the issues surrounding gender are given lower priority than other concepts such as class, the economy, the nation, the state, the (male) citizen, the (ungendered) individual, or political parties. These are the areas which have been of major concern to most social scientists, who have been predominantly male in any case. The traditions, furthermore, were developed by men in the first instance. For this reason,

Demonstration in the early 1970s

therefore, a specifically feminist perspective of writing, research and policy oriented work has been developed during the 1970s and 1980s so that questions concerning women could be made central. Feminists, especially radical feminists who insist upon gender being made central to any analysis of modern societies, have argued that the position of women as subordinate to men under patriarchal conditions cannot be made the central concern, as it should be, in any of the four traditions. The debate may well continue, for although the four basic traditions can and do each say something about women and society, none of them have made it a central concern in its own development. This means that the central concepts in these four traditions often remain either ungendered, or they refer primarily to men — the property owner, the citizen, the voter, the capitalist, the workers, even though up to half of the latter group may be women.

There is another large area of social and cultural importance in the eyes of some social scientists which lies primarily outside the four traditions: religion. You may recall that religion was mentioned as a major source of values and beliefs in many, if not most, societies in the world. Religion may sometimes be related to the traditions in some contexts, as you saw in Unit 27, but it retains a degree of autonomy from them. Religion remains a source of ideas, values and action in the world which some social scientists study and research. But as with the four traditions and feminism, not only do some social scientists study religion, some of them may accept a religious framework in guiding them in the work they choose to do. This may or may not be in the areas of researching religion itself. Social scientists in Western societies, who are religious believers in an explicit way, may concentrate their research upon the poor, upon child rearing, or education as areas of research, because from their moral and religious perspective such areas are of central concern. In other words, the moral values they hold as a consequence of their religion may lead them to research and write about the oppressed. This is true of some 'liberation theologians' in Latin America, some of whom are influenced by marxist ideas, who do social scientific research on such issues as urban and rural poverty, the oppression of children, poor housing, or bad food and water supplies.

Others combine a religious commitment with either Conservatism or Liberalism. An example of this is given in an article by Brian Griffiths, a Professor of Economics and government adviser in the UK:

> Some years ago, Milton Friedman posed me a challenge 'How can you be a Christian,' he said, 'and advocate the market economy? After all, didn't Jesus say it is more difficult for a camel to pass through the eye of a needle than for a rich man to enter the Kingdom of Heaven?'

> This question proved a turning point for me.

> …On the basis of biblical evidence, I advocate seven guidelines as of contemporary importance. They are: the legitimacy of wealth creation; the necessity of private property rather than state ownership as the norm for ownership; the ability of each family to retain a permanent stake in the economy; the mandate on the community to relieve poverty rather than pursue equality; the requirement for government to remedy injustice; the caution against materialism; and the importance of accountability and judgement in the whole of life.

> These mean that a Christian perspective is distinct both from secular capitalism and Marxism. I would characterize such a world as a market economy bounded by biblical principles of justice…

Most people who advocate socialist policies and who attempt to underpin them theologically do so by using a social gospel based either on the theology of the Kingdom of God or liberation theology. I have serious reservations about the way both deal with the biblical text itself. Instead of allowing the text to speak for itself, liberation theology accepts uncritically an economic and political ideology based on Marxism, then interprets the text within this framework.

More significant in this country are those who make the Kingdom of God synonymous with a rather vague concept of a sharing and caring community which, when linked to the Incarnation, drifts into a political programme of equality, at the expense of individual freedom, and large government spending, at the expense of wealth creation.

The Kingdom is relevant to personal ethics...

By contrast, the theology that underlies my view is based on creation ethics — the search for those universal moral principles and structures which are part of the creation order and are expanded on in Old Testament law. Despite the problems in relating the Old Testament to the modern world, there is a wealth of material relating social structures (marriage, ownership, family, law) to the moral law (the Ten Commandments, etc.).

[A second issue is...]

...what Edmund Burke called 'the little platoons' of society. They are those institutions — family, school, workplace, village, trade union, professional association, church — that allow people to pursue interests and to participate in the life of different communities. They *mediate* between the private life of the individual and the megastructures of society.

Burke saw them as not just helping people in their private lives but as fulfilling a political function. 'To be attached to the subdivision, to love the little platoon we belong to in society, is the first principle (the germ as it were) of public affections. It is the first link in the series by which we proceed towards a love of our country, and of mankind.' Public policy needs to protect and foster such structures and, wherever possible, use them in the pursuit of social policy.

B.Griffiths, *The Times*, 2 June 1989.

Not only does religious commitment motivate some people to undertake social scientific research into issues of social, economic, political or cultural oppression, it also produces a 'world view' which gives greater weight to religion than do those traditions of thought which derived from the Enlightenment. A 'world view' contains an underlying set of assumptions which social scientists, like other people, make about the nature of the universe, and of the place of human life within it. A religious world view is one which includes at some point a reference to a belief in a supernatural element at work in the universe, and on the planet earth, specifically. The traditions of thought which emerged from the Enlightenment have (with the possible exception of Conservatism) generally excluded this supernatural element. The Enlightenment of the eighteenth century, whilst it contained some writers who were religious in the conventional sense of belonging to a Christian church, was primarily based upon the assertion that humanity could advance through the use of reason, through scientific research and its application to agriculture and later, to industrial production. Enlightenment writers held the view that human beings could advance in this life without religion. This viewpoint, therefore, tended to underplay the role of religion in modern societies. The social sciences, influenced by three of the traditions whose roots lie most centrally in the Enlightenment — Liberalism, Social Reformism and Marxism — have tended to underplay the role of religion in human societies, especially in modern industrial societies. The fourth tradition, Conservatism, did have a place for religion, as a bulwark against some Enlightenment ideas, which in Burke's view of the French Revolution of 1789 had led to violent conflict.

From the nineteenth century, the assumption that religion would decline or disappear altogether in modern industrial societies, an assumption derived from the philosophy of the Enlightenment, has been challenged. Some social scientists (who may have broken with Enlightenment views and values, yet who are not necessarily Conservative), hold that one, or all, of the major world religions have remained important philosophically, both in industrial and in industrializing societies. Their importance is not only of a social, political, economic or cultural kind, depending on specific circumstances. It is also philosophical. That is some social scientists hold that religious positions offer viable philosophical world-views.

Secular world-views, based upon the claim that God is dead, or that there is no God, or there are no gods, are no more scientific, it can be argued, no more rational, no more guaranteed to be true, than older religious world-views. Some social scientists now take this position. They hold that one, or more, of the world's religions is as viable a basis, or a better basis, from which to do social science as that provided by any of the traditions which grew out of the Enlightenment period's faith in science, rationality and progress. With the questioning of the Enlightenment project's faith in progress through the application of reason and science, which emerged after the tragic events of the twentieth century — the two world wars, the Final Solution, the Gulag, nuclear weapons, Vietnam, environmental pollution — some social scientists and philosophers have concluded that a sense of humanity's dependency and humility is badly needed. They find these values in one or other of the world religions.

Finally, you should remember that there is another strand of philosophy, almost another tradition, that of positivism, whose roots also lie in the Enlightenment, which has led many to claim that social science should be value-neutral, politically neutral, and neutral, or hostile, towards all ideological views, including religious world-views. It is not possible to argue in detail here about the merits or otherwise of positivism as a philosophical position. Suffice to say that positivism claimed that only empirically testable propositions were to be considered 'scientific', together with propositions in logic or mathematics. The problem with this claim was that it was paradoxical — too paradoxical for many contemporary social scientists. The central claim of logical positivism, given above, is itself not a proposition which is empirically testable — it can be neither verified nor falsified. Nor is it a proposition in mathematics, nor one in logic as normally understood.

There are more mundane reasons why many social scientists no longer claim the almost infallible role of value-neutral, philosophically neutral, reporters on the social world. Their reports and observations are inevitably written in a verbal language, not in a mathematical one. This is so because they are, in part, concerned with the meanings of social events and social actions, and these meanings can only be conveyed in verbal language. Language, however, is never completely free from value overtones. Hence, it came to seem as more honest for social scientists to acknowledge that they were coming from a 'tradition', or from a mix of more than one, which did contain values and a specific way of seeing the world. To be explicit about these world-views now appears to be the more intellectually honest course to take. This position has been taken seriously in D103 — hence our emphasis on the four traditions and the brief discussion of alternatives: environmentalist positions; feminism; and religious world-views. This should help you to recognize one of the traditions when you meet one, or one of the alternatives. In turn, such recognition may help you to sort your own ideas more coherently. This issue will be addressed in Unit 30.

The reasons why a social scientist chooses one tradition rather than another are not just connected with technical issues in the areas of research in which they are working. Indeed, the reasons they adopt one of the traditions as a framework rather than another may not be based upon technical issues in a research project at all, but upon a mixture of factors derived from outside of the formal research process. These factors may include quite wide-scale, long-standing influences upon a person, such as the nation, regional, or class background of a particular social scientist, and the historical period and events which they have witnessed. For example, social scientists who were alive during the period in which Nazism and fascism were dominant forces in Europe were often interested in issues of particular relevance in that period, such as the notion of the authoritarian personality. An authoritarian personality type was defined as being predisposed to *follow* strong political leaders such as Hitler (the term did not refer to those who desired to be such leaders). This research interest derived from a commitment to an alternative political and philosophical tradition from that of fascism — authoritarian leadership was seen as a danger to democratic processes, not as an admirable quality.

There are also more individual personality factors which may influence a social scientist to adopt one framework rather than another. Some people who become social scientists seem to like working with quantitative data more than others; some like the more applied, practical areas of social research; others work upon more purely theoretical, or social philosophical, issues. These preferences seem to fit with particular individual types of personality. There is little point in claiming that one kind of work is necessarily intellectually superior to another, or the only type that should be done in social science, especially if people are unlikely to be persuaded to change their minds about the style of research they prefer by rational arguments alone. None of these influences, however, need be seen as fixed for all time — they may and do vary over a social scientist's lifetime.

The ways in which you might begin to sort out your own ideas about the traditions and alternative perspectives will be discussed in Unit 30.

ANSWERS

POSSIBLE SET OF ANSWERS TO QUESTIONS 1 TO 4:
FROM ROBERT LOOKER'S ESSAY

Marxism on	
Question 1: problems	• inter-related capitalist crises: involving the relative decline of the UK economy, the crisis of the Keynesian-welfare state, and the crisis of social and industrial unrest. • crisis too of social reformism, and of the Labour Party as the main political vehicle of that reformism. • shift in the balance of forces against the working class under the Thatcher Governments (growing inequality and social deprivation, anti-union laws and strengthening of the state). Thatcherite ideological assault on ways of thinking of particularly elite groups.
Question 2: causes	• rooted in capitalist character of both global and local economy, and in the relationship between the two. • UK decline rooted in openness of local economy to global forces and in defensive strength of organized labour. Gives UK politics a 'corporatist bias'. • stresses global crisis too; and the way interlocked nature of national economies blocks national solution of either a social reformist or free market kind.
Question 3: solutions	• lies in a socialist reconstruction of UK society by political forces based in the organized working class • asserts this in spite of unpopularity of idea of socialism and of profound restructuring of contemporary proletariat • argues that dynamic of world capitalist system will create conditions for socialist alternative again, this time as international class struggle.
Question 4: strengths of the tradition	• quality of marxism as analysis: holistic, dialectical, materialist • way forward offered by marxism out of contemporary barbarism.

POSSIBLE SET OF ANSWERS TO QUESTIONS 1 TO 4:
FROM DAVID DENVER'S ESSAY

Social reformism on	
Question 1: problems	• a vast list of specific and general problems could be given. • from these, prefers to concentrate on problems that can be solved — include here concerns of particular interest groups and general questions of economic management and welfare provision. These last two are the key problems. • recently these two problems tackled too much by market-based policies — generating inequality and selfishness. Sees liberalism's solutions as social reformism's problems.
Question 2: causes	• the main short-term cause is government policy itself. • the long term causes of any problem are complex — if one important common cause, it is the failure to achieve adequate levels of sustained economic growth. • social reformism failed, in its period of political dominance, to solve basic economic weakness — and so let in the New Right.
Question 3: solutions	• no simple solutions: but must pursue incremental practical solutions that move towards equality. • this is primarily the job of government. • governments must balance (in the economy) the market and the plan, (in welfare provision) private and state care. The trick is to get the balance right.
Question 4: strengths of the tradition	• its focus on practical solutions and manageable problems. Anchored in the caring middle classes — moral outrage fused with hard-headed realism. • the way it balances free-market individualism and full-blooded collectivism. • its concern for the general welfare of the people.

ACKNOWLEDGEMENTS

Grateful acknowledgement is made to the following sources for permission to reproduce material in this unit:

Photographs

p.74 and p.79: John Sturrock/Network; *p.81*: Mansell; *p.84*: Neil Libbert/Network; *p.89*: Topham Picture Library; *p.98*: Sally Fraser/Format.

UNIT 30 CHOOSING EXPLANATORY FRAMEWORKS

Prepared for the Course Team by Elaine Storkey

CONTENTS

INTRODUCTION

As the Block VII Introduction has already indicated, the position of this unit in the block might make it difficult for you immediately to identify it, or recognize its function. It is, in fact, one of the review half-units which normally comes at the end of each block. So the aim of Unit 30 is both to review the block and to continue the investigation into key aspects of social science thinking. It will in fact complete the cycle of enquiry initiated in Units 4 and 5 and continued in Units 9, 13, 18, 22 and 26. But, because this is the last of these review half-units, it has also a broader task. It will be trying to draw things together, especially with regard to the four Traditions of Thought used throughout D103 and central to this block. So, in reflecting on what has already been investigated about the nature of social science concepts, methods and approaches, it will need to apply some of these ideas to the Traditions themselves.

I shall be drawing on the material in each of the review units and shall work from the basis which they have already laid: for example, the discussion of concepts and conceptualization which first came in Unit 4 and Unit 9, the role of models and metaphors which you came across in Unit 13; and the interrelationship between theories and evidence analysed in Unit 18. My particular starting point will be to raise those same questions which were raised in connection with explanations in psychology at the end of Unit 22. But now I want to refer them to the four Traditions. So I shall begin by asking: what is the status of these traditions, and how do they relate to each other? Are they truly competing positions, or are they simply offering different but compatible kinds of insight into understanding society? I also want to look back to the discussion in Unit 26 about what constitutes an explanation and how explanations can be compared. What sorts of 'explanation' are we looking at when we focus on these Traditions? *What would be involved in choosing between them as explanatory frameworks*?

But in reviewing the block itself I hope we can also think about the ways in which the Traditions are more than theoretical positions articulated by social scientists. In fact they play many other roles. As we have seen (most recently in Unit 27 and TV14), the Traditions have influences in society independently of their impact on social science. They find expression in political parties and government policies, in social movements and in popular culture. And the ways in which theory becomes practice, and practice then further reinforces, refines and disseminates the theory, is a process which affects us all, day in and day out. What is more, as our four external consultants in the last two units have shown us, *what we are calling 'Traditions' can also be positions of personal commitment.* They can be orientations towards reality, frameworks of meaning in which everyday life is lived and understood. So for many people they are articles of faith. People 'believe in' liberalism or marxism; they are 'committed to' social reformism or conservatism. These frameworks influence the value systems which people hold, and in turn the values themselves become part of the very process of analysis. In that sense the Traditions 'live' in people's awareness and understanding of themselves, as well as 'living' in institutions and structures which impinge on the lives of all of us.

Yet they are not the only frameworks which influence or direct our lives or help us understand society. Even though their influences are enormously pervasive, there is more to life than liberalism, conservatism, marxism and social reformism. So I want to look beyond these four Traditions which have been central to D103, and ask about *other frameworks which greatly influence people in the UK in the 1990s.* And in asking this, I am of course aware that what I select will necessarily be partial. But I hope that you will recognize the significance of those other bodies of thought which have already been mentioned in Units 27 and 29. For instance, amongst the more recent frameworks of analysis which occupy a prominent place in many people's understanding of social reality today, environmentalism has had a striking impact. The Green Movement has thrown up sets of concerns and ways of evaluation which are slowly being disseminated throughout popular culture.

'You can't beat the seaside for taking your mind off the world's problems!'

In a similar way, as we saw in Units 8 and 29 some forms of feminism might also be seen as posing a contemporary alternative to the four major traditions which have provided our focus in this course.

'Does a feminist perspective offer a better explanation of the development of gender roles than the Traditions?'

Finally, there is the age-old challenge of religion as expressed in, for example, Christian, Jewish or Islamic traditions. They offer their own understandings of the problems of the UK in the 1990s, as well as the origin and meaning of these problems. One of the final tasks of this unit then will be to review some frameworks of meaning other than the four Traditions, and to investigate whether there are any underlying questions and issues which they all share in common.

2 SO WHAT ARE THE TRADITIONS ANYWAY?

In the light of what was said in Units 22 and 26, it seems important to be clear about the status of the four Traditions. By now you may have picked up several different notions as to what they are all about:

- In Unit 27, the Traditions were presented as 'ideologies' which underpin institutions and practices in society. In that sense, they are part of the *subject matter* of the social sciences.

- At other times, for example in Units 28 and 29, the Traditions were seen as 'grand theories' that we can use to understand society. And here you were given the task of being a social scientist trying to evaluate their usefulness as explanatory frameworks.

- Sometimes the Traditions have been talked of as personal frameworks of meaning involving values and commitments. They are what we use to orientate ourselves towards the social reality of which we are also a part.

However, these divisions are in many ways more imaginary than actual. For, wherever the Traditions 'exist', they do so as theoretical constructs; they inevitably use a 'network of concepts'; they generate a line of reasoning, and they involve values. These values themselves interact with the concepts and arguments in a complex way as we shall see later in the unit.

Thus, whilst noting their expressions in social science or in society more widely, we do need to avoid the temptation to 'reify' the Traditions or treat them as 'things'. We cannot talk of them as real entities in society in the same way that, for example, we might speak of the Open University or the Houses of Parliament as 'real' (although, of course, even when we describe these institutions, we would have to use concepts and ideas as part of our descriptions, and we might even make reference to the Traditions!). To talk of the Traditions existing in society is still to talk of them existing as bodies of ideas. So, even though we can see how liberalism has for example been influential in the Adam Smith Institute or the Institute of Economic Affairs, liberalism itself remains a theoretical construct.

Therefore, in answering the question 'What are the Traditions?', I do not want to draw a wedge between Traditions as ideology, Traditions as 'grand theory', and Traditions as frameworks involving values. Instead I want to offer these as closely interrelated, as three aspects bound together and informing each other. They have been separated in this block more for ease of analysis. Unit 27 looked at one aspect of the Traditions: namely as sets of ideas, beliefs or assumptions which influence the attitudes and actions of groups and institutions. In Unit 30 I am more interested in another aspect: in the Traditions as explanatory frameworks. So there will be more focus on their attempts to *explain or unpack the meanings* underlying the social world, or, in the language of Unit 22 Section 5.1, on their 'hermenuetic' task.

I have mentioned already that the Traditions each use a network of concepts. In fact they could not do their job of unpacking meanings without using concepts, and without using them in such a way that the meaning of each concept is derived from the network which provides the context. For example, as you will have realized from earlier units (e.g. Units 5, 9 and 13), words such as 'class', 'freedom', 'rights', 'choice', 'oppression', or 'exploitation' can only be understood in relation to the whole cluster of concepts of which they are a part. So the concepts 'free and equal' in the liberal framework mean something different from when they are used by someone writing in a marxist framework. The precise meaning of concepts varies according to the 'concept network' to which they belong.

So we could borrow a phrase from Unit 26 and say that the Traditions are bodies of thought 'comprising a network of concepts which generate a line of reasoning, which can tell us why something happened'. And, whenever such networks of concepts are strung together for the purpose of explaining something, we are producing *theory*. But in talking about the Traditions as theories or theoretical constructs, you need to remember that the Traditions are different from what we have been talking of as specific or particular *theories* in, for example, Unit 26. As the unit unfolds we shall see that they are different in both *level and scope*.

─────────────── ACTIVITY I   SOME REVISION ───────────────

Before we think about choosing between Traditions, you might remember that Units 22 and 26 brought out several reasons why it might not be appropriate to compare or try to decide between some theories. What would you suggest as the most important reasons?

1   We have seen that theories are not always concerned with the same issues. As a very obvious example, it would be pointless to try to compare theories about the development of human languages with theories about the origins of colonialism. In this case they would be not so much in a dialogue with each other as trying to explain quite different things.

2   Alternatively, theories might be concerned with the same overall issues, but addressing different aspects of them. For example, they might all look at nineteenth century colonialism but one might analyse it using theories about racial stereotypes, another using theories about the economy, yet another using theories about nationalism, and so on. So here we would have a whole set of partial theories or 'sub-theories' which might be in dialogue but equally might be 'talking past each other'. We would need a larger framework to see the picture in fuller perspective.

3   This reminds us that theories may be attempting different *levels* of explanation as we saw in Unit 18 for example. So it would be inappropriate, for instance, to compare a general theory about the history of social developments with a specific theory about the impact of advertising.

That all sounds fairly clear-cut. In practice, of course, it is not always that easy to sort out, and even social scientists who have worked with theoretical issues for many years will not necessarily agree about the level of generality of a particular theory, and whether it is in 'competition' with another or merely saying something different but compatible.

2.I   TRADITIONS AS 'GRAND THEORIES'

These kinds of questions are pertinent to our four Traditions. For example, are they really alternative frameworks, or simply offering different insights to be melded together for a fuller grasp of the meaning and history of society? Is there in fact a real *choice* between the four, or are they like brands of soap powder masquerading as being different and yet all basically the same?

I shall return to this question later, but at this point it can be answered simply. The four Traditions are very similar in that each is a 'grand theory' about the nature of society. That is why it was possible to ask their proponents in Units 28 and 29 to address the same central questions: what are the main problems of contemporary UK society, what are the causes of those problems, and so on. But the fact that we receive different answers to these questions, and again answers at the same degree of generality, indicates that they are indeed *big theories competing for our approval and acceptance. They each provide broad orientations to aspects of reality. They are alternative, and in some respects mutually exclusive, frameworks of analysis.*

Curiously, however, there is another way in which they are all similar. They all have their roots in the 18th century European Enlightenment, and it is within this context that their concerns are articulated. In this sense, they have a great deal in common. For example, they all start from an Enlightenment assumption of the importance of human freedom and the need for human autonomy (although conservatism does challenge the Enlightenment faith in 'progress'). Marxism and liberalism both have this as a common starting point. Neither, for example, starts with a belief in the need for divine revelation, or in the fundamental inability of human beings to produce a free society. It could be said that they differ simply in the way they see this freedom and autonomy to have been restricted or exploited, and how it can be best realized in social relationships.

David Hume, 18th century Enlightenment philosopher

Yet, in spite of this enormous underlying common area of interest, it is generally the *differences* between the Traditions which are central in social science. For their common starting-point of human autonomy, of freedom from any higher authority, has become all-pervasive. This very starting-point has a taken-for-granted status both in social science theorizing, and in popular thinking. Yet this in itself is simply an indication of its success as an ideology. For, even though the tenet of freedom and autonomy could be challenged as a sweeping assumption, it is instead something which frequently goes without question, because most of us live also within a culture and worldview which has thoroughly absorbed an Enlightenment perspective.

I shall be dealing more with this point later in the unit. But, at this stage, I want you to leave aside their common origins and focus on the Traditions as competing frameworks of explanation.

3   CHOOSING BETWEEN TRADITIONS

These review units have been concerned throughout with giving you some tools for handling and appraising theories and explanations. For, as we have seen, theoretical explanations in the social sciences are complex. They are certainly not simply about 'testing hypotheses' by looking at 'the facts', or gathering all the evidence. For the question of what constitutes the facts, or what counts as evidence, is a matter of debate and controversy. It is itself part of theorizing. And the answers to these questions are often couched in terms of the clusters of concepts or interpretive models which we looked at earlier. It is easy to see therefore why there is disagreement amongst social scientists, and why some people can hold a marxist explanation, or some a conservative explanation, and still be looking at the same society. Nevertheless, as we have also seen already, there might still be reasons for choosing one account or theory rather than another.

─────────── ACTIVITY 2   SOME MORE REVISION ───────────

In Unit 26, three categories were offered to help choose between different theories. Thus the *explanatory power* of a theory was associated with such concepts such as 'coherence', 'ability to reason', 'holding together', 'vulnerability to the facts', 'interpreting of evidence'. What would you include under the *explanatory reach* and the *explanatory openness* of a theory?

It would be interesting to read what you had come up with. In fact a variety of sentences could have been equally accurate, but they each would have needed to contain certain concepts. For example, the *explanatory reach* of a theory would be more concerned with its 'empirical scope', with how much the theory can explain, and with what is left out. The third category *explanatory openness* would involve a theory's 'adaptability', its responsiveness to change — both in the sense of fresh evidence or changes in the subject matter being analysed. In that way it is about the ability of a theory to 'keep the debate open' and to 'recognize limitations'.

Choosing one account over another, then, involves accepting its power to persuade, its coherence, its handling of evidence, its scope or comprehensiveness, its resolution of contradictions. It involves respecting the theory's ability to adapt to changed circumstances or new lines of research, and being prepared to use the same network of concepts. In other words, it involves both accepting the 'intellectual integrity' of the theory, and also being able to live with its implications.

So far, these criteria have been used to examine *specific* theories. But what would happen if we applied these criteria to the Traditions themselves; to develop in effect the task begun in Units 28 and 29? There you were invited to compare the Traditions in terms of their relative 'strengths and weaknesses' in accounting for the evidence and coping with new ideas, but we could see if these further categories offer greater help in evaluating them.

3.1 THE PERSUASIVE POWER OF THE FOUR TRADITIONS

We could for example look at each of the four Traditions using the notion of 'explanatory power'. We might decide that in terms of internal *coherence* there was little to choose between each position. They each, in fact, possess a self-standing quality. Every time, we are provided with a step by step account of what is seen to be the main problems of contemporary UK and the causes of those problems. And each works with its own network of concepts which holds together, as an interpretative whole. For example, marxism locates its understanding of the problems in the nature of the local and global capitalist economy. Such concepts as 'capitalist crisis', 'economic decline', 'inequality', 'social deprivation' 'forces against the working class', 'socialist reconstruction', 'international class struggle', all fit together to provide a coherent explanatory framework, which gives meaning and weight to the central arguments. The steps in the argument seem to follow compellingly from the earlier ones, and the reasoning does not pull rabbits out of hats, or make any sudden leaps.

Similarly, liberalism holds together as coherently, with its starting point in the primacy of individual freedom and development. The main problems of the UK then stem from what it sees as the restrictions on this freedom by state activity. Its own concepts of 'state intervention', 'bureaucratic encroachment', 'heavy tax burden', 'need for voluntarism', 'interference in private affairs', draw their meaning from one another and suggest certain connections between the role of the state and changes within UK society. The argument again is presented as an interrelated whole, underpinned by a strong network of concepts.

 ACTIVITY 3

Try doing a similar exercise for the internal coherence of the other two Traditions. List the concepts which predominate in social reformism and conservatism and compare them with those I have suggested above.

It is evident then that a theory's coherence cannot be the full measure of its effectiveness or its power to persuade. It can only tell us whether the ideas hold together as a logical whole. And we would expect each of these theories to be reasonably coherent, because they have already withstood the test of time, and been subject to much examination and even revision over the years. The problem is that a theory could be completely internally consistent, yet still not begin to relate to the reality which it is purporting to explain. In fact in some cases its very coherence could be the problem: creating a circular and self-contained process of reasoning which has no reference point outside the theory itself. That is why we can often experience such a theory as 'overpowering', yet still fail to be convinced by it!

It could be, then, that we need to put more weight on identifying how well the theory stands up to external examination: in other words we need to look again at the fit between the theorizing and the evidence. Yet this itself can unfortunately be very problematic. For at the level of a grand theory we may have no way of assessing the evidence, other than by hearing it presented through a particular theoretical position. So it could leave us somewhat in the position of a jury in a court room. We have bare details that a crime has been committed, but we do not know when, or how, or by whom, or for what reason. And the only way we will find out is by listening to the evidence presented to us first from one side and then from the other; we cannot go and find out for ourselves. And it is no good relying on the newspapers or television either, because they will only be reporting what is said in the court room. So the very process of 'getting the evidence' often means hearing it presented already through the cluster of concepts and framework of meaning of one position (or Tradition) or another, i.e. already *interpreted*.

'Who decides what counts as evidence?'

What is important, though, is that this does not mean we end in mere circularity. To start with, there is no suggestion that the evidence does not actually exist 'out there'. In the courtroom story the actual events were real enough. The crime did take place, someone committed it, on a definite date and by a specific method. And, in a similar way, the social data which the Traditions are working on does exist 'out there' in, for example, balance of payments deficits, the decline of Sunday observance, the growth of BUPA, and people sleeping rough in cardboard boxes. And, as it was put modestly in Unit 26 'what happens "out there" can tell us something, the evidence is not entirely without a voice of its own.'

If we were to take the other two categories offered in Unit 26, '*explanatory reach*' might lead us to ask what was inadequate or partially explained, or what had been left out of any account. For example: liberalism has been criticized because its notion of equality is a formal, legal one, but leaves out the economic dimension; marxism has been criticized because of its identification of 'classes' with 'actors'. Some questions are also important: how does social reformism explain the long-term continuation of inequality, or liberalism tackle the question of persistent poverty? How does marxism explain the growth of the middle classes, or conservatism handle economic questions?

And finally '*explanatory openness*' would direct us to the sense each Tradition makes of new situations, such as changes in Eastern Europe in the late 1980s. How would it adapt to new research findings, or broaden its canvas to include new issues?

3.2   THE LEVEL OF THE TRADITIONS

As I have been applying Unit 26's criteria of evaluating theories to the Traditions, you may have been aware of something rather unexpected. To some degree or another, they all seem to pass the test. Each has shown an apparently high level of coherence, explanatory power, relevance to the evidence, comprehensiveness, empirical scope, adaptability and openness. In fact, on this last point each Tradition seems so broad as to include and interpret almost any new development. There is certainly every possibility that you may have come down fairly conclusively in favour of one of the four Traditions. But, even if you have, you will also have noticed that in terms simply of the criteria we have outlined the choice was not an inevitable one. And, if you talk to other students in the study centre who have made different choices, you may find that their reasons too are as cogent as your own (well almost!)

This reinforces the point that the Traditions are more than theories, and involve several levels of explanation: big theories which in turn have spawned specific theories which in turn have generated specific hypotheses. And, even though there might be a rigour to the individual hypothesis or specific theories, the Traditions themselves are more general and over-arching.

It is therefore the very scale and level of the Traditions that contributes to their effectiveness and persistence. Their lack of 'vulnerability' and their durability as ways of seeing the world are all partly derived from the sheer scope of what they are attempting to do. And that is why, in choosing between Traditions, much more is entailed than weighing up arguments and sifting through evidence. It includes also becoming orientated to a *worldview*.

At the same time, the accumulated weight of explanatory power, reach and openness should not be dismissed. Nor should the impact of the 'big picture' be underestimated as part of the rhetoric of persuasion. For, as it develops, the grand story can itself exert a powerful persuasive influence because it convinces us that this is indeed a picture of reality as we know it.

3.3   WHAT PRICE A DECISION?

In Unit 29, you were asked to make a provisional judgement between these four Traditions on the basis of what you had read and how you judged their persuasiveness. I wonder how long it took you, or indeed if you found you could do it all. More important still, I wonder what impact such a judgement had on you.

I ask this because every year at Summer School I meet some students who have enjoyed the Social Science Foundation Course, have written some very good (and not so good) essays, can use concepts with skill, handle complex arguments about social class, give a dozen good reasons why the facts don't speak for themselves, and in any group debate speak cogently about the strengths of, say, marxism or liberalism and the weaknesses of conservatism or social reformism. Yet despite this many of us, both students and tutors, find that we don't fully take any Tradition 'into our lives'.

' … and in any group debate speak cogently
about the strengths of marxism or liberalism'

The reasons for this are in fact quite complex. Some of them were indicated in Unit 29, which reminded us that there is more to life than the Traditions! We saw in particular how some feminist positions saw themselves as lying outside the four 'grand theories', and only loosely or very partially connected with them. But, even when we do feel more or less convinced about a particular Tradition, it does not necessarily mean that it becomes 'integrated' into the way we live. For very often, when we are asked to choose between theoretical positions, we can sit down methodically and work out the pros and cons of each, feeling more or less intellectually convinced that one of them is stronger (more coherent, open, adaptable, persuasive, comprehensive, accounting better for the evidence, etc., etc.). We might even construct our own theoretical account, using for example insights from within and outside the four traditions: some marxist critique, some social reformism but directed by an environmentalist perspective for instance. And yet any of this can remain just an intellectual exercise, more or less divorced from the 'real world' of our personal lives, beliefs and actions. This is all the more remarkable, of course, because the very subject matter of the social sciences is the social and personal world in which we live and interact.

Several factors contribute to this distancing, some of which are central to this very unit. An obvious one is the presence of what we might call a personal 'time-lag'. After nearly a year of D103, many of you will be beginning to feel fairly competent at handling social science analysis. Yet, looked at in the context of your whole lifetime so far, this is probably still a relatively new (and very academic) enterprise. In fact, compared with the time you have spent being exposed to and absorbing ideas from the different Traditions, the time you have now spent in reflecting on those Traditions is very small indeed. Your mental time-clock does not start at zero at page one of D103! So what we are actually asking you to do is a much bigger task than has ever been spelled out. We are asking you not simply to read, learn and evaluate the Traditions as they have been presented in the Reader, or by the four consultants in this block. We are also asking you to take part in reflecting on your own experience of think-

'A need to reflect on decades of cultural involvement meshed in with personal history'

ing, conceptualizing and absorbing ideas from the Traditions which has come from decades of cultural involvement meshed in with personal history. So it should not surprise us when the naked arguments, persuasive though they might be, accepted though they might be, nevertheless do not impact more vehemently on a person's personal life. For this to happen, the concepts would need to take root and 'live' in that person's daily experience.

3.4   CHOOSING INVOLVES VALUES

There is another related point, however. Choosing between Traditions does not include only 'cognitive' processes. We have already noted, when we looked at the four consultants' essays, that choice can entail commitment. And involved in using concepts, and accepting arguments, is also an awareness of the values implicit in those concepts or embedded in those arguments. So our own systems of values which have themselves been built up over a lifetime are also a crucial part of what we bring with us when we make a choice. The question is, however, where those values come from. And, again, we have to acknowledge that (as was argued in Unit 5) very often our values come from the legacy which the Traditions have left on our social fabric, as they have taken root in social structures, social practices and popular culture.

If you followed all that was argued about concepts in Unit 9, you will realize that it would be a mistake to think of them as being somehow 'value-free'. This is no less true of those we have been examining in relation to the Traditions. For the very concepts themselves are laden with assumptions about what is good or desirable, or what is bad and should be rejected. The entire network builds up both a descriptive and a moral evaluative framework. Another way of putting this is to say that the concepts used within the Traditions are not only attempting to define or describe what *is*, but also prescribe what *ought to be*.

I could illustrate this by focussing again on some of the concepts which were listed under 'Liberalism'. Look for example at the idea of state *interference*. That is certainly not simply a descriptive term; implicit in the very choice of the word is the suggestion that interference is bad, over against non-interference which is good. A similar moral undergirding is given by other words such as 'encroachment' or 'private property'. But the reason why interference, or state encroachment is seen as unacceptable, and private property is approved of, is because of the *value* put on the notion of the free individual (notice the value-laden quality of the word 'free') who ought (another value term) to suffer as little restraint on this freedom as possible. The whole business of using concepts to build up a (grand) theoretical position is therefore inescapably caught up in making explicit or implicit value-judgements.

We can see this very clearly when we try to describe a marxist position using the same concepts. The concepts either become meaningless (e.g. 'state interference' has all the wrong connotations for marxism; the 'role of the state' would be a more appropriate concept) or they are used with the opposite moral overtones (e.g. 'private' ownership of industry is bad), because they fit into a very different normative system.

———————————————— ACTIVITY 4 ————————————————

Take a set of concepts from one of the other two Traditions and look at the values evident in those concepts. What would you say was the key concept of the Tradition which directs or typifies its value-system as a whole? (You might find this easier if you go back to the essays on conservatism and social reformism in Units 28 and 29).

Thus, just as values are part of the fabric of the theorising about society, so values are part of our own judgement framework which we bring to assess that theorizing. And some of our own values will have been formulated within practices and institutions which embody aspects of the Traditions of thought at their very centre. And they, as much as anything else, might make us resist allowing a newly discovered 'stronger' argument to redirect the meaning we give to our daily lives.

For, in a similar way to the one we noted above, we can ourselves become caught up in assessing the arguments of one Tradition from the value position of another. For example, if we have a deep commitment to social equality, yet fear rapid or unpredictable change, we are likely to remain 'unconvinced' by the positions of either liberals or marxists, but feel drawn towards social reformism as a more acceptable theoretical framework. Or, if we feel very strongly that selfishness is wrong, and that community and consensus are values to be pursued, we may approve of conservatism, and see some liberal ideas about 'free individuals' and the market as nothing less than immoral. In a similar way, if our moral framework endorses private enterprise, private property and freedom from restraints, we might think that marxist collectivist policies would be little short of theft. And if we look at capitalist society from a marxist perspective we might think that private property and profits were already legalized forms of theft.

So, when we are being asked to compare or choose between Traditions, we are often being asked to do more than assess persuasive arguments. For, a real choosing involves not just a mental assent, but a provisional commitment to the value-network of that Tradition. And the part played by values is complicated. Sometimes, the fit of the evidence and the power of the arguments themselves can involve us in a reappraisal of the values we have previously espoused. But, in other situations, we might suddenly realize that our own sense of what is just and morally defensible fits with the value system undergirding a particular Tradition, and so we become ready to reconsider its argu-

'Legalized theft or individual freedom?'

ments in the light of that discovery. There is a dialogue in fact between the power of argument and the tenacity of values; a complex interplay between being convinced of the persuasiveness of a theory, and being committed to certain beliefs which themselves contribute to the building up of a framework of meaning and evaluation.

Whatever form it takes, then, choosing between Traditions can be a complex and difficult task. It might well involve us in exposing our own value-framework; to ask why we believe certain things to be valuable, and even to rethink some of our most cherished and fundamental ideas of morality.

SUMMARY

1   The Traditions of Thought are involved in more than describing society; they are 'grand theories', incorporating clusters of explanations, which attempt to unpack the meanings underlying the social world.

2   They are competing 'grand theories', alternative conceptions of society and human nature, each addressing similar central questions. Because of the similar scope and level of their theoretical analysis, they can therefore be compared with each other.

3   Each of the Traditions has its own network of concepts through which it represents social reality.

4   Beneath all the differences between the Traditions is a shared set of basic post-Enlightenment assumptions, which are often taken for granted as an unexamined starting-point.

5   In comparing and choosing between Traditions we need to evaluate their relative explanatory power, explanatory reach and openness. They need to meet criteria of coherence, ability to account for evidence, breadth of scope and adaptability.

6   Theory is not value-free and underlying values are implicit in the task both of describing and explaining. Theoretical concepts themselves may incorporate both 'is' and 'ought' elements.

7   Each Tradition has its own value-network, and when we come to choose one Tradition in preference to another, we are also involved in assessing and evaluating our own systems of values.

4 BEYOND THE TRADITIONS

We have seen that the four Traditions have played a vital part, both in directing and shaping social movements, social institutions, ways of life, and also in providing the tools for analysing society. We have also glimpsed something of the depth of what is involved in trying to make a choice between these Traditions; and of the interplay between accepting the explanatory power of arguments, and the values undergirding the framework of meaning.

One very strong mark of commitment to a theory is a *belief* that it will be able to explain future events, and respond to unpredicted changes. And this *'openness'*, this ability to rework its position in the light of new movements or ideas has been seen as an important criterion in assessing the power of an explanation. In Units 27 and 29, we glimpsed some of the ways in which these big theories have moved in this direction, making connections with feminist thought, with new ecological analysis, and with debates in religion. And even where we might have expected there to be no obvious links, such as in debates within the Church of England or other religious bodies, we can still see the presence and influence of the Traditions.

Although it is very evident that the various Traditions and alternative explanations often court each other, marry and produce very interesting offspring, it is also important to acknowledge that there are explanatory frameworks which are separate from the Traditions. So, in working out strategies for choosing between explanatory frameworks, we need to recognize that there are other options which we have not outlined fully in this course. For, the central concerns of feminism, environmentalism or religion for example, cannot be reduced to a liberal, marxist, social reformist or conservative framework. It will be evident from what you have read elsewhere in the course (Units 5, 8 and 29) that a radical feminist analysis, whilst it might accept many insights from the Traditions, would nevertheless reject each of them as being fundamentally patriarchal. Although they each address the meaning of social reality and provide a coherent analysis of social history and contemporary issues, none of them identifies the underlying structure of patriarchy as the fundamental problem. In fact, the failure of the Traditions to examine their own patriarchal assumptions would be seen as a closing off of the analysis from a whole dimension of experience which crucially affects women. In that sense, feminism stands alone as an alternative body of thought and framework of values.

Similarly with religion. Although there might be divisions between groups within Christianity, or Judaism, or Islam along conservative, marxist, liberal or social reformist lines, the fundamental *meaning* of those religions would lie outside the Traditions. For even though there might be assent to the explanatory power of marxism, for example, amongst many contemporary Christians, for most of them the deepest underlying meaning framework would go back beyond and outside the beginnings of the Traditions of thought. It would go back in fact to biblical writings, and especially to the New Testament. But it would see these in a contemporary context as an alternative view of life. For, it is not only the Islamic fundamentalism or Papal Catholicism referred to in Unit 27 which would reject the common Enlightenment starting-point of the Traditions. At the heart of most religious belief systems would be a questioning of the central tenet of Enlightenment humanism: the assumption of autonomous human freedom. And, whatever later levels of assumptions would be incorporated into the overall framework of analysis, this fundamental starting point would remain different. For basic to most religions is the acknowledgement that there is a God who has some responsibility for the world, and with whom human beings also are in relationship. There is an acceptance therefore of 'external' norms by which people relate to the rest of the world and to each other and which also provide a basis for analysis and evaluation. So Christianity and other religious positions ultimately stand as alternative world-views, although often in dialogue and undeniably influenced by the Traditions, whose own 'religious' roots lie in the Enlightenment.

A distance learning course, understanding a Christian world view in a day-to-day context

5   A CONCLUDING POSTSCRIPT

I have been arguing for the ultimate non-reducibility of certain other frameworks of analysis to the four Traditions. And yet, the sense in which these positions are closely linked together remains significant. They are all bound up in the same process of addressing central questions about the meaning of social reality and human existence, and coming up with an interpretative response.

The differences between them are of course reflected in their clusters of concepts, and framework of values. But, most of all, these differences hinge on what assumptions they start with and what implications for living follow from those assumptions. And in this process there is no difference in status between those explanations which are normally labelled 'religious' and those which are not. For each of them begins with a point of commitment, however tentative, to a direction or framework of meaning, and each is struggling with basic questions about human personhood, the meaning of the self and of human relationships, and the nature of society. What remains the central point of difference is where they go for answers.

ACKNOWLEDGEMENTS

Grateful acknowledgement is made to the following sources for permission to reproduce material in this unit:

p.107 (top): Taffy Davies and Third Way; p.107 (bottom): Ulrike Preuss/Format; p.110: Mary Evans Picture Library; p.113 and p.115: by kind permission, Alexis West; p.116: Amos by Alan; p.120: by permission, Oak Hill Extension Course, Southgate, London.

UNIT 31   COURSE THEMES AND REVISION

Prepared for the course team by Diane Watson and Neil Costello

CONTENTS

1   INTRODUCTION

In the preceding units of Block VII, you have started to think about revision processes and the structure of the examination. Already you may have begun to review your notes and your essays, and started to find ways of summarizing the contents of units and blocks with a view to assessing your overall understanding of D103. As the course draws to a close, you will be aware that there are some overarching issues which cross the boundaries of units and blocks and give D103 an overall sense of coherence and integration. For example, as the Block VII Introduction points out, the *'social science methods'* half-units associated with each of the blocks form one mechanism through which this integration is achieved, as does the *'UK Society'* strand. Another such mechanism is the analysis of the influence of *'traditions of thought'* on personal and social science perspectives on the world. And, in these final two units, we are going to conclude your work on the *'study skills'* strand by concentrating on revision and exam skills, and exploring further the role played by the *three course themes*; the *'public and private'*, the *'local and global'* and *'representation and reality'*.

At this stage in your study of D103, you will certainly be familiar with their names and will have seen them referred to and used in a variety of ways by the unit authors in each of the blocks. It is likely that you have already made use of them yourself in your note taking and essay writing and may have noticed that, although all blocks make use of each of the themes, some blocks and units concentrate upon one theme more than the others and sometimes they use them in different ways. Now is the time to give some detailed attention to these issues. Not only will time to reflect explicitly on these themes and issues aid your understanding of the themes themselves, but it will also help you to develop your revision skills by taking you back over the course and encouraging you to reflect upon where and how the course themes are used. In addition, by linking this analysis in to a consideration of specific examination questions, we (Neil Costello and I) aim to help you move forward with your exam preparation and help you deal with the broader 'part two' questions on the examination paper.

The aim of this unit, together with the final unit of D103, is, therefore, to engage you in an *active* review and revision of the course through a focus on *themes, revision strategies* and *examination technique*. However, as the 'Revision Skills' section of Unit 28 suggested, you will probably have insufficient time or inclination to revise every unit of every block in D103. This would involve you in an almost impossible task in constructing your revision programme and it is not the best way to help you consolidate your understanding of the course. A sound revision strategy involves decisions to be *selective* about which issues, blocks and units to focus on at this point in your studies. We have kept this constraint in mind in writing these final two units and it has informed our decision to deal in depth with one theme at a time in relation to selected blocks of the course. Consequently, although we look at all three themes in Block I (and Blocks II and VI in Unit 32), in this unit Block III will be used to examine the use of the *public and private* theme in depth and Block IV will be used to focus upon the *local and global*. In Unit 32, Block V will be used for a review of *representation and reality*. This is not to imply that the other themes do not play an important role in each of the selected blocks. On the contrary, all of the blocks make use of all of the themes in some way or another (and it has already been suggested that you can use the *Glossary Index* in your own revision work to follow through how a particular theme or other important concept is used in the different blocks and units). However, to help you with the principles of revision, and yet still allow you scope to be selective and active in your choice of blocks for revision, we too have chosen to be selective in our focus. In so doing we hope that we have set the framework for you to use and apply the themes flexibly and imaginatively in situations where you judge them to be most relevant.

This revision exercise inevitably involves the use of a number of different units and study materials. Consequently, before you settle down to study, leave for the library, or embark on a journey in which you intend to study, check first that you have all the materials which you will require with you.

2 WHY HAVE COURSE THEMES?

———— ACTIVITY I ————

Let us start by returning to the very beginning of D103. In the Block I Introduction and Study Guide and in Unit 4 Section 2, there are a number of suggestions about the value of having course themes in D103. Return to these sections now and make a few brief notes on the ways in which the themes are useful. You may already have some notes made on these sections. Have a look at these too and consider how helpful they are to you at this stage.

How did you get on?

The following are the points which I noted down:

- Each theme helps us to *organize* and structure ideas and factual material.
- Each theme consists of a pair of concepts which may be *applied* to aspects of society.
- The themes enable us to *ask* a wide range of open-ended *questions*.
- They point us towards interesting questions about *tensions* and *relationships*.
- They provide *links* between blocks of the course giving overall unity and integration.
- The themes have flexibility and we have choice in how to apply them.

I also noted the following potential dangers:

- Because the themes are flexible, the same 'label' may be applied to a range of different things. This introduces the possibility of confusion and inconsistency.
- We may be tempted to 'mis-apply' the themes where they are irrelevant or unhelpful, and risk the over-simplification of social science analysis.

From these few brief notes, I think that we can come to some conclusions about the role of course themes in D103. Our themes were selected, from a range of possibilities, to help us make sense of the material in D103 and give the course an overall integration. They are *'tools'* which we (students and unit authors) *use to organize and make sense of the vast amount of material we acquire about society.* They enable us to *'extract'* or *'abstract'*, from the wealth of empirical material available to us, those issues which seem to be of importance and warrant further attention. By guiding us in our decisions about what we should focus on and what things we should omit, the themes have helped us make the task of studying 'Society and Social Science' more manageable. In addition, the generalizing nature of the themes has helped us to make connections across the boundaries of each block and to see similar tensions at work in apparently dissimilar areas. In short, they have helped us to clarify what the course as a whole, rather than a particular unit or block, is about.

The word 'tensions' in the above paragraph is vital here. As outlined in Unit 4, the themes are ways of *conceptualizing* particular aspects of society. However, they are more than this. Because the themes consist of *pairs of concepts* they suggest complex relationships between social phenomena and have the capacity to assist us in the formulation of questions about these tensions and relationships. For example, it is not a matter of trying to 'fit' some things into the 'public' sphere and some things into the 'private'. The two areas are linked and interconnected and the boundaries between them are continually shifting. Complex social life does not fit easily into neat categories and to attempt to make it do so would hamper our understanding rather than assist it. The 'public and private', 'local and global' and 'representation and reality' are pairs of concepts which have been chosen because of their value in helping us to conceptualize certain dynamic tensions between those aspects of society we have chosen to study.

Finally, the choice of themes has been influenced by their relevance and applicability to contemporary issues. We could have chosen other themes, and other writers might well have done so. Other themes were raised and debated but, ultimately, these were chosen because they were the ones which appeared to have most relevance to the important debates of the 1990s. We have chosen them as a means to the end of understanding more about the nature of society. The danger would be if they became an end in themselves. We cannot fit everything we choose to study into one of the course themes. Sometimes a given theme is helpful but sometimes it is not. And sometimes more than one of the themes may be applied to a particular aspect of society with a view to highlighting different aspects of the same phenomenon. In other words, we have the choice to use them flexibly and creatively as a means to the end of coming to a fuller understanding of 'Society and Social Science'.

SUMMARY

In answer to the question of why have three course themes, *public and private, local and global,* and *representation and reality,* the preceding section suggests that they play a positive role in:

- Helping us to organize our material.
- Helping us to decide which issues to focus upon.
- Helping us to integrate the course as a whole.
- Helping our analysis and understanding by suggesting relationships and interconnections between social phenomena.

---

3   COURSE THEMES REVISITED

In the previous section I have outlined briefly some of the reasoning behind the course team decision to have three, overarching course themes and why we have chosen to use these three themes in particular. A major characteristic of all three course themes is that they each consist of a *pair of concepts* which are linked together to constitute the theme. On one level, the separate concepts (public, private, local, global, representation, reality) are everyday words which are familiar to us. There is a general level of agreement about what we mean when we use the words 'private' or 'local', for example, and we can take it for granted that we broadly understand one another. However, as soon as the two separate concepts become linked together in a pair, a new set of relationships and interconnections is suggested. And it is in this that the value of the course themes lies. By directing our attention towards two linked and interrelated areas or dimensions, the themes suggest interesting issues for investigation which might otherwise be overlooked or seem irrelevant. Furthermore, the linking of two concepts within a theme highlights the ways in which dimensions or areas are in tension with one another, give rise to conflicts and are constantly changing. Consequently, the themes enable us to examine *dynamic* relationships and shifting balances between the dimensions of the *public and private, local and global, and representation and reality*. These processes are summarized in Table 1.

Table 1

PUBLIC	PRIVATE
Open to view.	Secret. Confidential and intimate.
Concerning the public domain of state and civil society.	Concerning the private domain of home and family.
Involving public sector employment.	Involving private sector employment.
LOCAL	GLOBAL
Confined to a limited area.	Concerning the wider world.
Limited to a particular area or space.	Comprehensive and large scale.
REPRESENTATION	REALITY
Common or widespread images or portrayals (verbal or visual) of the world which have *social effects*.	The social context
	The social and physical world in which people find themselves.
The ways in which individuals 'make sense' of the world through ideas and images.	

Take the *public/private* theme for example. Not only are we able to conceive of the 'public' as encompassing the world of work, economy and politics and the 'private' as involving the sphere of home, family and household, but we are also able to examine the boundaries between these two spheres and the ways in which these boundaries may change over time. How, for instance, does what happens in the world of paid employment influence the lives of individuals within the family? How have the boundaries between the public and private shifted one way or another, with the state taking more, or less, responsibility for health, education and social welfare than in previous times? Or, taking another facet of the public/private theme used in the course, we might ask questions about the world of employment and industry (conceptualized in the above example as the 'public') in the light of the role of government and the state in the ownership and management of companies in the public sector. In this example, the state becomes defined as the 'public' (managing public sector industries) and the wider, general sphere of work and employment becomes defined as the 'private', except where sections of it are owned by the state as a consequence of nationalization (Unit 1: Section 3.3). This *public/private sector* distinction serves to illustrate the ways in which issues in one area of the economy are intimately related to, and have implications for, issues and developments in other areas. Finally, another set of questions are brought into focus when the interrelationship between an individual's private inner world and the public context in which interactions occur and identities are constructed is explored (Block V Introduction). These are the types of questions brought into focus when the two concepts become linked together to form a relationship.

The public/private theme may be represented as follows:

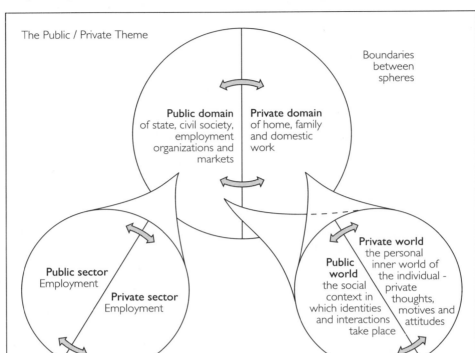

Figure 1

If we examine the *local/global* interconnection we find that our attention is focused upon the ways in which events and issues at the level of the locality are influenced by, and in turn influence, the wider national and international scene (see Figure 2). So, for example, we might use the theme to explore the processes involved in the rise and decline of particular local industries or in the structuring and restructuring of a local economy, and examine the ways in

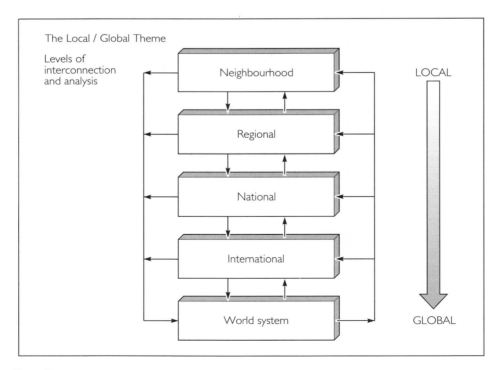

Figure 2

which these are linked with developments at the level of national government or the global economic order. And, as you will have learnt from your discussion of Lancashire and cotton in Block VI, this is a two-way process. Events in the locality are not mere reflections of global events but powerful influences in shaping and constructing outcomes at the global level. Furthermore, the terms 'local' and 'global' refer to different things depending upon our level of analysis. Sometimes, for example, the UK is defined as 'global' in relation to the community or region. At other times, the UK becomes 'local' when compared with a European or World-wide perspective.

Finally, the *representation / reality* theme focuses our attention upon the ways in which those sets of ideas which we hold about aspects of the world around us (our representations) both reflect the ways in which we experience the world and play a part in the 'construction' of that world. It alerts us to the fact that individuals do not merely experience an external world which exists independently of their experience. On the contrary, they construct and reconstruct sets of images and ideas about the world as they experience it and, in so doing, they shape and change that world. So, for example, widespread and taken-for-granted media and advertising images of the role of women within the family and at home, both build on existing perceptions of women in society and shape and influence future perceptions. However, women do not necessarily passively accept such definitions of themselves and their 'proper' role in society and the family, and may act together to resist such representations and find ways of raising alternative images in the public consciousness. Ideas and images are not just passively internalized by individuals, and groups of individuals, but are also actively used to make sense of experience and, where possible, to re-present ideas and images to others in the process of enhancing the position and status of those individuals or groups. The success, or otherwise, of groups in resisting unfavourable representations and asserting favourable ones is clearly linked in to processes of power in society and the theme plays a useful role in alerting us to this relatively hidden dimension of social structure and process.

The representation and reality theme may be presented as follows:

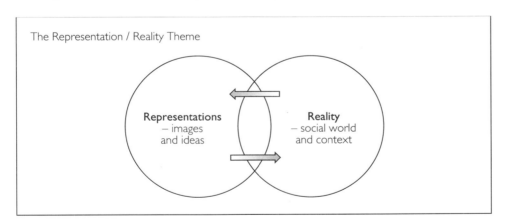

Figure 3

———————————————————— ACTIVITY 2 ————————————————————

Before you complete this section, it would be helpful, for revision purposes, to return to the Block I Introduction and Study Guide (pp.6–7) where you will find a brief outline of each of the themes in turn. Look over these now, make a few notes of the main features and compare them with my discussion above. If you keep these notes by you as you work through these units they will help you know what to look out for as we go back over some of the early material in the course.

SUMMARY

MY NOTES ON THIS SECTION:

- The distinction between *public* and *private* areas of social life is one frequently used in everyday language as well as in social science analysis.

- The labels 'public' and 'private' are used to apply to several different things.

- Examples so far are the private sphere of the household or the public domain of the market; private charity or public aid; private enterprise or public sector economics.

- The *local/global* theme is especially valuable in dealing with different levels of analysis.

- The 'local' refers to social processes at the small or local level. The 'global' to the large scale, national or international context.

- The social scientist can move between levels. For example the UK might be seen as the global level compared with a region or locality within the UK. Or it may be seen as the local level when compared with the European or international context.

- The *representation/reality* theme examines the ways in which individuals and social groups experience the world, and images and portrayals of the world, and interpret it to themselves and to others.

- The theme may be applied to everyday commonsense interpretations, images and popular stereotypes or it may be applied to social scientific forms of understanding.

- The distinction between 'ideal' images and the 'reality' of experience can be very fruitful in exploring the role and influence of ideas however 'inaccurate' those ideas may seem to be when examined from the perspective of an outsider.

4   USING COURSE THEMES: BLOCK I

Before leaving Block I, I would like to take you back to Activity 1 of Unit 4 and have a look at the table which you were asked to complete there. I found this activity really quite difficult. However, working my way through the units with the themes in mind was invaluable revision and, after reading through the summary in Section 2 following the table, I settled on the following points:

REPRESENTATION AND REALITY

A striking example of this theme in the block is the discussion of the ideas behind, and images suggested by, the notion that 'there is nothing so English as a cup of tea'. Think back to the picture which is at the start of the unit and the suggestion that this is *representation* which has 'knitted itself into our idea of ourselves as a nation' (Unit 1, p.14). Exploring that image further raised issues and questions surrounding the tendency to equate *Englishness* with *Britishness* and all this means for glossing over the internal variety within a society such as the UK. It also raises the question of why it is that some ideas are more salient and more influential in society than others.

A traditional English setting.

The timeless quality and craftsmanship of Royal Albert fine bone china has set the scene for perfect summer days since the 1800's.

Gracing the tables of royalty and gentle-folk alike, Royal Albert's distinctive gilt edged fluted curves and rich floral patterns embody everything that is English. This example of

Moonlight Rose is only one of the many traditional patterns that have made the name Royal Albert synonymous with high teas, garden parties and polite society.

You couldn't find a better assurance that when you cherish Royal Albert you hold a little piece of England.

ROYAL ALBERT

For a free Royal Albert brochure showing our full range of china visit your local department store or china shop. For a full list of stockists write to
Royal Doulton, Dept. WHF, London Road, Stoke-on-Trent ST4 7QD.

A second representation I thought of in Block I was associated with the discussion of hunger in Unit 2. There the unit examined ideas put forward to explain hunger in the Third World, such as 'over-population', 'food shortage' or 'natural forces', and illustrated how this theme suggests lines of inquiry which dig beneath the surface of popular conceptions of hunger to examine underlying causes. And finally, in Unit 3, representations encountered through the mass media and advertising were examined for their capacity to appeal to existing images and self-definitions held by individuals and groups, and for their role in shaping our perceptions of ourselves, and promoting our perceptions of products made available through the market. Examples of representations explored there were those relating to social class, health, fitness and fatness and purity and pollution.

PUBLIC AND PRIVATE

If we return to Unit 1, we can see how the discussion of the making of 'afternoon tea' throws up a distinction between the *public domain of paid work* within the formal economy and the *private arena of unpaid work* within the household. This distinction emerges again where a second, and different, usage of public and private occurs. This is where a distinction was made between the *private and public sectors of the economy* in relation to the production of sugar. The value of the theme in these contexts is that it gives us a framework within which to examine changes in the organization of work in society and the economy over time, such as a shift in emphasis from the private to the public, and suggests ways of exploring the boundaries between public and private 'worlds'. In particular, it provides a tool for examining the potential role of the state, both in protecting certain parts of society and in enabling things to happen, and in interfering in certain areas and placing constraints upon what happens.

Public or private ownership

LOCAL AND GLOBAL

This third theme is fundamental to our discussion of food in Block I because it encourages us to focus upon economic, political, social and cultural relationships at a world wide level (Unit 1, p.30). In doing this we are better placed to explore the impact of *global changes*, such as the expansion of trade in the eighteenth century and shifts in world trade patterns, upon the local, regional geography and social structure of the UK and other individual countries (Unit 1, Section 3). Similarly, Unit 2 examines the 'degree to which local vulnerability to famine is shaped by global forces' (p.87) and uses the theme to highlight the complexity of the interrelationship between factors at different levels. In Unit 3, these factors are again explored in relation to the development of major supermarket chains and their impact on local patterns of shopping (the closure of small, corner shops). The developments are connected to the global search for food supplies and the domination of supermarket shopping by a small number of food retailing organizations (Unit 3, pp.129–33). The theme enables us to focus our discussion more closely upon relevant factors and the links between them and raises useful questions about the types of explanation put forward to account for real world issues such as hunger and famine.

Check through your notes to see that you are clear what the course themes are and how they have been used in the course so far. If you have the opportunity, why not discuss ways of 'reviewing course themes' with your tutor and fellow students at the study centre? A cooperative approach often has advantages, especially where you can share out tasks, pool ideas and argue through problems and uncertainties. But don't worry if this is not possible. The aim of this unit is to work with you to help you to find ways through the material to arrive at a firmer understanding of the themes and their applications.

If you now look over the examples of the course themes which we have extracted from Block I, you will see that the specific examples we have chosen to highlight raise some wider and more general issues about the role and value of the course themes in D103. What I want to do now is explore each of the themes in more depth by concentrating on one theme at a time in relation to Blocks III and IV. But remember the point I made earlier about being selective. In doing this, I have made a decision to focus on a given theme in relation to a particular block. I could have swapped the themes around and chosen different themes for Blocks III and IV and it would have worked equally as well. You might consider doing this as you revise your chosen blocks, either alone or with your tutor and fellow students at the study centre. For each theme Neil will then take an examination type question and help you through the plan of an answer for each question thereby developing your examination technique. I shall begin with Block III and the *public and private* course theme.

5   BLOCK III: THE PUBLIC AND THE PRIVATE

You will remember from the 'Introduction and study guide' to Block III that the public and private course theme features in each of the units in the block. It is developed in Unit 10 in the discussion of the ways in which work is regarded differently depending upon whether it takes place in the 'public' domain of the economy or the 'private' domain of home and family. It occurs again in Unit 11 where the role of the state in economic markets is explored and in Unit 12 where the role of the state in planning and directing the economy is considered in depth.

One of the first things which I noticed on returning to my notes on Block III was that this theme is used in two distinctly different ways across the three units. You may remember at the beginning of this unit I noted that the flexibility of the themes meant that the same 'label' could be attached by different authors to a range of different things. This certainly occurs in the units in Block III. Let us explore this further.

———————————————— ACTIVITY 3 ————————————————

How you approach this particular activity will depend in part on the extent to which you intend to revise Block III for the examination. Remember the advice given in the Study Skills section for Unit 28 about how to select topics for revision and, where relevant, refer to notes and ideas which you have already assembled. Look through the contents page of this unit and consider the amount of time you have to devote to each particular block. Consult the Study Guide for advice on time allocation. This will enable you to plan a timetable of study to fit in with your wider revision needs. For Block III, you may have decided to work through each of the units in depth because you hope to answer a question on that block.

Alternatively, you may wish to skim through the Introduction and Summary sections as you think about the themes. In any event, it is worth bearing in mind that a focus on course themes will highlight some aspects of the unit and the block at the expense of others. If you have the opportunity to work with your tutor-counsellor and fellow students at the study centre, you may find group work and discussion very beneficial to remembering issues and debates more clearly. Whatever the attention you propose to give to Block III, now is an opportunity to practise some general revision techniques. For example:

- Check over the contents pages of each of the units to get an overall picture of the shape of the block.

- Give close attention to the introductions to the block, the units and the specific study sections to remind yourself of the structure of the discussion. Similarly, go to the Summary sections and work through the conclusions.

- Sort out the central questions of the units and the block.

- Think about the sort of TMA questions you have been set on the units.

- Attempt to condense the arguments into note form.

- Review your existing notes and decide whether you can condense them further.

- Review the relevance of other components of the course such as the TV and radio, cassettes and set books.

You may already be well into your own preferred way of revising but, if not, there is still plenty of time to work on this. This review of course themes will help you to integrate the course and draw together some of your ideas on the blocks and the course as a whole.

Now think about how you are going to deal with Block III and the *public and private* theme. Go back to your notes, look over the units and, as you do this, make a note of some of the ways in which the public and private theme has been used by the unit authors. From your examples are you able to pick out two different usages of the public and private distinction?

——

The first use of the public and private theme in Block III which I found was in Unit 10 on 'Work and the economy'. There, a distinction is made between the public domain of the world of paid employment and the private domain of the family and household. In spite of differences in the type of work people undertake, work which takes place within the public domain is formally recognized as economic activity by being paid. Paid work gives the individual independence, status and access to scarce and valued goods and services. It achieves social and public recognition. People have a status and identity because of the job of work which they do. However, people who do not work within the public domain of the formal economy are not so rewarded. Even though the work they do within the home and family may be necessary and important (rearing children, cleaning, cooking, nursing) it does not attract the same social and public recognition because it does not produce products which can be sold in the public arena. Hence the housewife apologizes that she is 'only a housewife' and the long term unemployed, like Jim Jarratt, feel that they are 'one of the untouchables of the British Caste system'. Work within the private sphere of home and family tends to be invisible precisely because it takes place within the 'private' arena and, as a consequence, has tended to be neglected by both economic theory and policy making which have generally concentrated upon full-time, paid employment (Unit 10, Section 3.3). Moreover, ideas about the type of contribution made in the private sphere, and especially by women, are carried over into the public sphere of paid work. Consequently, women tend to occupy work which is regarded as of lower status, is more poorly paid and tends to confirm the image of women as nurturing providers of services to men.

A second major use of the 'public and private' dichotomy is in Section 3 of the same unit where the nature of 'real' work is discussed. Here the distinction is made between the public and the private but this time the discussion takes place *within* the public sphere of paid work, markets and the economy. Within the public domain, different sectors may be distinguished. There are the privately owned industries and companies within the *private sector* of the economy and there are the *public sector* services and publicly owned utilities and industries. This public/private sector distinction is one common to everyday discussions of the economy and is one you are likely to be generally familiar with. The relationship between these two sectors of the economy, and the relative balance between them, is the focus of much economic and political activity. You may remember that this was explored in some detail in TV06 where the 'privatization' (the transfer of services from public to private sector control) of transport, gas and hospital cleaning services is examined. If you have time, refer to your TV notes and remind yourself of the issues raised there.

Unit 12 takes the debate further, making use of the same public and private distinction. One of the main aims of Unit 12 is to illustrate the ways in which a public body, such as the government, is able to shape the private economic activity of firms and individuals which is conducted within the private sphere. What is illustrated in Unit 12 is the fact that these two sectors are not separate but are intimately interconnected. Choices about the proper role of government in intervening in the 'market' and in managing the economy involve value judgements and political positions. This is illustrated by the unit discussion of the influence of liberal and social reformist ideas on the development of the monetarist, corporatist and Keynesian 'packages'. These 'packages' were developed by different governments in the post-war period with the aim of achieving economic competitiveness (Unit 12, Section 2). The distinction between these public and private sectors of the economy has drawn our attention to the implications, for groups and individuals, of such trends as the decline in the private sector manufacturing base, the growth of public sector service employment, government intervention in the planning and provision of welfare needs or government reluctance to intervene in the operation of 'market forces'. This public/private distinction is valuable in highlighting the shifting boundaries between, and the interconnectedness of, these two spheres.

133

These two different uses of the public and private theme are not new to Block III. If you return to your notes for Blocks I and II, you will see those same uses appearing there too. Unit 1 looked at the public arena of paid work and the private domain of unpaid work in the household but also examined the role of the government, and the public and private sectors, in the production of sugar. Unit 8 examined the implications for black women of the separation of the public world of production from the private world of reproduction.

Now the question you are probably asking at this moment, if not before, is whether this matters! Has the course team fallen into the trap of introducing confusion and inconsistency?! Well, I don't think so. Provided that we are clear about the ways in which we are using terms and concepts, then the flexibility in the use of the theme can enhance its value. For example, the use of the theme at the broadest and most general level enables us to examine what sociologists have defined as the distinction between 'personal troubles' and 'public issues' (Wright Mills, 1959). Wright Mills argued that 'personal troubles' were private matters related to the individual and their relationships with others in the immediate and limited social setting. 'Public issues' on the other hand are matters of public interest which transcend the localized experience of the individual and are to do with organization at the level of the wider society (*ibid*, p.6–7). Consequently 'private' matters such as marriage, suicide, the experience of unemployment or mental illness all have public dimensions when rates of divorce, suicide, unemployment and mental illness become such that they register as public, social problems and issues. If you refer back to your notes on Unit 6, you will see that these issues were raised in the discussion of the 'nature of the social'. So, in the first instance the public/private theme highlights the complex interrelationship between the individual and social structure and sets up the comparison between the public and private spheres of experience.

Furthermore, if we begin with this broad and general perspective on the public and private, we are likely to be wary of the temptation to lose sight of the private sphere of domestic life and family relationships in which much of women's experience is located. As Gamarnikow and Purvis (1983, pp.1–6) have argued, the domination of men in the development of Sociology has resulted in a concentration upon the public sphere of male concerns associated with the realm of work, economy and politics. By and large, women have been excluded from these social and institutional activities and 'consigned and confined to the private realm of the family' (*ibid,* p.1). They have been actively excluded by men from the social and physical space occupied by men. This argument may be familiar to you from your reading of Chapter 22 of the Course Reader which cites Pateman's observation that, in the sphere of politics, liberal thought 'divided the world into private and public spheres, and prioritized the first over the second' (Reader, Chapter 22, Section 2.1 'Power and the State'). And, as Pateman herself has argued, although the private sphere is part of civil (i.e. public) society, it tends to get 'forgotten', with the focus of discussion being upon divisions 'within the "civil" realm itself, between the private capitalist economy or private enterprise and the public or political state' (Pateman, 1988, p.12). A focus upon the private sphere brings with it an awareness of otherwise neglected issues. For example, instead of focusing largely upon official recorded statistics of violent crime, we direct attention towards hidden forms of violence within the family. The idea of what is regarded as 'work' becomes more broadly conceptualized to include 'invisible' work within the family. Furthermore, the role of 'reproductive' work within the family is explored and an understanding of the relationship between 'reproductive' work and 'productive' work within society is developed. These are just some examples from the course which illustrate the value of the broad usage of the public and private theme.

SUMMARY

Provided that we are aware of this broader division into the public and private spheres and of the fact that the two are intimately related, with events in the private sphere influencing and being influenced by events in the public arena, then the different uses are not likely to be problematic. Discussion of public and private distinctions within the public domain (public and private sectors, public services and private enterprise, the role of the state in shifting the boundaries between the two, the intervention of the state in providing welfare services) are of value in themselves but they must be located within the *wider framework* of the whole society, both public and private.

Now over to Neil Costello for a discussion of an actual exam type question on Block III related to the public and the private. Neil will provide a plan of an answer then hand it back to me for comment.

The purpose of these sections, which are interspersed with Diane Watson's analyses of the use of the themes in D103, is to try to help you to produce good examination answers. I described the skills needed for this in the revision section of Unit 28 as 'the ability to think quickly and to respond concisely and in a relevant way'. Such skills are immensely valuable outside the exam room and I expect we would all like to have more of them for many reasons. For now, though, I would like to concentrate specifically on using them in the examination. One of the things I tried to emphasize in the revision section was the value of planning examination answers as an aid to revision, and this is where we can pick up that idea again. The activities we are going to go through in a moment are things you should carry out as part of your revision as well as adapting them for your use in the examination itself. There are just a few more preliminaries before I make an attempt at a specific question. They are important preliminaries and I shall mention them again later. They are also raised in Chapter 7 of *The Good Study Guide*, and near the end of Unit 32 we shall ask you to look at the later sections of that chapter. The first preliminary is one which appears in almost every external examiner's report I have seen: the need to answer the question set and not the question you hoped would be set! The remaining points relate to this, namely, how we can try to ensure that we do tackle the real question, particularly under the pressure of examination conditions.

The first thing we must do is read the question. This involves more than simply scanning. It is important to read the question thinking: 'What does the examiner really want me to do with this question?' There are no trick questions and the examiner will be trying to give you the opportunity to illustrate your understanding of the course. Usually, this will involve some kind of debate between alternative interpretations or explanations. We must read the question carefully and avoid slipping into the error, which I am sure we have all made at some time, of seeing a concept or phrase in the question and jumping straight into a debate about that phrase without checking the context in which the phrase is used. The question will be asking you to *use* what you know, not simply to write down all that you know. This might sound obvious in the clear light of several weeks before the examination but, in the exam room itself, in my experience, failure to tackle the question which is on the paper is the biggest source by far of low scores.

All questions are open to interpretation and it is not unknown to find an interpretation which the examiner had not expected. In such cases, scriptmarkers would try to assess the unexpected interpretation. That is why scriptmarking is a challenging job involving many skilled people and not something we can simply pass over to the computer! It is not the unexpected interpretation which is likely to cause disappointment, however. Indeed for the scriptmarker it could be delightfully refreshing. But we do need an interpretation of the question and not simply a list of everything which might have some relevance to the question. Most people try to give relevant answers, of course, but there is a strong temptation after a period of revision to throw everything in, because it seems to be relevant. The most common topic of conversation after an examination tends to be about what was included in an answer and the worry that something might have been forgotten, not about interpretation. We have therefore to devise some method of preparing examination answers which allows us to indulge our impulse to write down everything that we can think of, whilst at the same time trying to ensure that the answer itself does focus on the question set.

How can we do that? The system that has worked reasonably well for me is to break the activity down into three phases:

1   To pick out the key words and phrases in the question.
2   To list, very briefly all the things I consider connected in some way to the question.
3   To organize the list in such a way that it directly tackles the question.

This has to be done quickly in the exam and that is why it is worth practising as often as possible before the exam.

Let me try to do this now for a particular question. It is a question from Block III set by the Block authors, and I know that it has some connection with the public and the private theme because it was set specifically to that brief (an advantage which you will not be given in the examination!). I am going to think aloud about what I am doing as I attempt this question so that you can get a grasp of how I approach an exam answer. I shall also try to carry this out in circumstances as near as possible to examination conditions rather than try to polish a perfect model. Diane will then comment on my answer. We think you should find this more helpful than the two of us trying to compose a perfect example. My background is in economics and Diane is a sociologist, so that should ensure some difference of perspective.

The question is: '*Real work takes place only in the public domain.*' Discuss.

───────────────────── ACTIVITY 4 ─────────────────────

Before you look at the way I have attempted this question, write out a brief plan yourself. Even if you do not intend to revise Block III, I think it is worth having a stab at it so that you can make more sense of the suggestions I make below.

───

Key words and phrases here are: real work, public domain and the 'doing' word — discuss.

How do I go about this question? I have first to define the two concepts 'real work' and the 'public domain' and then to 'discuss' their relationship. There are different perspectives on the nature of work. I know an important issue is the distinction between work in the public domain and work in the private domain. I can remember too the way in which the article by Jim Jarratt in Unit 10 talked about the problems of those without work in the public domain, although he didn't put it that way. There is also the issue of what is *real* work and this is related to different philosophical views, from the Physiocrats on agriculture through to Bacon and Eltis, on marketed output being real. I wonder if there is a difference here between profit-seeking work and work which is not for profit? And, I must ensure I include something on work in the private domain. This is important because the question seems basically to be challenging the view that work in the private domain is real. It isn't asking me to examine only public domain work. I must contrast this with private domain work to assess what we mean by the term 'real work'. This will involve the distinction between production and reproduction.

This rather jumbled paragraph is the equivalent of the rather more cryptic notes I would make in trying to list all the things I thought might be connected with the question. In an exam, the notes might look rather like this:

- Define work
- Define public domain
- What is meant by *real* work?
- Real work — Physiocrats
              — Bacon and Eltis etc.
- Public and private domain (and unemployment?)
- Profits/non-profits
- Is private domain work real?
- Production and reproduction

I find it very helpful to let my thoughts flow in this way. At this stage, I am not trying to answer the question directly but, rather, to put down all those things I see might be relevant. It is a quick mind clearing exercise. It enables me to put something down on paper straight away and to get my thoughts onto the question. It also goes some way in coping with the 'blank sheet of paper' syndrome; the problem of not knowing where to start when faced with a blank sheet of paper. Essentially I begin by noting very briefly everything which I think might be relevant.

The idea then is to use these notes to produce an outline for the question. Before I do that, however, one aside is worth making. The jumbled paragraph, if written out in full, does not look very much different from many examination answers. It contains most of the relevant bits of information but is disorganized and, apart from the definitions of the concepts of work and the public domain at the beginning, and the reflection on work in the private domain at the end, does not really seem to make any true recognition of the specific things the question is asking for. That kind of jumble will not score very well even though it contains most of the elements of a good answer.

Now I must try to put these pieces together into an answer to the specific question. The question is asking me to look at the relationship between work and the public domain. I know that the relationship is not an entirely simple and straightforward one, and that the question must be asking me to look at some of the complexities involved: I must problematize the relationship. What are the complexities here? From my notes, I realize that they draw in some part from the distinction between the public and the private domain, which has also been taken up in the long-standing debates about what constitutes 'real' work. There are some examples of these things in the unit which I can probably draw on too, for example, the issue of domestic work and the position of women and perhaps something about unemployment. I feel I am beginning to get somewhere and I can begin to plan an answer.

I have a basic structure for an answer which I modify to suit the question involved. The basic structure assumes the question requires some kind of debate:

- I begin with an introduction which defines the main concepts and sets out the kind of debate which I hope to undertake in the answer.
- This is followed by a section which picks up one side of the debate: usually the one which is most prominently signalled in the question.
- The next section takes alternative perspectives to the one(s) set out in the previous section and sets them out.

- Then an important section. It tries to compare the different points raised in the previous two sections. I will not have carried out that comparison as I have gone along. I try to leave it until the different ideas have been set out fairly clearly.
- Finally I will try to set out a short conclusion which summarizes what has gone before.

I am not suggesting this structure as a perfect model for critical writing! I do find it useful, however, when under pressure to have a basic framework to get me started. Let me see how well this model suits the Block III question we have been considering. In fact, it suits it very well. What we are asked to do — the 'doing' word as I called it — is discuss, and that is precisely what this structure helps us to do. It is basically a framework for discussion, setting out one side of the argument first, then the other and finally trying to compare and contrast the arguments. Thus an answer to this question could be structured as follows:

INTRODUCTION

I need to define 'real work' and 'public domain'. I should also set out briefly what I think the question is asking me to do, and how I intend to do it. Public domain isn't too difficult to define, but real work is a problem. In trying to define this I shall be raising all the issues the question asks me to cover, so I would problematize it rather than define it precisely. What I mean by this is that I would say something to the effect that the debate over real work is the core of the question, that the concept cannot be defined unambiguously and that my answer is going to explore various interpretations of the term.

SECTION 1

I would lead straight out of the introduction into a discussion of real work in the public domain. I would point out that there has been a continuing debate about what is productive and what is unproductive work. Examples would be necessary here but not explored in great detail. I would show how the early views on productive work based around agriculture have shifted, that there is a perspective which sees only manufacturing as productive and that there has more recently been a discussion of the distinction between marketed and non-marketed output as the main dividing line between productive and unproductive work. Thus, even within the public domain there is room for debate on what constitutes real work.

SECTION 2

Following from Section 1, I would now put the other side of the argument. In this context, I see that as a need to raise the issue of work in the private domain. If non-marketed work in the public domain is in some sense unproductive then, since all private domain work is non-marketed, on that argument it is not real. Whilst this logic is impeccable (I think!), it begs the question. Is there real work in the private domain? The answer is, of course, yes. The work is real. The work is demanding and is often much the same as work in the public domain but carried out without pay. (I would give a couple of examples here such as child care/nursery provision and voluntary work for a charity/committee membership.) It is also different from work in the public domain. It relates to the reproduction of society as well as to production. It is important too, not trivial. Why then is there a debate about real work in the private domain? This moves us on to Section 3.

SECTION 3

This section, then, challenges the assumptions on which work is recognized. Now we need to look at the distinction between the public and private domains. Is work in the private domain any less important or any less demanding? The answer in general is no. But such work is less recognized socially. This relates to the kind of society we live in. In a capitalist society, things which are bought and sold are recognized because they appear in public in a visible way and have values attached to them, values which connect with the main means of valuation under capitalism, namely market prices. Thus, the main point here is that work exists in a very real sense in the private domain but it is valued differently.

Those differences are ideological rather than related to the nature of the work itself. As we will have seen, from examples in the previous sections, the work itself can be almost exactly the same in physical terms in both domains. The distinction is important, however. It is not simply an academic debate. It is important because the valuation we put on things has real effects on status, employment opportunities and the provision of public and private investment in facilities, for example. It is also, in general, a gendered distinction.

CONCLUSION

In the conclusion I would try to summarize very briefly what had gone before. I would emphasize the ideological importance of the distinction between real work and non-work, stating again that this comes down to the valuation the market puts on work rather than the intrinsic worth of the activity itself.

I have set out my train of thought on this question in as full a way as I felt I could, consistent with helping you to see the way in which I would plan an answer to an examination question. If I had been sitting in an exam room my plan would have been very brief. One method I have adopted is to draw a line down the middle of the page. On the left-hand side I make brief notes, such as those I set out above, and on the right-hand side (and taking up about as much space) I would set out the plan. It would look something like this:

Notes	Plan
Define work	Introduction: Definition of public domain and difficulty of definition of work
Define public domain	1 Debate over work in public domain. Productive and unproductive work etc.
What is meant by *real* work?	
Real work — Physiocrats	
— Bacon and Eltis etc.	2 Work in private domain. What is it? Examples showing similarities plus production/reproduction distinction.
Public and private domain (and unemployment?)	
Profits/non-profits	3 Ideological nature of these distinctions. How we value work in capitalist society.
Is private domain work real?	
Production and reproduction	Conclusion: Review plus emphasis on ideology and market.

Once I have a plan like this and, through constructing it, my thoughts are beginning to concentrate on the question, the writing out of the answer becomes much more straightforward. I would recommend that you think about adapting this to your own needs so that you have a clear set of tactics to adopt on the way to realizing your exam strategy.

Now, I'm going to hand you back to Diane so that she can say what she thinks about this outline and move us on the local and the global.

What I think is interesting about this question is the extent to which such a short statement has the potential for generating a wealth of interesting material for discussion. At first sight, what might appear to be a fairly limited question about the nature of 'real work' turns out to allow the scope to explore the *public and private* course theme in the context of examples of paid and unpaid work, production and reproduction. The question is interesting in that it is as much about issues which are *implied* by the question as it is about those specifically stated. So, to make sense of the question, Neil has taken on a discussion of the private domain as well as the public one and explored work associated with reproduction in the home as well as production in the public sphere. His initial thoughts on the question are a useful illustration of the value of giving time to think over

the implications of a question in an exam context. Only by doing this can one begin to draw out the subtleties and nuances associated with the particular question and the range of possibilities available in the process of constructing an answer. In the anxiety of the examination, it is so easy to launch into an answer by picking out the obvious and stated aspects of the question, and neglecting to think through fully those other relevant but less obvious dimensions.

I like the way Neil focuses upon the specific wording of the question to help him organize his ideas and materials. Isolating 'process' words, such as 'discuss', are vital in helping us to decide what we should *do* with an answer, whereas 'content' words indicate the type of content an essay should include. In this case we are focusing on concepts such as *public domain* and *'real work'*. I saw the use of the word *only* as a helpful indicator that I should not merely confine myself to 'real work in the public domain' but widen my discussion to make comparisons with the type of work which takes place in the private domain. It encouraged me to ask a series of questions just as Neil has done. For example, it suggested to me that I should consider whether there are domains other than the public domain and whether any kind of work is carried out there. Since I decided that the answer to those questions was 'yes', I realized that I would need also to consider whether that work was different in some way from the work taking place in the public domain and, if so, why? Is work only defined as 'real' if it takes place within this public domain, and are there distinctions even there about the values placed upon different types of activity? Clearly, neither Neil nor I are advocating that we break down the question into parts in such a way that we lose its overall meaning. However, taking time to explore exactly what the question wants of us, even when we feel very pressed for time, is a valuable way of sorting through ideas and deciding what is particularly relevant to a given question.

In this case, it happened that the plan which I had constructed was very much along the same lines as Neil's. I thought about the question in such a way that I arrived at similar content and a very similar line of argument. I think anyone reading Neil's plan and answer could understand why he had included what he had included and placed it in that order. However, I think that the most significant point which I would emphasize is the importance of an integrated and coherent line of argument. This Neil has summarized in his plan on the right-hand column at the end of his notes, and this plan gives the bare bones of an answer. Having got to this stage, you can make a variety of choices about what to include and what to leave out, but the basis of a good answer is outlined there.

ACTIVITY 5

Before concluding this discussion of the public and private theme in Block III, look back over the notes you made for this answer and compare them with the outline which Neil has worked out. How do they compare? Can you see in what way they are similar and different and why? If possible, exchange your notes with a fellow student at the study centre and discuss how and why you arrived at the answers you did, and whether, in the light of the discussion in this section, you would now want to make any changes to them.

Finally, before we leave Block III, this is an appropriate time to finish off the activity begun in Unit 3. Activity 7 in Unit 3 asked you to look out for five or six items of commonly purchased food where the price did not vary with the seasons. You were asked to repeat the exercise during your study of Unit 12 in Block III, when the topic under consideration was inflation. It is now time to complete the operation to calculate your own rate of inflation. The activity is on page 133 of Unit 3.

In a sense what you have done is to calculate your own retail prices index. This is the index, usually referred to as the RPI, which is what commentators usually mean when they talk about the rate of inflation in the UK.

My guess is that the inflation rate measured by your index is different from that announced by the government at the end of last month. Does that mean your rate is wrong? No, it doesn't. We have a good example here of the need to interpret evidence. The RPI is a particular representation of inflation. It is calculated to give as good a guide as possible of what is happening to prices, on average, in the economy.

Think back to Unit 3 when you first began this exercise. Why did you decide to choose one good rather than another to feature in your index? For an accurate measure of inflation, we need to choose a selection of goods which in some way represents the typical purchasing pattern of consumers. The RPI is constructed by collecting the prices of around 600 items on a specified day each month based on the typical buying patterns of the population as a whole, but excluding those dependent on state benefits (except pensioners) and the wealthiest 4 per cent. Those items are shown in the pie chart.

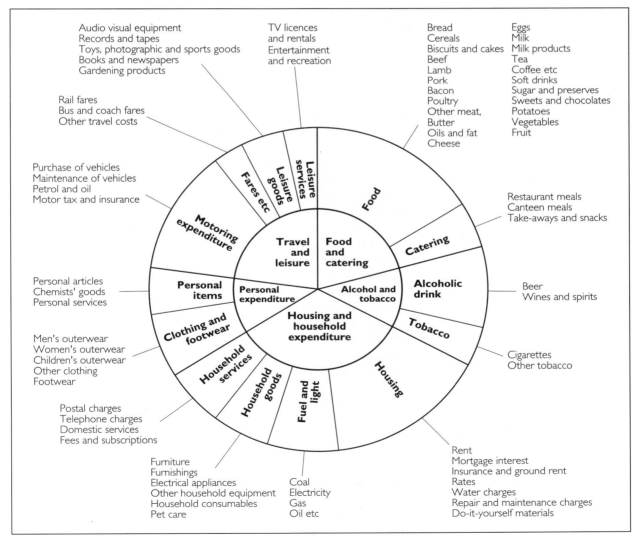

Figure 4   Pie Chart: Structure of the RPI

But it is not enough just to average the price increases for all the goods as we have asked you to do. If we do that, we are saying a 10 per cent increase in the price of, say, records and tapes is just as significant as a 10 per cent increase in the price of, say, footwear or bread. To get round this problem, the different goods are given 'weights' where the most important have the highest weights and therefore count most in the calculation of the inflation rate. The weights are calculated each year from the Family Expenditure Survey, which asks how each of a large sample of households spends its money every month.

Finally, there is one further point which you may find helpful in interpreting the inflation rates which are announced every month. We asked you to avoid goods whose prices vary with the seasons. Obviously, if our index was full of seasonal items, such as vegetables, we would find it varied according to the time of year rather than saying something about the state of the economy. To get round this problem, the RPI is usually expressed as the change since the same month in the previous year. That way the effect of the seasonal items should be roughly the same in each month.

I hope you can see that the RPI is, at root, a simple idea. Your own personal retail prices index is essentially the same as the more complex version announced each month. It is important which items are selected for inclusion, however, and how they are combined together — weighted — to produce the final figure. These selections are based on judgements and surveys. The inflation rate which affects you will depend upon your own purchasing pattern, and this is likely to be different for all of us.

Now, on to Block IV and the next course theme, the *local and the global*.

6   BLOCK IV: THE LOCAL AND THE GLOBAL

If you return to the notes we made on the Introduction and Study Guide for Block I, you will see that we concluded that one of the major values of the *local and global* theme is that it enables us to undertake analysis at different levels and allows us to make links and interconnections between these levels. As is so clearly illustrated in Block VI, the term 'global' does not always refer to factors operating at a world level. From a *community* level or *regional* point of view (Lancashire, South Wales and Central Scotland in Unit 23) the UK level may be viewed as global. Alternatively, from a *European or international global* viewpoint the UK may be perceived as *local*. Block VI explores these *local / global connections* in some depth and, since you have quite recently dealt with this material, I anticipate that it should be quite fresh in your mind. Let us return now to the structure of Block IV (leaving for the moment Unit 17 which is more closely connected with the *representation and reality* theme) and consider the relevance of this local and global theme.

——————————————— ACTIVITY 6 ———————————————

To help you in your revision, and using the advice above, return now to Units 14–16 and list some examples of processes and events which may be seen to be operating at the *local* level. Do the same for those which appear to operate at the *global* level. Can you see how in some situations the UK, for example, is regarded as the global level, whereas in other instances it is represented as the local in relation to the international or transnational context?

These three units are a good illustration of a variety of processes operating at a number of different levels but which are quite clearly intimately connected to one another. For example, Unit 16, 'Power and the People', begins the analysis of democracy from a personalized and localized level. The *local* encompasses the local community, the neighbourhood, the parish and local government. It is about 'who gets what' at the local level. However, the focus of discussion is on the extent to which individuals can shape and influence the operation of politics at the national level. UK politics may be influenced by the actions of individuals as voters and as members of interest groups. Politics in the broadest sense is seen to operate in the home and in the workplace, and changes consequent upon individual human action ultimately have their impact on the shape of politics at the national level. This is the local in relation to the global.

In Unit 15, 'Power and the State in the post-war UK', the discussion is centred on the *global* level of national political decision making and the extent to which 'UK governments can achieve their objectives at home, by examining their relationship to certain important local institutions and processes'. In this unit, the interconnections between the local and the global and the global and the local are drawn out through an examination of two case studies. In the one case, the actions of governments in the making of economic policy were related to the cooperation and resistance of other key institutions such as UK manufacturers, trade union groups and financiers. In the case of equal opportunities legislation, the reluctance of government to intervene in the issue of equal pay served to delay legislation on this front, even though there was a forceful campaign by sympathetic groups at the local level to have the issue placed on the national, global political agenda. What emerges from the debates in Units 15 and 16 is the need to locate local and national issues within the wider global context and framework. For example, the case study of the making of economic policy highlights the ways in which the UK political agenda was shaped and constrained by forces operating beyond national boundaries. Now the UK becomes the 'local' and the wider international context becomes the 'global'. To understand political events in the UK, it is clearly necessary to take account of the *wider context* in which the UK is placed. Developments in the international division of labour, the growth of new industrial economies, the proliferation of multinational corporations, the connectedness of world financial institutions, the erection of national protective trade barriers and competition for new and changing markets all work to impose certain imperatives on government at the level of the UK. As the unit points out: 'In the sphere of economic activity by the 1970s, local freedom of action was being drowned by global developments' (Unit 15, p.67).

These pressures are further highlighted in Unit 14, where the sovereignty of the UK is examined. There, the UK is placed within the context of the global political arena and the extent of national power in shaping political events within the nation is explored. In arriving at a definition of 'sovereignty', Unit 14 concludes that it is a 'legal and political concept' which is broadly understood to mean 'that a state, which is independent, possesses the exclusive and sole authority over a specific people and territory' and where 'the government of this state exercises the final and ultimate, or sovereign, authority within its borders' (Unit 14, p.7). Here, then, we have a conception of the UK as the global context in which other, local events and processes occur. However, as the unit — and the whole of D103 for that matter — illustrates, it is problematic to conceive of the UK in this way. A legal and political definition of sovereignty may serve to obscure international and global economic forces which act to constrain national governments in their choices and options. The study of the European Community in Unit 14 illustrates the difficulties facing national governments when they choose to isolate themselves from the pressures of the world economy. Furthermore, the development of the UK independent nuclear deterrent, also examined in this unit, shows how it is necessary to place such apparently national issues within the international and world wide context. Economic and political relationships extend beyond the boundaries of the nation state. For example, economic decisions affecting firms within the UK are frequently taken by companies whose headquarters are located in countries such as Japan, Germany and the USA, and financial developments are influenced by fluctuations in exchange rates in Hong Kong and on Wall Street. Clearly, an awareness of the global context is necessary if we are to achieve a fuller understanding of the range of factors involved in localities.

SUMMARY

How then has the *local and global* course theme helped us in our study of politics and in D103 more widely?

First and foremost, I think that the value of the theme is that it encourages us to be constantly aware of the need to place events, institutions and processes within broader *contexts*. It alerts us to the fact that what appears to be a localized issue may need to be placed within the global context if we are to fully understand the influences which are shaping and directing the course of events. We need to be aware that local issues are part of wider global processes.

Second, the theme highlights the extent to which the global context *constrains* local developments. To a greater or lesser extent, local occurrences are coloured, shaped and even determined by the wider global context. This is not to downplay the influence of individuals and groups in shaping outcomes, but it is valuable to be aware of the wider, though perhaps less obvious, factors which are outside the control of such individuals and groups.

Third, the theme encourages us to *compare* the specifics of the local in one area with what is local in another. We are alerted to those aspects which are similar and those which are different. In particular individuality and local character are placed within a wider framework and otherwise unobserved similarities are isolated.

Finally, the theme illustrates that things which happen at the local level can create outcomes at the global level and vice versa. So for example, the actions of individual voters, local government and pressure groups may influence the national economic framework, which in turn influences the decisions of multi-national corporations to locate plants in the UK. Thus the *local* is *constitutive* of the *global*. On the other hand, the decision of a multinational to locate a plant in the UK has profound implications for the nature of the local economy and is an illustration of the *global* as *constitutive* of the *local*. Furthermore, the relationship is not *unidirectional* but a two-way process of interaction.

In short, the *local/global* theme enables us to conduct four operations more adequately. It enables us:

• To *contextualize*

• To examine *constraints*

• To make *comparisons*

• To see the local as *constitutive* of the global and the global as *constitutive* of the local.

The hidden dangers of UK entry into the Common Market
Source: Punch, 15 August 1962. Reproduced by permission.

─────────────────── ACTIVITY 7 ───────────────────

Before moving on from this course theme, check your notes on Block IV and, if possible, discuss with your tutor and fellow students at the study centre examples of these four ways in which the local and global theme is helpful in isolating and understanding the links between events and levels of analysis. Then move on to consider the following notes which Neil has prepared in relation to an examination question on Block IV.

Diane has reviewed the local-global theme in the context of Block IV. It would be timely, therefore, for you to attempt an essay plan for a Block IV question linked to that theme.

─────────────────── ACTIVITY 8 ───────────────────

Have a go at this one:

'To what extent is the government of the United Kingdom constrained by external factors and developments both in Europe and in the rest of the world?'

Let's assess your plan by looking at the way in which it deals with the main issues addressed by the question. What is this question asking you to do? I think it is asking you to debate the importance of global factors as influences on the UK government. A key phrase is 'to what extent ... '. Does your answer focus on that phrase, weighing up the extent to which the government of the UK is constrained by global factors? For me, the weighing of these factors would form the whole basis of my answer. The answer would not be as complete a list as I could muster of the 'external factors and developments both in Europe and in the rest of the world'. I would try to choose examples of these external factors and I would compare them with other influences on government in order to get a picture of the *extent* to which external factors were important.

My plan would have a structure something like this:

INTRODUCTION

The question is about the importance of the global on the government of the UK: how much is government constrained by the global? We need to look at the balance of influences on UK government to assess the extent of the importance of the global. Then a brief outline of the rest of the essay.

SECTION 1

This section would highlight perhaps two major global factors and describe the way in which they appear to have influenced the UK government.

SECTION 2

In this section, the influence of local factors on the examples used in Section 1 would be discussed.

SECTION 3

Here the focus would be on the interplay between the local and the global. The point would be that we cannot easily isolate one factor from another and that the different levels of explanation will vary depending upon the example. In every case, it is important to recognize the way in which both global and local factors depend upon each other. Sometimes one will appear pre-eminent but it is unlikely that we shall ever be able to point to one level as completely determining an outcome.

CONCLUSION

This would be brief review of what has gone before, emphasizing that we cannot understand the local, namely the government of the United Kingdom, without considering the wider context.

So far, you have probably noticed, the plan is totally devoid of any substantive content! I need to select relevant content from Block IV. What did you think were the most appropriate examples to use? I think there are many places in Block IV from which examples can be drawn, and we certainly do not need to select them all. We need to use those examples we think are most suitable, or about which we feel most confident. We should resist the temptation to write down all the examples. Material could be drawn from Unit 14 or Unit 15. Unit 14, remember, is on sovereignty and the local/global theme is central to it. There is a discussion of the UK's relationship with the European community, the loss of sovereignty associated with admission and the further loss anticipated by the movement towards political and economic integration. The material on the 'independent' nuclear deterrent, from Unit 14, could also provide the basis of an answer. From Unit 15 the treatment of economic relationships is another example which illustrates the interplay of local and global factors.

You may well have chosen different examples and that is fine, but I hope you used the phrase 'To what extent ... ' as an important organizing focus of your essay, or that you can see now why it is important to think carefully about what such phrases mean when you begin to plan out your answer.

Before leaving the local/global theme, I think we should consider it in the context of Block VI. Diane has not reviewed Block VI yet, so we are on our own rather more. Block VI is very much centred on the local/global theme. A question which considers the theme and the block together should help you in your revision of the block, and it gives another opportunity to practise planning examination answers. I would like to follow a similar pattern to that which we followed for Block III: you and I make an attempt at an essay plan and Diane makes a comment on mine. You can then compare your plan with mine and Diane's view of it.

The Block VI authors came up with the following question:

'The UK's international pre-eminence in the early nineteenth century was built on the labour and enterprise of the people of Lancashire.' Discuss.

─────────────────── ACTIVITY 9 ───────────────────

Write an essay plan for that question now.

As someone who spent most of his formative years in a Lancashire cotton town, and who still thinks of himself as a Lancastrian, this question has a particular appeal for me. I must be especially aware, therefore, that I do not let my enthusiasm for the subject, and my detailed personal experience of life in the cotton towns, draw me away from the question into anecdotal meanderings. Personal experience can add a richness and vividness to an answer if handled carefully, but it can also drift off the point and imply that one person's experience proves an argument if it is used as more than an illustration. Do use your experience if you can. It is one of the great assets which you possess (unlike most 18-year-old undergraduates) but use it to illustrate and illuminate, not as proof-perfect that something must be true. Be careful about the way you use personal anecdotes.

The course material (as against personal experience) relevant to this question is primarily in Unit 23, Section 2. In that unit, Doreen Massey puts the position of Lancashire into a global context. Let me try to use that part of the unit and the wider appreciation of the local/global theme which I have picked up from the course to attempt an answer.

The question asks me to *discuss*. That means the basic structure I mentioned earlier in the Block III section will work well. I need an introduction which defines terms and sets out the essay structure. Section 1 of the essay will present the case which supports the argument that the UK's pre-eminence was built on the labour and enterprise of the people of Lancashire. Section 2 will question this and present alternative arguments. Section 3 will attempt to compare the previous sections, and for this comparison the local/global theme will be an ideal vehicle. Finally, the conclusion will summarize the arguments of the essay, emphasizing in this case the fact that local/global relationships are complex and work in both directions, from local to global, and from global to local. In fact, even that way of expressing the relationship is too simple since both levels are also changing in response to changes in each other and are not independent of each other.

The essay plan then looks like this:

INTRODUCTION

Explain that the UK was the first nation to industrialize and that in the early nineteenth century a high proportion of its success depended on cotton. Quote some figures (if I could remember them under exam conditions):

Around 1830 more than half Britain's total domestic exports, by value, consisted of cotton yarn and cotton goods, while imports of raw cotton made up a fifth of total net imports.

Virtually all the cotton goods were produced in Lancashire.

The essay is about the extent to which the UK's success was built upon this part of Lancashire, therefore, or whether the position was more complex than this.

Set out the essay structure briefly.

SECTION 1

Factory production took over from production in the home in a way unknown elsewhere in the country. A new division of labour was established and new social classes emerged. Capitalism was born in the cotton towns of south-east Lancashire. The long-term impact of this in the rest of the country was enormous in stimulating ironfounding and engineering to produce the new machines, railway development, shipbuilding, etc. There was a huge accumulation of capital which was used by owners to invest in other sectors.

Some commentators argue that the effects of cotton on the rest of the economy were not of such enormous importance. The basic raw materials for the cotton industry came from abroad and a significant part of its output was exported. However, even such analyses do not disagree with the basic point that the developments in the Lancashire textiles industry were an important part of the UK's economic pre-eminence during that period. The disagreement is about how important they were.

SECTION 2

Section 1 implied that there was a clear un-dimensional link between changes in Lancashire (local), changes in the UK (global) and changes in the world economy (even more global). We do need to ask why it was that the textiles industry developed in Lancashire and why it was so successful, i.e. the global influences on the local.

Comment on the wider position of the UK economy — colonial commerce, the slave trade and the expansion of overseas markets.

Comment on the changes in other continents, both as suppliers of raw materials — the West Indies and Southern States of the USA, and as markets — Latin America and Asia.

SECTION 3

Put Sections 1 and 2 together to discuss the links between the local and the global. Social processes happen unevenly — to some extent the UK's pre-eminence was built on Lancashire because that was where developments were moving rapidly — but the fortunes of the local and the global are linked so that we cannot separate Lancashire from its suppliers, its markets nor its place in world economic history. The big global changes can also have different effects locally: thus Liverpool and Manchester have very different histories even though they are only 35 miles apart and developed in response to the same economic factors.

CONCLUSION

Briefly summarize the points made in the essay.

Now over to Diane for her comments on both these essay plans.

At first sight I thought the essay question on Block IV quite straightforward in that it appeared to focus on one major issue, that of global constraints upon the government of the United Kingdom. However, the inclusion of the words 'to what extent …' makes the essay more of a complex challenge than it appears at first sight. To weigh up the *extent* to which the UK government is constrained by international factors is potentially so huge a task that Neil could have found himself lost in a mass of detail. To this extent, I think it was a wise move to adopt the strategy of selecting one or two illustrations to explore the links and argue the case. This approach seemed to keep the essay located at a manageable level where the overall structure and argument could clearly emerge.

The selection of examples taken from Units 14 and 15 with a view to exploring one side of the question, namely the influence of European and world-wide factors on the UK government, is very helpful. However, in addition to these examples of *global* influences on the *local*, I would have been interested to see some examples of the influence of *local* factors on *global* contexts. For example, the actions of the UK government deliberately to affect outcomes in Europe or the world may be perceived as local influences upon the global. Or there may be other *local* issues, such as those explored in Unit 16, which concern the actions and interests of voters and interest groups. These local influences may well constrain the government in what it can or cannot do in a way which compares with the global influences of Europe and the world. These examples would balance up the other side of the question explored in Section 2 of the essay, and enable a fuller evaluation of the *extent* of the local influence on the global and the global influence on the local. One issue which is highlighted by this essay question is the extent to which we can, at times, conceive of the UK government as an aspect of the global whilst in other contexts the UK government becomes a local influence. I thought section 3 of the essay, and the conclusion, excellent in acknowledging the complexity of these relationships.

Neil's essay on Block VI is a good illustration of the problems of definition which relate to levels of analysis with the global and local. In the case of the Block VI question, the level of analysis, Lancashire, is below that of the UK. Consequently, the *local* (the UK government) in one of our questions is different from the *local* (Lancashire) in the other of our questions. This is recognized by Neil's use of the term 'even more global' in Section 2 of his essay plan. I thought his discussion of uneven development, in Section 3 of the essay, illustrated the *interactive* nature of the local/global links admirably. In fact, both of these essay questions on Block IV and Block VI highlight the ways in which the theme helps us to make *comparisons* about the extent to which developments are *constrained* in certain *contexts* and the processes whereby the local and the global are *constitutive* of each other.

Both of the Block VI examples should prove helpful to you when you move on to the next unit, where you will be asked to work through the block to produce a grid of where the three different course themes appear. These essays will give you a start.

7 CONCLUSION

In this unit, we have spent time reviewing the three course themes and exploring the ways in which they are put to use in Block I. In addition, we have looked in some depth at the public and private theme in relation to Block III and the local and global theme in relation to Block IV, and we have done this in the context of considering the structure of the examination and examples of examination questions and answers. We have also begun to review Block VI by looking at a specific examination question on that Block. Before you complete your work for this week it would be helpful if you could find time to review your revision activity thus far. You might do this by going back to the 'revision skills' section of Unit 28 and the relevant sections of *The Good Study Guide*, and reflecting on your progress. You might consider whether you have found your approach to revision useful or whether you might need to change your approach in any way. If you feel that you are having difficulties in some area, raise this with your tutor by telephone or at the study centre. They may be able to suggest ways of helping you with your difficulties. Check that you understand the broad outline of the three course themes, and have a note of some examples from your revision which you might find useful in illustrating examination answers. Then move on to Unit 32 which explores *representation* and *reality* in more depth, returns to the three course themes in Block II and encourages you to use all three themes in relation to Block VI. In that unit, Neil Costello will also help you to finalize your revision plans and think about how to approach the examination.

REFERENCES

Anderson, J. and Ricci, M. (eds) (1990) *Society and Social Science: a Reader*, Milton Keynes, The Open University.

Coates, D. (1990) Chapter 22, *Traditions of thought and the rise of Social Science in the United Kingdom* in Anderson, J. and Ricci, M. (eds).

Gamarnikow, E., Morgan, D., Purvis, J., Taylorsan, D. (eds) (1983) *The Public and the Private*, London, Heinemann.

Pateman, C. (1988) *The Sexual Contract*, Cambridge, Polity Press.

Economic Briefing, HM Treasury, No.1, December 1990.

ACKNOWLEDGEMENTS

Grateful acknowledgement is made to the following sources for permission to reproduce material in this unit:

Figure

Figure 4: H.M. Treasury (1990), 'Structure of the RPI', *Economic Briefing*, December 1990, No 1. Reproduced with the permission of the Controller of Her Majesty's Stationery Office.

Illustration

p.129: Courtesy of Royal Doulton (UK) Ltd.

Photographs

p.130: John Sturrock/Network; p.131 (left) Raissa Page/Format; p.131 (right), Brenda Prince/Format; p.135 (left), Jenny Mattahews/Format; p.135 (right), Denis Thorpe/The Guardian.

Cartoon

p.145: Punch.

UNIT 32   COURSE THEMES AND THE EXAM

Prepared for the course team by Neil Costello and Diane Watson

CONTENTS

I   INTRODUCTION

In this final unit of the course we shall be completing the work on reviewing the course themes and preparing for the examination which we started last week. In Unit 32 our aim is to look more closely at the third course theme, *representation and reality*, in the light of some of the material on identity and interaction which is presented in Block V. In addition, we shall return to Block II to examine the ways in which the three course themes are used there and we shall be setting you up with a revision exercise of a similar kind for Block VI. Finally, you will be spending some time on the last study skills section of the course which is devoted to exam preparation. In the preceding unit we reviewed the themes as they appeared in Block I and used both the *public and private* and *local and global* course themes to revise aspects of Block III and Block IV respectively. In covering Blocks II, V and VI in this unit we shall have touched on each of the Blocks, and each of the themes, in some way or another. In doing so we hope we have assisted you in your revision programme and in consolidating your overall understanding of the course themes.

2   BLOCK V: REPRESENTATION AND REALITY

This theme is particularly rewarding as a means of exploring the ways in which people make sense of their lives through their perception of images and representations of the world, and drawing our attention to forms of *qualitative evidence* about society which we might otherwise overlook. You may recall from the 'Introduction and Study Guide' to Block I that 'representations' are defined as the *'various portrayals or interpretations of social reality which are common and widespread in society'* and which are socially important *'whether or not they are accurate'*. This relationship between ideas and the social world is complex and vital to our understanding of the ways in which people interpret the social context. For example, if you return to the notes which we have already made on Block I, you will recall how it was argued that manifestly 'physical' phenomena such as hunger and famine involve groups and individuals making use of sets of ideas about, or 'representations' of these aspects of 'reality'. These representations are drawn from the stock of ideas available within a culture and are reworked by individuals to make sense of their own situations, to represent themselves to others and construct representations *of* others. Aspects of the world external to individuals cannot be seen to exist independently of the ways in which those individuals subjectively experience that world. Individuals use existing frameworks of ideas to make sense of their experiences and at the same time construct and reconstruct new understandings of that reality. As the Introduction to Block V points out, individuals select what is important and relevant to them and impose their own interpretations upon it.

 ACTIVITY I

Pause for a few moments and quickly jot down some of the representations which you have encountered in the course of D103. This could be a useful activity to do at the study centre where you can share ideas and compare notes with your tutor and fellow students.

When I made my own list these were some of the examples of representations I came up with:

'Englishness'	poverty	hunger	'the happy family'
famine	the body	health	sickness
mothers	black people	masculinity	femininity
society	social class	work	unemployment
markets	the nation	community	sovereignty
identity	regions	Britishness	middle class
places	local character	working class	

The above are, of course, very generalized representations. They involve a much more detailed working out of images and assumptions, and may mean quite different things to people in different social positions. There are many varied examples in D103, both in the written materials and in the TV programmes, and there are many varied examples which you could select from your own experience.

'Local heroes' or 'vast tartan monster'?

ACTIVITY 2

Again, pause for a moment and think about the ideas and images you hold about yourself. Go back to the activity in the 'Introduction to Block V' and look over any notes you made there. Where do these images of yourself come from? Can you identify the influence of the processes of socialization and institutions involved in education and the transmission of ideas (family, school, community, workplace, media)? How important are these representations to your sense of self and identity? Do you feel that you have been passively moulded and shaped by factors external to yourself, or do you feel that you have played an active role in choosing from the range of images available to you? These are all issues relevant to the discussion of identity and social interaction in Block V, where it is argued that 'Identity is very much about representation, about our capacity to make sense of the social world and our place in it' (Block V, Introduction, Section 1, p.5).

Let us turn to the units in Block V and undertake a review exercise to establish where the *representation and reality* theme occurs and its value in helping our understanding of the ways in which individuals actively make sense of their place in the world and become aware of shared, collective representations.

———————————— ACTIVITY 3 ————————————

As before, work through the units in Block V and your notes on these units and note down examples of the representation and reality theme and some of the issues raised by its use.

You will remember that Units 19, and 20 have as their focus the study of personal and social identity. In Unit 19, it is argued that 'the experience of identity is essentially a representation in itself' (Unit 19, p.19) which is rooted in subjective personal experience, in biological and physical characteristics and is influenced by time and the life stages of individual development. To talk about our 'identity' is to say something about our sense of 'self', who we feel we are, how we see ourselves, how others see us and how we would hope that others see us. In Unit 20, the analysis is extended by an exploration of the ways in which personal identity and social context are interconnected. Social factors have a powerful influence on an individual's sense of identity and yet, at the same time, individuals have some choice in the way that they present them- selves to others and in the ways in which they make use of shared representa- tions to make sense of their lives in the social context.

In the notes which you took on Unit 20 did you pick out the way in which social categories (wife, father, working class, unemployed worker) have associated with them sets of representations about the type of person you are likely to be and the characteristics you are likely to possess if you belong to such a category? Sometimes the relationship between these sets of representations and any real knowledge of people within social categories is very tenuous and the way is open for one-sided, exaggerated and stereotypical representations to be constructed and imposed (stereotypes of ethnic groups, criminals or devi- ants would be examples). This is the distinction between 'representations' and 'reality' highlighted by the course theme.

Did you also note the crucial role played by language, symbols and communica- tion in the construction, transmission and sharing of representations? Through the use of shared symbols we are able to build images of ourselves and to imagine ourselves as others would see us. However, although there is always scope for individual choice in the construction of identity and representations, we do generally make use of ideas and images which already exist before us in society and are acquired by us through the processes of socialization mentioned earlier in this unit. So, for example, however much we might choose to view ourselves as unique individuals, we are still shaped and moulded by prior conceptions about the appropriate forms of behaviour associated with someone in a particular role or social category. And this has a major impact on our sense of identity and the range of representations available to us.

In exploring the relationship between representation and reality, Block V has examined further the implications, for individuals, of images associated with such things as gender, race, class, work, unemployment, family relationships and deviancy. The value of the theme is evident in the way it encourages us to dig beneath the surface of popular representations and examine the processes at work in the construction of shared experience and identities. Our ideas and perceptions of the world are not merely the outcome of our individual, subjective experience. They are socially structured and defined, in part, by the existing stock of representations available to us. Representations play a major role in defining for us what 'reality' is. Furthermore, the representation/reality theme highlights the ways in which *some representations take a dominant role in society* over others and have the capacity to persuade and influence individuals and groups and shape and frame the reality which they experience. When representations have the power to convey that things are 'natural' and 'inevitable', then we are into the area of 'ideology'. For example, if you think back to Unit 17 on the *Power of Ideology,* you may remember the 'baseline' definition of ideology which was outlined there. Ideology was defined as: *'sets of ideas, assumptions and images by which people make sense of society, which give a clear social identity, and which serve in some way to legitimize relations of power in society'* (Unit 17, p.114).

Note how similar this definition is to the definition of 'representations' referred to at the start of this unit. There, we referred to the notion that representations may be regarded as commonly held portrayals and interpretations which have a social significance and social implications. Exploring this further, we may note that one social implication of major significance is the linking of a given set of ideas, or representations, to the nature of *power* in the existing social structure. In one sense, all socially shared representations act to support and serve the interests of those groups in society which hold those ideas. However, when these sets of ideas become systematically linked together, and systematically used by some groups to make legitimate an existing power structure and social order, then we are firmly within the realms of 'ideology'. The concept of ideology alerts us to the processes through which sources of power and sets of ideas, or representations, are related and work to further the interests of some groups over others, such as one class over another, men over women, one race over another or parents over children. Consequently, representations serve a whole range of functions, from making sense of ourselves and our personal situations right through to legitimating dominant interests within an existing power structure in society.

Finally, because the theme encourages a focus on ideas, perception and experience it brings our attention to *qualitative forms of social science evidence* which can add richness and depth to our understanding of social processes. It tends to discourage a view of the world as factual and unproblematic, and brings into focus the complex nature of the inter-relationship between the individual and social structure.

Now over to Neil again for the examination question on this block.

Let's get straight into the question which the Block V authors set.

———————————————— ACTIVITY 4 ————————————————

Write an essay plan for the following question from Block V:

'Cultures differ in their representations of human nature. How might the representations found in our culture influence our sense of identity?'

I find this a challenging block because much of the material is very new to me. However, I think the Block V team have been kind with this question because, on the face of it, it is relatively straightforward. The question is asking me to write about the mechanisms by which representations influence identity and it asks about representations with particular reference to 'our culture'. The key issues then, for this question, are firstly to discuss what is meant by representations and by identity, secondly to show how these representations vary between cultures and thirdly to relate the representations to our sense of identity. The assertion that 'Cultures differ in their representations of human nature' sets the scene. Assertions like this one, in essay questions, require us to question them, not to accept them as necessarily correct. Most of the material for the question can be found in Unit 20, 'Social identity'.

This question does not fit easily into the 'basic' structure I used earlier in Unit 31, because it requires me to explain something, drawing out the complexities and ambiguities in the explanation, rather than debate something. Here is my plan:

INTRODUCTION

Here I would define representations and identity. Both concepts are quite difficult to define and this is partly what the question is about—the debate about these terms and their interrelationships. 'Identity' I would define as our own sense of ourselves, but this definition is to some extent begging the question. Our identities may differ depending upon the circumstances we find ourselves in and the roles we are carrying out. We may have a different sense of ourselves 'underneath' than the public face we present. Representation is also a complex concept. It relates to generally accepted portrayals of the world we live in, which help us to make sense of that world by providing us with a framework of ideas from which we can construct meanings. A discussion of the source of these representations and their relationship with identity will then form the bulk of the essay.

SECTION 1

This section would concentrate on the way identity is influenced by the social. I would make brief reference to the physical/biological explanations outlined in Unit 19 and make reference to 'essentialism' but would concentrate almost exclusively on the way the social world affects our sense of our own identity. This would cover some mention of identity and work — the way unemployment changes one's sense of one's own worth and the way features of jobs (opportunities for control, skill etc.) affect a sense of identity — and identity and gender. The Zimbardo study in the Reader also indicates how social circumstances in the mock-up prison affected a sense of identity.

SECTION 2

This section would concentrate on the ways in which different cultures represent identity. It would quote examples of the ways in which different cultures define what is normal. Such examples would include the Roman attitude to homosexuality — that the moral distinction was between active and passive sexuality; definitions of Englishness; the importance of individuality in different cultures and the taken-for-grantedness of all these things in respect of our own cultural expressions.

I think it would also be a good idea to reflect on the fact that different theoretical traditions have different notions of what constitutes human nature. Thus a society, like the UK, which has been heavily influenced by the liberal tradition has in general an individualist representation of human nature, though social reformist and conservative conceptions have also been important in making the link a complex one.

SECTION 3

In this section I would try to relate identity and representations. This would include a brief reference to socialization — not a description of how it occurs but just a mention of what it means — and a short discussion of Mead's symbolic interactionism to explain how human beings are able to symbolize themselves or represent themselves to themselves. Symbols — or representations — then become a central feature of how we make sense of the world.

CONCLUSION

In the conclusion I think it would be worth emphasizing the plasticity or flexibility of human beings — that we can respond to our social circumstances and take on different identities, and the relativity of identity to the historical and cultural situation under analysis.

In an examination, of course, as before, my plan would be considerably briefer than this but I have tried to set out the train of thought involved in devising this plan so that you can get a grasp of why I decided to structure the essay this way.

Let's see what Diane thinks about it.

I too thought this an interesting, though very challenging, question and I found Neil's plan of an answer both comprehensive and logical. Quite clearly he has a definite line of argument which he pushes home through a careful selection of examples and illustrations. Whilst he took up the 'different cultures' angle of the essay, I found the illustrations available from Unit 20 on that issue were not very many. However, I did think the question raised an interesting point about the *unitary concept of 'culture'*. It brought to my mind the extent to which there are sub-cultural differences within the overall society, with some groups having the power to impose their own particular representations upon others. For example, if we were to examine the list of representations in Section 2 of this unit, we would see that many of them do indeed imply a division within the overall UK culture. I think that I might have found this angle quite fruitful in relation to questions of worth, power and social value and how these questions tie in with the concept of 'identity'. I suppose that this goes to illustrate the extent to which all examination questions may be interpreted from a slightly different angle whilst at the same time requiring the inclusion of some basic common points of explanation and illustration.

--- ACTIVITY 5 ---

1   Here is another question from Block V based on the representation-reality theme. If this is a block you intend to revise have a go at this on your own and discuss the results with your tutor-counsellor or fellow students. Unit 20, Section 6 is a useful starting point for ideas and content.

'Explain the role which representations play in the development of a sense of identity in Mead's theory of Symbolic Interactionism?'

2   You will probably have attempted to plan answers to the questions on the Specimen Examination Paper by now. If you have not yet done that, take the specimen exam paper and plan out answers to the questions on those blocks you have decided to revise. Try to do this fairly soon so that you have time to discuss your outlines with your fellow students and tutor-counsellor and can learn from each other's ideas.

3   Now is also the time to go through the units and make up your own questions. Use the Summaries and concluding sections as a guide to possible topics and, on the basis of your TMA questions and the Specimen Examination Paper, construct other possible or likely questions. Then plan answers to the questions. Just because you made up the question yourself does not make it a less worthwhile activity! Thinking of appropriate questions is one good way of working out the focus of the unit or block and can help a good deal in revision. This is also something which is worth sharing with fellow students and your tutor-counsellor if you can.

Now back to Diane to continue the review of Course Themes.

3   USING COURSE THEMES: BLOCK II

At this stage in the unit, it would be helpful to undertake the same kind of review exercise with Block II which you completed in Unit 31 for Block I. Block II is concerned with the nature of the 'social' and the ways in which social scientists go about the study of society. Block II builds on the themes as they were introduced in Block I.

──────────────── ACTIVITY 6 ────────────────

For this activity you will need to return to the units in Block II, and any notes which you have made on them, and look for examples of the course themes. You might also note down any issues or questions which you think are raised by the use of the themes in the block. The overall aim of this activity is to help you to think about the themes by completing the grid which follows. To do this it is best to take the task in separate stages, taking each theme in turn and working through each of the units of the block before moving on to the next theme. Let us begin with *representation and reality* as we have been exploring this theme in the previous section.

Course theme	Examples and definitions	Issues and question raised
Representation and reality		
Public and private		
Local and global		

How did you get on?

Here are some of my ideas on how to complete this grid. I found that exercise quite difficult and time consuming but discovered that, by looking through the units for examples of the course themes, I have also reminded myself of the broad structure and content of the block as a whole. So it has been a wider revision exercise too. Here are my examples.

REPRESENTATION AND REALITY

Examples and definitions	Issues and questions raised
Unit 6 argues that, although the body is a physical entity, it is also 'socially constructed'. Individuals attach meaning and significance to the way they experience their bodies and in doing so make use of 'representations' available to them from culture. The body is represented in culture in a variety of ways; medically, anatomically, in advertising and in fashion. Individuals act to 'present' themselves to others, and to themselves, through the use of language, dress and other forms of expression (Unit 6, Section 1.4.)	The recognition of a tension between *representation* and *reality* directs our attention towards qualitative forms of data. Qualitative data complements quantitative data by concentrating upon symbols, meaning and experience. It gives us a 'feel' for a situation. For example, Barbara's account of her illness in Unit 6, Section 1.4, gives us insight into the ways in which she 'makes sense' of the biological and physical process she is experiencing. The theme highlights the dynamic relationship between the 'natural' and the 'social'.
In Unit 7, contemporary social class divisions are examined, as are social science theories which have been advanced to explain them. One valuable source of information about class which is available to social scientists is popular, 'commonsense' beliefs and representations of social class (Unit 7, Section 2). Examples given were Hillsborough, teenage girls talking and three weddings.	The representation and reality theme encourages the social scientist to examine popular representations as evidence of the ways in which social class is perceived, mediated and experienced by individuals in different positions in the 'objective' social class structure. By 'digging beneath the surface' of popular images and stereotypes, we can learn more about class divisions and obstacles to change.
Unit 8 examines the stereotypes and everyday concepts surrounding race, ethnicity and gender and argues that 'words are not neutral'. On the contrary, they are one of the major ways through which we 'represent reality' (Unit 8, p.90). Some words have negative and offensive overtones and can be used to represent some groups in society in a negative way. The reverse is also true. The discussion of 'black' in Section 1 is useful here.	The tension between subjective experience and 'objective' reality can be further explored by examining the role of language and images in the active construction of stereotypical images and the role these play in relationships between different groups in society.

THE PUBLIC AND THE PRIVATE

Examples and definitions	Issues and questions raised
In Unit 6, the relationship between the public and private is explored. It is argued that apparently 'private' and individual issues such as marriage and suicide have important 'public' dimensions. (Unit 6, Section 2.2). Marriage is a 'social institution', with public and legally sanctioned rules, and not merely a private and intimate affair between two individuals and their families. Suicide, though arguably the ultimate individual act has, according to Durkheim, a distinctively social explanation (Unit 6, Section 2.1).	One value of the public and private theme in this context is that it draws the attention of the social scientist to social factors which exist over and above the experience of individuals. Activities within the private arena of home and personal relationships cannot be fully understood without rooting them in the wider, public context of society and social structure.
In Unit 8, the public/private theme is used to analyse the historical separation of the public world of the economy and production from the private world of reproduction and domestic life (Unit 8, Section 5.2). The tendency for women to be located within the private sphere is linked with their economic dependency and vulnerability. Furthermore, the public/private divide is explored in relation to the discussion of public and private images of violence. The point is made that, despite massive media coverage of public forms of violence, little attention is given to violence against women in the privacy of their own homes. This private face of violence is less open to public scrutiny and rarely features in any official statistics on violence against the person (Unit 8, Section 2.5)	The use of the public/private theme in relation to the role of women, and particularly black women, highlights the difficulties involved in separating the private world of home and family from the public world of work and the economy. The role of women as 'reproducers' is linked in a fundamental way to the requirements of the national and international economy. An awareness of the tensions between the public and private spheres helps us to guard against the danger of isolating women in the private sphere and keeping important issues which affect them off the public agenda. It also raises questions about the adequacy of quantitative data and official statistics (Unit 8, Section 2.5).

THE LOCAL AND THE GLOBAL

Examples and definitions	Issues and questions raised
This third theme is touched on in Unit 6, where the local relations and rudimentary form of society which exist between Crusoe and Friday are located within the wider, global framework of the development of commercial contexts of colonialism and capitalism. In Unit 8, the specifics of black women's experience within the UK may be linked to the experiences of other women throughout the world. What happens in the UK economy is crucially influenced by events in Europe and internationally. The 'global system' of patriarchy suggests common experiences of oppression between women throughout the world (Unit 8, Section 3).	The local/global theme has usefully drawn our attention to the need to locate what happens in the local context to wider structures and processes. Crusoe and Friday did not relate to one another merely as isolated individuals but as 'master' and 'slave' in the context of 'New World' slave plantations. An understanding of this global context sharpens our awareness of the factors influencing relationships in the local context. More than this though the theme highlights the complex interrelationship between events at different levels. Events within the UK can have effects locally (at the small scale, regional level) and globally (outwards to the wider world). It helps us to focus on those factors which seem most important.

4 USING COURSE THEMES: BLOCK VI

In this final week of D103, Block II may seem an awfully long way off. Maybe you had already begun to look again at the units, your existing notes and your marked essays, and this review of the themes will have added to, and consolidated, the work which you had already done. However, it may be that you do not intend to revise Block II in any great depth. In this case, the work which you have completed on the grid should assist you in dealing with the 'course-wide' type questions which you will find in Section B of the examination paper. By contrast, Block VI has been studied relatively recently and was supported by the Module work which you did at summer school (or your Summer School excusal pack). It should, therefore, be relatively fresh in your mind. You will need to make a personal decision about the extent to which you intend to revise the content of Block VI, and you may find it useful to talk this over with your tutor when you are discussing your revision strategies. The following activity is there to assist in your revision of Block VI, and you are free to use it in any way you find helpful. You may wish to look at one unit or one course theme only, or you may decide to revise Block VI in depth, in which case it will be a useful guide to highlighting the themes as you progress. As the Unit 28 Study Skills Section on Revision points out, you have to be selective in choosing what to revise and this will depend on your interest in some topics and your relative success in dealing with the Blocks and TMAs. In any event, see what you can remember of the themes in Block VI by referring back to Summer School (or your excusal pack) and any notes you may have made on the units. You will see that I have begun to complete the grid in parts to start you off with the exercise. Good luck with completing the rest of it! Remember, it could be a helpful focus for part of a study centre session, or a self-help group meeting, so raise this with your group if you think it would be useful.

———————————————— ACTIVITY 7 ————————————————

COURSE THEMES IN BLOCK VI

Course Theme	Examples	Issues explored	Unit references
Local and global	Regional fortunes relate to the international economy. The growth in Swindon's local economy linked to international processes. The impact of the oil industry in Scotland — local effects. Local and Regional Councils can take action to by-pass national government and forge direct links with the European Community.	Highlights the complex inter-relationship between events in a local economy and other parts of the world. The 'local' varies according to our particular focus — whether a region or the UK overall. Illustrates that the *local* can be *constitutive* of the *global*. The direction of influence is from the local to the global. It is a two-way process.	Unit 24, Section 2 and the Reader, Chapter 19 'Global local times' and Chapter 20 'Economic and social change in Swindon'. Unit 25, Section 4, especially 4.2. Reader, Chapter 19 'Global Local Times'. TV12 'Regions Apart'.
Public and private	The influence of private decision making on levels of investment. The influence of the international market on public state policy. Regional policy as an aspect of state involvement in the 'welfare state'.	The theme provides a focus for examining the inter-relationship between the state and the regions and the state and Europe. The efficacy of local campaigns are linked to views about state provision and self-help.	Unit 25, Section 2.2, 'The politics of regional decline'.
Representation and reality	Local character and identity e.g. a Scot or a Cockney. Competing images of place — e.g. Hackney. People share the same locality but inhabit 'different worlds'. Places are seen differently depending upon whether you are insider or outsider.	Images of place as interpretations. The theme highlights a qualitative dimension and focuses on experience. It also highlights the social construction of landscapes and places and illustrates that dominant images serve dominant interests.	Unit 23, Section 2.1 on 'Representations of places'.

5 'WRAPPING UP THE THEMES'

In this concluding section of Unit 32, I want to say a few final words about the course themes before handing over to Neil for some advice on preparing for the examination. You have almost completed a challenging and lengthy period of study, and I have no doubt that you will have experienced some difficult moments along the way as well as the excitement of learning about new things and looking at familiar issues from a social science perspective. If you feel at this stage that this discussion of course themes in D103 is overwhelming, stop for a moment and think about the points which I raised with you at the beginning of Unit 31.

As you may remember, I argued that, in dealing with the complexities of the social world, social scientists find ways of handling the material which makes it more manageable. The course themes are among the mechanisms the course team have used to help you in this. I suggested that the value of having these course themes was that they could be used as social science 'tools' to enable us to simplify complexities, to organize our material, to make connections between topics and blocks, and to reflect on real issues and problems as they occur in the social world which is the object of our study. In short, the themes are there to help you. There is nothing mysterious about them and you should not let them intimidate you. If they raise complexities and inconsistencies, it is because they are doing the job which was intended for them. If you have discovered that one of the themes is more appropriate to a given area than another, then the themes are really working for you. It is not possible to explain and understand everything in the course through each of the themes, and to try to do so would be to attempt to force the complex world into artificial categories and boxes. And finally, if you observe that more than one of the themes has value when applied to a given area, then you will have benefited from the fact that each of the themes approaches an issue from a slightly different angle, thereby giving a subtlety to our understanding which one of them alone might not have done. Refer back to the discussion about 'Combining themes' in Block I (Unit 4), where all three themes are applied to aid for famine relief, and consider whether you have noted any other examples as you have studied the course. This might be the point to listen again to the Block IV cassette on 'Reviewing the themes' (audio-cassette 4) where Neil and I discuss the use and relevance of the three course themes, and you should make sure that you listen now to audio-cassette 7 which concentrates on revision (side 1) and preparation for the exam (side 2). The final TV programme for D103 is also devoted to 'Wrapping up the themes'. That programme, in the form of a quiz show, challenges you to apply the themes to material which is outside of D103.

On that note I will wish you well for your examination and future studies and hand over to Neil for some final examination preparation.

STUDY SKILLS SECTION: FINAL PREPARATION FOR THE EXAMINATION

Prepared for the course team by Neil Costello

We often hear about students staying up all night to ensure success in their final examinations: however, the main thing to say about last minute cramming is don't! But that does not mean it is not important to spend the 3 or 4 days before the exam getting yourself into good shape, and that is what this section is about. The D103 examination is a bit like running a marathon. You have trained for months and have built up some weekly mileages which are very impressive. You have overcome the occasional injury, have sometimes been jaded and questioned the whole point of it, but now you are here on the brink of the race and it is important that you do yourself justice. You must put all that training to good use. The race is going to take three hours (a good time for a marathon by the way!) and so you will need to pace yourself. There is no point in going off too fast and blowing up before the end. Neither do you want to go off too slowly and find that you have not finished by the time three hours are over. The three or four days before the race are important, but the last thing you want to do is a lot of hard training. It will make you tired and probably confused. Rather, you should build on what you have already achieved and perhaps reduce your training slowly over a few days. Get plenty of rest. Eat well, and, at least for a couple of days before, avoid alcohol! I think the parallels are uncanny, and both running a marathon and completing D103 require a large amount of commitment and sheer determination.

The main point here is that in the few days before the exam there is little point in learning new material. What you need to do is to ensure that you can use the material you have already acquired effectively. It is probably more useful to plan outlines for a number of questions on topics you know than to try to learn new topics. It is also worth going through the exam in your head to think positively about how you are going to approach it on the day—what will you do first? How will you pace yourself through the questions? What do you need to take with you? And even more mundane things like finding out *exactly* where the exam room is and working out your travel plans on the day.

Most people are apprehensive about the exam itself, but careful preparation with the details worked out in advance so that you know exactly what you need to do and when, can take away a good deal of the pressure.

--------------------------------- ACTIVITY 8 ---------------------------------

Have a go at the following quiz which is intended to help you assess your attitude to the D103 examination. It is a based on a quiz designed by Andy Northedge and has been helpful to other foundation course students in the past.

YOUR ATTITUDE TO THE D103 EXAMINATION

Please tick the appropriate boxes:

		Yes	No
1	I'm looking forward eagerly to the exam	❑	❑
2	I've read every bit of the course material	❑	❑
3	I've thoroughly grasped everything I've read	❑	❑
4	I've done so many exams it's a well worn routine for me	❑	❑

5	I know exactly which questions to go for	❏ ❏
6	I think at my clearest when the pressure is on	❏ ❏
7	I find the way exam questions are worded a stimulating challenge	❏ ❏
8	My memory never lets me down in a crisis	❏ ❏
9	My background, general knowledge of social science subjects is so broad, I have no fear of being caught short of material	❏ ❏
10	I know exactly what's expected in exam answers	❏ ❏
11	I find it easy to plan an answer and write it out in 45 minutes	❏ ❏
12	Luckily I write stylishly and legibly when hurrying	❏ ❏
13	I like to relax and get plenty of sleep the last day or two before an exam	❏ ❏

1 *I'm looking forward eagerly to the exam*

If you said 'no' you are with the vast majority. However, some students are much more apprehensive than others. Indeed some get into a terrible lather, which can be very unhelpful. It's important to get exams into perspective. It isn't a life or death issue. Taking an OU course is a challenge from which you can gain a great deal whether you pass or not. And in any case you won't help matters by being over-anxious. So just accept that exams will create a certain amount of tension. And recognize that this *tension* can be *very valuable* in driving you to put in an exceptionally vigorous burst of work as you pull together the threads of the course. But make sure you *use* the tension constructively. Don't just wallow in despair. Make plans. Aim to build on your strengths. Be practical. And if you do get worried, talk to somebody about it: your tutor-counsellor, other students, family or friends, or even your doctor. Exams are an unpleasant chore, but they are only a small part of the course and only half of your assessment, so keep them in proportion.

2 *I've read every bit of the course material so far*

Most part-time students have to miss out some sections of any course and even the best students specialize in those areas which interest them. D103 contains a lot of material and you have done well just to get this far. It's no use worrying now about what you've left out. You'll do far better to consolidate on what you *have* done than to attempt any desperate catching up on what you haven't.

3 *I've thoroughly grasped everything I've read*

I'd say you're a genius if you've understood everything in D103. If the course is any good, it will have set all sorts of ideas whirling around your mind, some of which you will still be sorting out several years from now. Indeed it's hard to imagine what a 'final' understanding of, say, the economic system or the political system would be like. Naturally, the course team had plans as to the directions it wanted your understanding to progress. But you have been presented with some very broad and challenging issues, and on a foundation course you could hardly be expected to have arrived at a resolution of all of them.

4   *I've done so many exams it's a well-worn routine for me*

It's sensible to be wary of university exams if you're new to them. You need to find out as much as you can about them in advance. Read past papers if they're available; ask your tutor-counsellor and more experienced students; read the OU booklet of information for exam candidates. The basic facts are that the exam lasts three hours. You answer three questions from Section A, and one from Section B.

5   *I know exactly which questions to go for*

By the time you sit down to take the exam, you *ought* to have a fair idea of the questions you intend to go for. You can't afford to waste time in an exam dithering or changing your mind half way through a question, though, of course, you must tackle the question *on* the paper. One of your most important jobs between now and the exam is to form a clear plan of attack on the paper.

6   *I think at my clearest when the pressure is on*

It's easy to get into a flap in the later stages of revision or during the exam, such that you can't think straight. You become highly charged, which means that you have plenty of nervous energy and can get lots done. But it's hard to keep in control, to make sure that the energy is channelled in the best directions. Being highly charged makes you very good at focussing attention on concrete matters-in-hand, but conversely makes you less good at sorting out broad abstract issues. There is an obvious answer to this. You do your broad planning well in advance so that, by the final stages of revision and in the exam itself, you have clear cut strategies to guide you — strategies for tackling the revision, for allocating time in the exam, for taking exam questions apart, for structuring answers and so on. You need to become like an efficient exam-crunching machine. If you have a well developed sense of purpose — a framework within which to work — you may find you can think surprisingly clearly.

7   *I find the way exam questions are worded a stimulating challenge*

Exam questions are usually fairly abstract in form and can seem rather oblique in their wording. As a result your first look at a sample exam paper may give you a fright. The questions sound so broad and demanding.

However their obliqueness is usually because the course team wants to direct you to a specific section of the course without actually answering the question for you. So remind yourself that the exam *is a test of your reading of D103* and that somewhere within what you know of the units lie the makings of an answer to each of the questions. Carefully match what you know of the units against what the question seems to be asking. There is no mystery. The course team wants you to display an understanding of some parts of the material in the course. It's just a question of working out very carefully *which* bits.

8   *My memory never lets me down in a crisis*

University exams are not intended as 'memory' tests. University education aims primarily to develop your ideas. The purpose of exam questions is to provide you with the opportunity to show how you can *use* ideas in *arguing a case*. If you revise constructively before the exams, the role of 'pure' memory will be small. When you have an organized *understanding* of what is contained in the course material, and if you can see the *relationship* between the course material and a given question, you will have the core of an answer. Around this basis you will find it fairly easy to remember details of examples, and so on, from the text. So don't think about your memory. Concentrate on organizing your notes and let memory take care of itself.

9   *My background general knowledge of social science subjects is so broad, I have no fear of being caught short of material*

Forget this one. The exam is a test of your understanding of D103, not of your general knowledge. Don't search your general knowledge for material for answers—more likely than not it will fail to appeal to your script marker. At foundation level, the material required for exam answers is to be found in the course.

10 *I know exactly what's expected in exam answers*

If you worry about this, you may well be right. It's clear from past comments of examiners that many students are indeed uncertain as to what is required in exam answers. So please think carefully about the advice given earlier in this block about analysing the questions carefully.

11 *I find it easy to plan an answer and write it out in 45 minutes*

How long do you spend on a TMA? Six hours–ten hours? How on earth can you condense all those processes into 45 minutes? Clearly you can't. So exam answers do not look like TMAs. For a start they are shorter, usually more fragmented and much less polished than TMAs. But more important is that, whereas in TMA writing you can gradually work out a considered response to the question, in an exam you can only afford to spend a few minutes thinking out the line you are going to take. So you need to have done a good deal of your thinking prior to the exam. That is, you need to have the central issues of the relevant blocks clearly in your mind. Then in the exam you settle, after a few minutes, on a particular way of presenting a selection of these issues in relation to the question and stick to it, for better or worse. (Once again this calls for practice in tackling questions.) As far as writing at speed is concerned you need to be able to get down about 500–700 words in 30–40 minutes, for a high grade answer. The fact that you are highly aroused in exams will help you to reach such targets. But, if in doubt, give yourself some practice in writing at speed to get your hand limbered up.

12 *Luckily I write stylishly and legibly when hurrying*

Surely most people write below their best in an exam. One the other hand, if your writing style or your handwriting is particularly poor this may be a problem. Script markers have to work at speed through mountains of answers and, with the best will in the world, it is hard to do justice to judging an argument which is very difficult to read. On the other hand, it's not a problem to spend time *worrying* over. You will just have to *do your best*. You cannot do much to change either your basic style of expression or your handwriting at short notice. You can only work to improve them gradually over the years. But, of course, do try to remember your reader as your write. Don't be so over-whelmed by the need for speed that your writing descends to a desperate scrawl.

13 *I like to relax and get plenty of sleep the last day or two before an exam*

Yes, wouldn't it be great to knock-off from revision for the last couple of days before the exam and get plenty of rest. But life is rarely like that for students, especially part-timers. And in any case, in my experience, that last day or two is spent building up to a peak of preparedness. You can concentrate wonder-fully when it's too late to worry about the frills and all that is possible is to make the best job you can of marshalling what you know. But try to avoid becoming obsessed about the exam. You need to be fresh and lively for the exam itself. You need sleep! You may find it hard to be relaxed but you can be calm and unruffled. You may be keyed up, but like a tennis star or stage performer ready to give your big performance of the year you can transcend your normal limits by the force of all that nervous energy and your single minded concentra-tion. I know it is difficult to wind down revision over the last few days and my guess is that it is impossible for any of us to enter the exam room completely relaxed. We are bound to be keyed up and that is very useful because it enables us to perform well if we use that nervous energy effectively. However, it is my experience that we should try to relax, wind down and get a couple of early nights before the exam. Simple relaxation techniques, such as taking a few deep breaths just before the examination starts, work wonders for me and for other people with whom I have discussed these kinds of issues. I would also argue that the benefit we gain from two or three nights good sleep more than outweighs the (sometimes confusing) effect of cramming into the small hours.

I don't think anybody relishes the stress of an exam; but I know it is possible to get satisfaction and a real sense of achievement out of a job done well. This is true of exams as it is of other activities. So try to go into the exam room feeling very positive. This isn't just wishful thinking. If you go in there determined to do your best, then you are more likely to do well than if you worry about all the things you could have done but didn't have time. Make the best of what you've got. Don't worry that other people may have more, or that you could have done more. Use what you know to answer the question and you might surprise yourself. You might even enjoy the challenge.

=============== THE GOOD STUDY GUIDE ===============

is an excellent source of advice on the activities needed just before the examina-tion and in the exam room itself. You should read Sections 5, 6 and 7 of Chapter 7 now.

In Chapter 7, Andy Northedge gives very wise counsel, in my view. As you have seen, he repeats some of the things already mentioned in the quiz and he adopts an approach to question planning very similar to the style which has been used earlier in this unit. I hope you are able to adopt his advice. If you are, I am sure you will become an efficient exam performer as Andy suggests.

The D103 examination is a simple four question paper just like that described in *The Good Study Guide*. Your time plan could be exactly the same as the one outlined there.

Unlike Andy, I am one of the people who prefers to plan out each answer immediately before writing it. I find I lose track of the arguments if I plan several questions together and risk mixing them up in my answers. My time plan would look something like this:

10.00	Work out which questions to answer on both parts of the paper and get a sense of what is expected of me for the next three hours	(4 or 5 minutes)
10.04	Plan the first answer	(8 to 10 minutes)
10.13	Write out the first answer	(35 minutes)
10.48	Plan the second answer	(8 to 10 minutes)
10.57	Write out the second answer	(35 minutes)
11.32	Plan the third answer	(8 to 10 minutes)
11.41	Write out the third answer	(35 minutes)
12.16	Plan the fourth answer	(8 to 10 minutes)
12.25	Write out the fourth answer	(35 minutes)
13.00	Finish and breathe a sigh of relief.	

Clearly some of the timings here will vary a little depending upon the particular questions answered, but this is the broad strategy I would attempt to carry out and I would stick to it as closely as I could. I would also leave a little time at the end of the writing-up phase for each question to read back what I had written. Andy Northedge does not do this but some people (and I am one) find it a very useful activity in order to pick up occasions when, in the rush of writing, words have been missed out or some connection which was intended has not been signalled. The essay can be compared with the original plan. If it has drifted away from the point a little, it may be possible to add a phrase or two to pull it back round. You must not spend so much time on this, however, that you leave yourself with insufficient time for subsequent answers. It is impossible to rewrite the answer—avoid that wish!—but the answer can be polished and occasional lapses can be rectified. Alternatively or additionally, if you have time at the end of the exam, it is worth re-reading and checking your answers then.

You can do no more than your best. The important thing is to make sure you are as well placed as possible to give of your best. You shouldn't need luck but it always helps, so…Good luck!

POSTSCRIPT

James Anderson

Good luck in the exam. I'm sure you'll do yourself justice, particularly if you follow the advice in Block VII and *The Good Study Guide*.

An exam is a bit like a cold shower — you don't exactly look forward to it or enjoy being in it, but you feel much better once you've been through it. Exams can concentrate the mind wonderfully and they are usually an important part of the education process. So your experience of the D103 exam could stand you in good stead in the future.

Block VII naturally emphasized course revision and exam preparation, and how to go about answering questions in the exam itself. The exam is the culmination of D103, you owe it to yourself to get a credit, and at this stage of the year you could be forgiven for thinking that the exam is the be all and end all of the course. Education, however, is about much more than exams and credits. It doesn't end with exams, and exams are only one measure of it. You've already got TMAs under your belt, and just having stuck with the course for eight months or more is itself a considerable achievement (and it's one you may have noticed generally impresses independent observers). Also, you may remember that the three main aims of D103 as spelled out in the *Course Guide* and Block I did not hinge on the exam.

We aimed to enhance your knowledge of contemporary society in the UK and its wider international and historical context. We aimed to increase your understanding of social science, to appreciate the analytical strengths of its methods and approaches and also their limitations. We have given you opportunities and guidance in using these methods for yourself, and practice in making social scientific approaches part of your own thinking. Our third aim was to involve you in what university study is centrally about — developing your own ideas and study skills in a 'dialogue' with the course material and in debate with other students and tutors. I hope that you and we have achieved these aims, and that you now have a better foundation for whatever subsequent courses or career you choose to follow. Best wishes.

SUGGESTIONS FOR FURTHER READING

Previous blocks suggested some optional readings which you might wish to follow up after finishing the block or the course as a whole. You may welcome a complete break from study after the exam, but after a break you might want to learn more about some topic or topics which particularly interested you. If so check back to previous blocks, and if you want to find out more about the traditions here are some suggestions:

CONSERVATISM

Nisbet, R. (1986) *Conservatism: Dream and Reality*, Milton Keynes, Open University Press,

Norton, P. and Aughey, A. (1981) *Conservatives and Conservatism*, London, Temple Smith.

O'Gorman, F. (1986) *British Conservatism*, London, Longman.

LIBERALISM

Arblaster, A (1984) *The Rise and Decline of Western Liberalism*, Oxford, Basil Blackwell.

Gray, J. (1986) *Liberalism*, Milton Keynes, Open University Press.

Hayek, F.A. (1982) *Law, Legislation and Liberty*, London, Routledge and Kegan Paul.

MARXISM

Callinicos, A. (1983) *The Revolutionary Ideas of Karl Marx*, London, Bookmarks.

Harris, N. (1986) *The End of the Third World*, Harmondsworth, Penguin.

McLellan, D. (1973) *Karl Marx,* Basingstoke, Macmillan.

SOCIAL REFORMISM

Kavanagh, D. and Morris, P. (1989) *Consensus Politics from Attlee to Thatcher*, Oxford, Basil Blackwell.

Marquand, D. (1991) *The Progressive Dilemma*, London, Heinemann.

Williams, S. (1981) *Politics is for People*, Harmondsworth, Penguin.

ACKNOWLEDGEMENTS

Grateful acknowledgement is made to the following sources for material reproduced in this unit:

Illustrations
p.159: Jenny Mathews/Format; p.161: Mary Evans Picture Library.

Photograph
p.160: Topham/Observer.